QA184.H4 1974
[redacted]
Heal, G. M./Linear algebra and line
Whitworth College Library
S0-BKX-263

Linear Algebra and Linear Economics

DISCARD

LINEAR ALGEBRA AND LINEAR ECONOMICS

Geoffrey Heal
Gordon Hughes
and
Roger Tarling

AMERICAN ELSEVIER PUBLISHING CO., INC.

© Geoffrey Heal, Gordon Hughes and Roger Tarling 1974

All rights reserved. No part of this publication
may be reproduced or transmitted, in any form
or by any means, without permission.

First published 1974 by
THE MACMILLAN PRESS LTD
London and Basingstoke

Published in the USA
by *American Elsevier Publishing Co., Inc.*
52 Vanderbilt Avenue
New York, N.Y. 10017

ISBN 0–444–19520–3
Library of Congress Catalog Card Number 74–17255

Printed in Great Britain

CONTENTS

	Preface	vii
1	Sets, Vectors and Other Concepts	1
2	Convexity	11
3	Linear Dependence and Bases	26
4	Matrices	34
5	Linear Equations	50
6	Linear Transformations	61
7	Inverse Mappings and the Inverse Matrix	70
8	Determinants	83
9	Eigenvalues and Eigenvectors	90
10	Non-negative Square Matrices	110
11	Linear Economic Models	129
12	Linear Programming	145
13	Economic Applications of Linear Programming	160
	Appendix A. More General Vector Spaces	170
	Appendix B. Differentiation in Linear Algebra	173
	Some Test Questions	176
	Answers to Problems	186
	Bibliography	208
	Index	209

PREFACE

This book sets out the concepts of linear algebra frequently encountered in economic and statistical theory, and uses them to discuss some of the important models and techniques in linear economic theory. It is the product of our experience teaching both linear algebra and linear economics to undergraduates at Cambridge, which has impressed us with the advantages of combining them. We have aimed to provide a unified treatment of the field in which similar methods of proof are used throughout, and the results required in the discussion of linear economic theory are proved in the same book. Thus, as well as the traditional topics of linear algebra, we have included chapters on convexity, non-negative square matrices, and linear programming which introduce concepts and theorems used in many branches of economic theory.

The part of the book dealing with linear algebra adopts a rigorous approach to the subject but assumes little previous mathematical expertise. Care has been taken to separate the theorems and proofs from the discussion which provides the continuity. Hence all definitions and theorems have been italicised and the ends of proofs are clearly indicated. Operational techniques such as methods for finding the inverse of a matrix or solving a linear programme are illustrated by worked numerical examples. In proving theorems we have relied, as far as possible, on the use of the concepts of linear dependence and independence. We show that many results may also be proved by the use of the properties of linear transformations, but these play a subsidiary role. Wherever possible the use of determinants has been avoided, and their properties are only briefly discussed in Chapter 8.

Since it is desirable that the student should master the linear algebra before tackling the economics, problems have been provided for each chapter together with answers and outline proofs at the end of the book, so that the student may check his progress at each stage. Not all of the problems are numerical questions; about half of them require the student to develop proofs of important results which are not included in the preceding chapter, but which may be referred to in later chapters. A set of 25 test questions – mostly taken from past examination papers set for the original course – covering the topics discussed has also been included.

As well as its treatment of linear algebra, this book provides an introduction to a very substantial body of economic theory. The chapters on linear economics contain some of the most important results of the Leontief and Von Neumann models, and provide an introduction to the applications of linear programming. It is hoped, therefore, that it will prove a useful introductory and reference text for a variety of courses on linear algebra, linear programming, and linear economic theory.

We are indebted to the University of Cambridge for permission to include selected questions from past papers of the Preliminary and Part II Examinations for the Economics Tripos. We are very grateful to Miss Judy Barnes and Mrs Mabs Simmonds for their excellent work in the preparation of the typescript.

G.M.H.
G.A.H.
R.J.T.

1 Sets, Vectors and Other Concepts

1.1 Sets

D.1. *A SET is any well-defined collection of objects. The objects contained in a set are referred to as ELEMENTS of the set.*

In terms of this definition we could talk about the set of all books in a library or of all people in a room. A set need not be a collection of physical objects: most of the sets we shall be concerned with will be collections of mathematical objects, e.g. the set of all odd numbers. The significance of the term 'well-defined' is that it must be clear whether or not any particular object is an element of the set.

The usual notation for a set is to list all its elements within brackets or to enclose a definition of the elements between brackets: i.e. the set X of the integers 1, 2, 3 may be written as: $X = (1, 2, 3)$, *or* $X = \{x | x \text{ is an integer}, 0 < x < 4\}$. In general, $\{x | x \text{ is } P\}$ describes the set of objects having property P. Further, to say that 2 is an element of this set X we write: $2 \in X$. The use of the equality sign relies upon the following definition.

D.2. *Let* A *and* B *be two sets. They are said to be equal if they comprise the same elements; i.e.* A = B *if and only if every element of* A *is also an element of* B, *and vice-versa.*

D.3. *The set* A *is a SUBSET of the set* B *if every element of* A *is also an element of* B. *This is written:* A ⊂ B.

For example the sets $X_1 = (1, 3, 5)$ and $X_2 = (5, 25, 125)$ are both subsets of the set of all odd numbers.

Clearly on occasions we will wish to combine two or more sets. Formally this is known as taking their union:

D.4. *If* A *and* B *are two sets, then the* UNION *of* A *and* B, *written* A ∪ B, *is the set of all objects which are either in* A *or in* B.

Symbolically this may be written:

$$A \cup B = \{x | x \in A \quad \text{or} \quad x \in B\}.$$

The union of more than two sets is found by an obvious extension of this definition.

Another definition is prompted by our interest in objects which are simultaneously members of several sets.

D.5. *If* A *and* B *are two sets, then the* INTERSECTION *of* A *and* B, *written* $A \cap B$, *is the set of all elements in both* A *and* B.

Thus $A \cap B = \{x | x \in A \text{ and } x \in B\}$.

D.6. *If* A *and* B *are two sets which have no elements in common, then* A *and* B *are said to be* DISJOINT. *This may be written as:* $A \cap B = \varnothing$ *where* $\varnothing$ *is the NULL SET– that is the empty set or the set which contains no members.*

One final piece of notation often used is the symbol $\forall$ which stands for the phrase 'for all'.

1.2 Necessary and Sufficient Conditions

The concepts of 'a necessary condition' and 'a sufficient condition' are used extensively in logical arguments, and occur frequently in this book. It is thus very important to be clear about their implications from the beginning. In plain language *a necessary condition* is something which must hold for a result to follow, but it does not guarantee the result. On the other hand *a sufficient condition* guarantees the result, but the result may, perhaps, follow even if the condition is not satisfied.

To elucidate this more fully let us suppose that A and B are two propositions such that the truth or falsity of A is contingent upon the truth or falsity of B. Consider Figure 1 below: let the area shaded

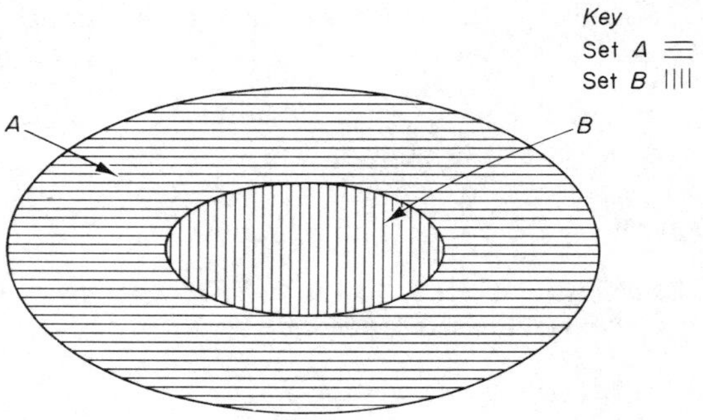

Figure 1

horizontally represent the set of situations where A is true, and that shaded vertically those where both A and B are true. In the figure A is true *if* (but not *only if*) B is true, whereas B is true only if A is true. In other words, the truth of B is *a sufficient condition* for the truth of A and the truth of A is *a necessary condition* for the truth of B. Alternatively we can say that the truth of B implies that of A, but is not implied by that of A.

If the two sets are equal, then the situation can be described by any of the following three statements:

(i) A is true *if and only if* (iff) B is true.

(ii) The truth of A is a *necessary and sufficient condition* (N.A.S.C.) for that of B.

(iii) The truth of A *implies and is implied by* ($\Leftrightarrow$) that of B.

In any of these statements A and B may be interchanged.

An important result to emerge from this is that in proving a result of the form 'A is true iff B is true' one has to prove two distinct results:

(i) 'A is true *if* B is true',

(ii) 'A is true *only if* B is true'.

The first may be expressed as:

$$\{x \mid B \text{ is true}\} \subset \{x \mid A \text{ is true}\}$$

and the second as:

$$\{x \mid A \text{ is true}\} \subset \{x \mid B \text{ is true}\}.$$

Together these imply that:

$$\{x \mid A \text{ is true}\} = \{x \mid B \text{ is true}\}$$

which, of course, is the desired result.

In establishing propositions we shall often use a method known as 'proof by contradiction'. This proceeds as follows: in order to prove the proposition 'A is true' we should start by assuming the validity of the proposition 'A is not true', and then show that this implies a result known *a priori* to be untrue. We would then claim to have established that 'A is not true' is itself not true. Assuming that 'A is true' and 'A is not true' are mutually exclusive and exhaustive possibilities, this proves the desired result. Alternatively a proposition can often be shown to be false by an example – e.g. assume 'A is true', then an example in which A is not true will suffice to demonstrate the falsity of this assumption.

1.3 Vectors

D.7. *A VECTOR is an ordered set of numbers.*

By an ordered set we mean one which is distinguished not only by the elements it contains, but also by the order in which they appear. Thus (1, 2) and (2, 1) are both vectors, but are not the same since their elements are listed in different orders. A vector with n components will be called an n-vector.

Notation: We shall denote the general n-vector by $(x_1, x_2, x_3, \ldots, x_n)$ where the x_i $[i = 1, 2, \ldots, n]$ stand for the n components. For convenience we may write $\boldsymbol{x} = (x_1, \ldots, x_n)$. However the notation $\boldsymbol{x}$ does not indicate the number of components of the vector concerned; therefore it will only be used when this is clear from the context.

Illustrations: Consider a man who consumes some of each of n different goods, label the goods $1, 2, 3, \ldots, n$, and let x_i be the quantity of the ith good that he consumes. If we list the quantities of each of the goods which he consumes we have $\boldsymbol{x} = (x_1, x_2, \ldots, x_n)$. We can refer to $\boldsymbol{x}$ as his consumption vector. If $n = 2$, x_1 = number of books read, and x_2 = number of sandwiches eaten, then clearly the consumption vector (1, 3) is very different from (3, 1). Similarly we could take as an example the prices of the n goods – $p_1, p_2, \ldots, p_n$ – to form the price vector $\boldsymbol{p} = (p_1, p_2, \ldots, p_n)$.

Alternatively we can give vectors a geometrical interpretation. It is well known that if we draw a pair of perpendicular straight lines (axes) in a plane then any point in that plane may be represented by a pair of numbers – its co-ordinates. Let the two axes be the x_1 and x_2 axes; then the pair (a, b) represents a point vertically above a on the x_1 axis, level with b on the x_2 axis. Clearly the order of the pair matters. In this way any point in the plane can be represented by a 2-vector, and every 2-vector can be interpreted as a point in some 2-dimensional space. Similarly for a 3-dimensional space and 3-vectors. By analogy the same idea may be conceptually extended to n-vectors representing some point in n-dimensional space.

Quite frequently in physics a vector is represented by a directed line segment. The usefulness of this in physical terms will be obvious if the example of motion on a plane surface is considered. Starting from the initial point, the vector tells us about the magnitude and direction of such motion by giving us the co-ordinates reached after some unit time-period. This interpretation of vectors can sometimes be useful in economics.

One final point about vectors must be noted. Later we will need to distinguish between vectors written as a row array of the components, and vectors written as a column array. Unless otherwise stated, in this book we will use the general vector notation $\boldsymbol{x}$ to denote the column vector

$$\begin{bmatrix} x_1 \\ x_2 \\ \vdots \\ x_n \end{bmatrix}.$$

Further, if $\boldsymbol{x}$ is a column vector, then $\boldsymbol{x}'$ – called the *transpose* of $\boldsymbol{x}$ – is the row vector $[x_1, x_2, \ldots, x_n]$.

1.4 Operations on Vectors

D.8. *EQUALITY. Two vectors with the same number of components are equal if and only if their corresponding components are equal.*

If vectors have different numbers of components, we do not try to compare them.

D.9. *MULTIPLICATION BY A SCALAR. Real numbers are referred to as scalars (and are denoted by small letters* – a, b). *The product of the vector* **x** *with the scalar* a *is defined to be the vector* **y**, *each of whose components is* a *times the corresponding component of* **x**. *Thus:*

$$\mathbf{y} = a\mathbf{x} = (ax_1, ax_2, \ldots, ax_n) \tag{1.1}$$

D.10. *ADDITION OF VECTORS. The sum of two* n*-vectors* **x** *and* **y** *is defined to be the* n*-vector* $\mathbf{z} = (x_1 + y_1, x_2 + y_2, \ldots, x_n + y_n)$ *obtained by adding corresponding components. Addition is only defined for vectors with equal numbers of components.*

If we take the last two operations together we get the idea of a *linear combination* of two or more vectors. Suppose we have two vectors $\boldsymbol{x}, \boldsymbol{y}$ and two scalars a, b then the vector $\boldsymbol{z}$ given by:

$$\boldsymbol{z} = a\boldsymbol{x} + b\boldsymbol{y} \tag{1.2}$$

is called the linear combination of $\boldsymbol{x}$ and $\boldsymbol{y}$ using the scalars or weights a and b.

Examples: (i) Suppose that $\boldsymbol{x}$ and $\boldsymbol{y}$ represent two different baskets of goods made up from n different commodities. Then, if a people buy the basket of type $\boldsymbol{x}$ and b people the one of type $\boldsymbol{y}$, it is clear that the total quantities of commodities disposed of is given by the vector $\boldsymbol{z}$ as defined in (1.2) above.

(ii) Consider the sum $\boldsymbol{z}$ of two 2-component vectors $\boldsymbol{x}$, $\boldsymbol{y}$, i.e. $\boldsymbol{z} = \boldsymbol{x} + \boldsymbol{y}$. Clearly $z_1 = x_1 + y_1$, $z_2 = x_2 + y_2$. Figure 2 shows $\boldsymbol{x}$ and $\boldsymbol{y}$, and also the point $(x_1 + y_1, x_2 + y_2)$, which is $\boldsymbol{z}$. It is easy to show that the line $\boldsymbol{yz}$ is parallel to $0\boldsymbol{x}$, and $\boldsymbol{xz}$ is parallel to $0\boldsymbol{y}$, so that $\boldsymbol{z}$ is found by completing the parallelogram that has 0, $\boldsymbol{x}$ and $\boldsymbol{y}$ as three of its vertices. This gives the parallelogram law for adding vectors which will be familiar to those who have studied physics.

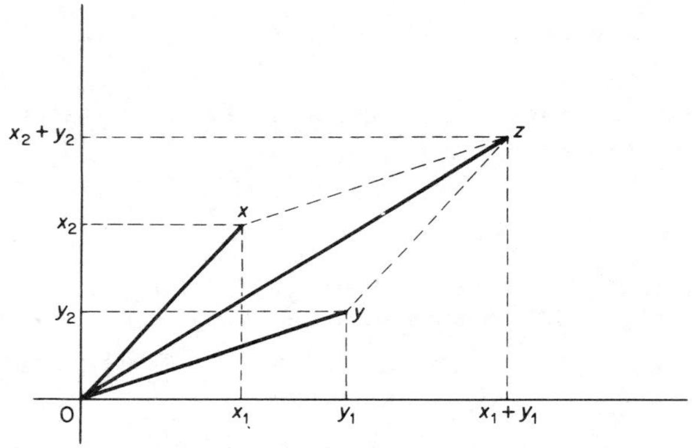

Figure 2

We can define *subtraction* of vectors by considering the linear combination of $\boldsymbol{x}$ and $\boldsymbol{y}$ using the scalars 1 and -1; then

$$\boldsymbol{z} = \boldsymbol{x} - \boldsymbol{y} = (x_1 - y_1, x_2 - y_2, \ldots).$$

The operations defined so far have the usual *associative*, *commutative*, and *distributive* properties. Thus:
Associative:

$$(\boldsymbol{x} + \boldsymbol{y}) + \boldsymbol{z} = \boldsymbol{x} + (\boldsymbol{y} + \boldsymbol{z}) \tag{1.3}$$

Commutative:

$$\boldsymbol{x} + \boldsymbol{y} = \boldsymbol{y} + \boldsymbol{x} \tag{1.4}$$

Distributive:

$$(a + b)\boldsymbol{x} = a\boldsymbol{x} + b\boldsymbol{x} \tag{1.5}$$

$$a(\boldsymbol{x} + \boldsymbol{y}) = a\boldsymbol{x} + a\boldsymbol{y} \tag{1.6}$$

D.11. *The SCALAR PRODUCT of two* n*-vectors* $\boldsymbol{x}$, $\boldsymbol{y}$ *is defined as:*

$$\boldsymbol{x} \cdot \boldsymbol{y} = x_1 y_1 + x_2 y_2 + \ldots + x_n y_n. \tag{1.7}$$

Note that $\boldsymbol{x} \cdot \boldsymbol{y}$ is a *number*. Once again associative, commutative, and distributive properties hold; i.e.

$$\lambda \boldsymbol{x} \cdot \boldsymbol{y} = \boldsymbol{x} \cdot \lambda \boldsymbol{y} = \lambda(\boldsymbol{x} \cdot \boldsymbol{y}) \tag{1.8}$$

$$\boldsymbol{x} \cdot \boldsymbol{y} = \boldsymbol{y} \cdot \boldsymbol{x} \tag{1.9}$$

$$\boldsymbol{x} \cdot (\boldsymbol{y} + \boldsymbol{z}) = \boldsymbol{x} \cdot \boldsymbol{y} + \boldsymbol{x} \cdot \boldsymbol{z} \tag{1.10}$$

Examples: As earlier let $\boldsymbol{x}$ be an individual's consumption vector and $\boldsymbol{p}$ be the vector of prices which he faces. Then the cost of his consumption will be:

$$C = x_1 p_1 + x_2 p_2 + \ldots + x_n p_n = \sum_{i=1}^{n} x_i p_i = \boldsymbol{x} \cdot \boldsymbol{p} \tag{1.11}$$

If the consumer's income was Y we could define his *budget set* as the set of all consumption bundles that he could afford to buy. If B is this set, $B = \{\boldsymbol{x} \mid \boldsymbol{p} \cdot \boldsymbol{x} \leqslant Y\}$.

1.5 Vector Spaces

D.12. *A VECTOR SPACE is a set of vectors which satisfies the following conditions:*

(i) The operation of addition is defined for any two elements of the set;

(ii) The operation of multiplication by a scalar is defined for any element of the set and any scalar;

(iii) The set is closed under these operations, i.e. the vector resulting from either of these operations is a member of the set;

(iv) The operations referred to in (i) and (ii) have the usual associative, distributive, and commutative properties.

Put symbolically we may say that the set V is a vector space if, given $\boldsymbol{x}, \boldsymbol{y} \in V$, for any scalars λ, θ the vector $\boldsymbol{z}$ formed as a linear combination of $\boldsymbol{x}$ and $\boldsymbol{y}$ is a member of V – i.e. $\boldsymbol{z} = \lambda \boldsymbol{x} + \theta \boldsymbol{y} \in V$.

It is clear that the set of all n-component vectors satisfies the above conditions and is thus a vector space.

D.13. *The vector space composed of all real* n*-component vectors is called an* n*-dimensional Euclidean space, denoted by* R^n *(or in some books by* E^n*).*

An example of 2-dimensional Euclidean space is the set of vectors on a plane defined by a pair of co-ordinate axes.

D.14. *A SUBSPACE* S *of a vector space* V *is defined to be a subset of* V *which is itself a vector space.*

In other words the subset S itself satisfies the condition of being closed under the operations of addition and scalar multiplication. If we consider a line through the origin in R^2 it will be seen that sums of scalar multiples of vectors on the line themselves lie on the line. Thus any line through the origin is a subspace of R^2.

When discussing vector spaces it is sometimes useful to have a measure of the length of a vector or a *norm* in order to compare different vectors. There are, in fact, many possible norms, but we will use one with an obvious geometrical interpretation. It is written as $|\boldsymbol{x}|$ and is defined by:

$$|\boldsymbol{x}| = (\boldsymbol{x} \cdot \boldsymbol{x})^{\frac{1}{2}} = (x_1^2 + x_2^2 + \ldots + x_n^2)^{\frac{1}{2}}. \tag{1.12}$$

In two dimensions this is the length of the hypotenuse of the right-angled triangle whose two other sides are the two components of the vector.

Extending this idea we may talk of the *distance* between two vectors $\boldsymbol{x}$, $\boldsymbol{y}$ written as $|\boldsymbol{x} - \boldsymbol{y}|$ defined by:

$$\begin{aligned} |\boldsymbol{x} - \boldsymbol{y}| &= [(\boldsymbol{x} - \boldsymbol{y}) \cdot (\boldsymbol{x} - \boldsymbol{y})]^{\frac{1}{2}} \\ &= [\sum_{i=1}^{n} (x_i - y_i)^2]^{\frac{1}{2}}. \end{aligned} \tag{1.13}$$

Now consider the two vectors $\boldsymbol{x}$, $\boldsymbol{y}$ in R^2. We will suppose that there is an angle θ between the lines joining them to the origin. Now if we consider $|\boldsymbol{x} - \boldsymbol{y}|$, using a little trigonometry it is possible to show that

$$\boldsymbol{x} \cdot \boldsymbol{y} = \sum_{i=1}^{n} x_i y_i = |\boldsymbol{x}|\,|\boldsymbol{y}| \cos \theta. \tag{1.14}$$

From this it will be seen that if θ is 90°, then the scalar product of the two vectors will be zero. Generalising this idea we get:

D.15. *Two* n*-vectors* **x** *and* **y** *are said to be ORTHOGONAL if their scalar product is zero; i.e. if* $\mathbf{x} \cdot \mathbf{y} = 0$.

1.6 Vector Inequalities

It will sometimes be useful to refer to inequalities between vectors – that is to know whether $\boldsymbol{x}$ is greater than $\boldsymbol{y}$. The criterion used for deciding this is a simple extension of the way we order numbers. Note that these comparisons can only be made between vectors with equal numbers of components. For $\boldsymbol{x}, \boldsymbol{y} \in R^n$, we will write:

(i) $\boldsymbol{x} \geqq \boldsymbol{y}$ if $x_i \geqslant y_i \quad \forall i$.

(ii) $\boldsymbol{x} \geqslant \boldsymbol{y}$ if $x_i \geqslant y_i \quad \forall i$ and $x_i > y_i$ for some i.

This is called a *weak inequality*.

(iii) $\boldsymbol{x} > \boldsymbol{y}$ if $x_i > y_i \quad \forall i$

This is a *strict inequality*.

For $\boldsymbol{x} \geqq \boldsymbol{0}$ we say that $\boldsymbol{x}$ is *non-negative*; for $\boldsymbol{x} > \boldsymbol{0}$, $\boldsymbol{x}$ is *positive*. Note the use of $\boldsymbol{0}$ to denote the *null vector* – that is the vector with each component zero.

It is important to realise that not all vectors can be compared by the ordering just defined – it is a *partial ordering*. Thus it is always possible to find two vectors in R^n such that neither $\boldsymbol{x} \geqq \boldsymbol{y}$, nor $\boldsymbol{y} \geqq \boldsymbol{x}$; for example, (1, 2) and (2, 1) in R^2.

Illustration. Consider a community with n individuals denoted by $i = 1, 2, \ldots, n$. Let the utility of the ith individual by u_i. Call $\boldsymbol{u} = (u_1, u_2, \ldots, u_n)$ the community utility vector. Now suppose that we are required to judge whether a policy change has led to an increase in the utility of the community. Suppose $\boldsymbol{u}$ was the community utility vector before the change, and $\hat{\boldsymbol{u}} = (\hat{u}_1, \hat{u}_2, \ldots, \hat{u}_n)$ that after it.

The Pareto criterion says that a change raises welfare if, as a result of it, no-one is worse off and at least one person is better off. By this criterion the change raises welfare if $\hat{u}_i \geqslant u_i$ for all i and $\hat{u}_i > u_i$ for some i. But this is equivalent to $\hat{\boldsymbol{u}} \geqslant \boldsymbol{u}$ – i.e. the Pareto criterion can be restated in terms of the vector ordering. It follows that the Pareto criterion gives a partial ordering; it cannot be used to order any pair of community utility vectors. In particular it cannot be used to compare points such that the move from one to the other makes some people better off and other people worse off. This is a source of much difficulty in welfare economics.

1.7 Problems

1.1. Consider the set A of prime numbers, the set B of odd numbers and the set C of even numbers for numbers from 1 to 10. Write down the intersection of (i) A and B, (ii) A and C, and (iii) A, B and C. What is the union of B and C?

1.2. Let Y be the set of numbers from 1 to 5. Consider the set

$A = \{x | x = y^2 + 2y + 2, y \in Y\}$, and the set $B = \{x | x = 2y^2 - 3y + a, y \in Y\}$. For what values of a between 0 and 20 will the two sets A and B not be disjoint?

1.3. Prove that a necessary and sufficient condition for set A to be a subset of set B is that the intersection of sets A and B is the set A. How might this condition be stated in terms of the union of A and B?

1.4. Let S be the set of all even numbers. Which of the following propositions is a necessary and/or sufficient condition for $x \in S$:

(i) x is divisible by 4,

(ii) x is divisible by 2,

(iii) x is greater than 1.

1.5. Illustrate graphically $A_1 \cap A_2 \cap A_3$ and $A_1 \cup A_2 \cup A_3$ where:

$$A_1 = \{(x_1, x_2) \mid x_1 - x_2 \geqslant 0\}$$

$$A_2 = \{(x_1, x_2) \mid x_1 x_2 \leqslant 1\}$$

$$A_3 = \{(x_1, x_2) \mid 3x_1 + 2x_2 \geqslant 0\}.$$

1.6. (*a*) Consider the vectors $\boldsymbol{x} = (1, 2, 3)$, $\boldsymbol{y} = (5, 0, 1)$ and $\boldsymbol{z} = (2, 2, 4)$. Write down (i) $\boldsymbol{x} + \boldsymbol{y} + \boldsymbol{z}$, (ii) $\boldsymbol{x} - \boldsymbol{y} + \boldsymbol{z}$, and (iii) $9\boldsymbol{x} - \boldsymbol{y} - 2\boldsymbol{z}$.

(*b*) Find a and b such that $(10 + a, a + b, b - 1) = (5, 9, 3)$.

1.7. Prove that, if $\boldsymbol{x}$ is a vector and a is a scalar, $|a\boldsymbol{x}| = |a|\,|\boldsymbol{x}|$.

1.8. Let $\boldsymbol{y}$ and $\boldsymbol{z}$ be vectors orthogonal to vector $\boldsymbol{x}(\neq \boldsymbol{0})$ and a and b be scalars. Suppose that $\boldsymbol{v} = a\boldsymbol{x} + \boldsymbol{y}$ and $\boldsymbol{v} = b\boldsymbol{x} + \boldsymbol{z}$. Prove that $a = b$ and $\boldsymbol{y} = \boldsymbol{z}$.

1.9. Prove that the set of vectors orthogonal to the vector (1, 2) forms a vector space. What is this vector space?

1.10. Prove that the set of vectors

$$X = \{\boldsymbol{x} | \boldsymbol{x} = (x_1, x_2, \ldots, x_{n-1}, \sum_{j=1}^{n-1} a_j x_j), a_j \neq 0 \text{ for some } j = 1, \ldots, n-1\}$$

forms a vector space. Show that this is a subspace of R^n which does not include all vectors in R^n. If another set is defined as $Y = \{\boldsymbol{x} | \boldsymbol{x} = (x_1, x_2, \ldots, x_{n-1}, \sum_{j=1}^{n} a_j x_j)\}$, show that this is also a vector space and that it is actually R^n.

2 | Convexity

In Chapter 1 we introduced and used sets in a quite general manner. However, much of modern economic analysis rests on theorems dealing with a particular type of set, known as convex sets. The purpose of this chapter is to prove certain fundamental theorems relating to convex sets and to illustrate briefly the role they play in economic theory. Before we do this it is necessary to introduce a series of concepts and results from set theory which will be required in the discussion.

D.16. *A HYPERSPHERE in* R^n *with centre* $\mathbf{a} \in \mathrm{R}^n$ *and radius* $\varepsilon > 0$ *is defined to be the set* X *given by:*

$$\mathrm{X} = \{\mathbf{x} \in \mathrm{R}^n \mid |\mathbf{x} - \mathbf{a}| \leqslant \varepsilon\}.$$

This definition uses the distance norm defined in 1.5, and so the equation of a hypersphere is:

$$\sum_{i=1}^{n} (x_i - a_i)^2 \leqslant \varepsilon^2. \tag{2.1}$$

When $n = 2$ this gives a circle with centre $\boldsymbol{a}$, radius ε; for $n = 3$ it gives a sphere.

D.17. *The INSIDE OF A HYPERSPHERE centre* **a**, *radius* ε, *is defined to be the set:*

$$\{\mathbf{x} \in \mathrm{R}^n \mid |\mathbf{x} - \mathbf{a}| < \varepsilon\}.$$

D.18. *An* ε*-NEIGHBOURHOOD about* $\mathbf{a} \in \mathrm{R}^n$ *is defined as the set of points inside the hypersphere centre* **a**, *radius* ε (> 0).

D.19. $\mathbf{a} \in \mathrm{A}$ *is an INTERIOR POINT of* A *if for some* $\varepsilon > 0$ *there exists an* ε*-neighbourhood of* **a** *containing only points of the set* A.

D.20. $\mathbf{a} \in \mathrm{A}$ *is a BOUNDARY POINT of* A *if for every* $\varepsilon > 0$, *the* ε*-neighbourhood of* **a** *contains points in* A *and points not in* A.

D.21. A *is an OPEN SET if it contains only interior points.*

D.22. A *is a CLOSED SET if it contains all its boundary points.*

Consider the real numbers between 0 and 1, and two sets A and B defined as: $A = \{x|0 \leqslant x \leqslant 1\}$, $B = \{x|0 < x < 1\}$. Clearly the points 0, 1 are boundary points of both sets while $\frac{1}{2}$ is an interior point. Since 0, 1 are both members of A, A is a closed set, while B is an open set. Note that there are sets which are neither open nor closed: for example $C = \{x|0 \leqslant x < 1\}$, which contains some but not all of its boundary points.

D.23. *The COMPLEMENT of* A *in* R^n, *written* C(A), *is the set of all points in* R^n *not in* A.

Thus: $A \cup C(A) = R^n$,
$A \cap C(A) = \emptyset$.

Further A and $C(A)$ have the same boundary points, so that if A is closed then $C(A)$ is open, and vice-versa.

D.24. (i) *A set* A *is BOUNDED if there exists* $\mathrm{r} > 0$ *such that for every* $\mathbf{a} \in \mathrm{A}$, $|\mathbf{a}| < \mathrm{r}$. (ii) *A set* A *is BOUNDED BELOW (ABOVE) if there exists* r *such that* $\forall\, \mathbf{a} \in \mathrm{A}, \mathrm{a}i \geqslant \mathrm{r}\ (\leqslant \mathrm{r})\ \forall i$.

D.25. *A set* A *in* R^n *which is both closed and bounded is said to be COMPACT.*

D.26. *The LINE passing through* $\mathbf{x}_1, \mathbf{x}_2 \in \mathrm{R}^n$ $(\mathbf{x}_1 \neq \mathbf{x}_2)$ *is defined to be the set:*

$$\mathrm{X} = \{\mathbf{x} \in \mathrm{R}^n | \lambda \mathbf{x}_1 + (1 - \lambda)\mathbf{x}_2 = \mathbf{x}, \textit{ all real } \lambda\}.$$

If we restrict the λ *in this definition to values between 0 and 1, i.e.* $0 \leqslant \lambda \leqslant 1$, *then the set is called the LINE SEGMENT.*

D.27. *A HYPERPLANE in* R^n *is the set:*

$$\mathrm{X} = \{\mathbf{x} \in \mathrm{R}^n | \mathbf{c} \cdot \mathbf{x} = \mathrm{z}\}$$

with $\mathbf{c} \neq \mathbf{0}$ *a given vector in* R^n *and* z *a given scalar.*

When $n = 2$ this gives the equation of a straight line in R^2; when $n = 3$ it gives a plane in R^3. A hyperplane goes through the origin iff $z = 0$; in this case it is a subspace of R^n – as we have already noted for R^2.

For a line in R^2 the coefficients multiplying the elements of $\boldsymbol{x}$ tell us about the slope of the line. This use is generalised by the next definition:

D.28. *Given the hyperplane* $\mathbf{c} \cdot \mathbf{x} = \mathrm{z}$ *in* R^n $(\mathbf{c} \neq \mathbf{0})$, *the vector* $\mathbf{c}$ *is said to be* NORMAL *to the hyperplane. Any vector* $\lambda\mathbf{c}$ *is also normal to the hyper-*

plane, provided $\lambda \neq 0$. *The two vectors of unit length* $\mathbf{c}/|\mathbf{c}|$, $-\mathbf{c}/|\mathbf{c}|$ *are called the unit normals of the hyperplane.*

Note that if $z = 0$, c is also orthogonal to all vectors in the hyperplane. Further we can say that two hyperplanes are parallel if they have the same unit normals.

Another familiar notion which we must formalise is the idea of a line dividing R^2 into two distinct sets of points on either side of the line.

D.29. *The sets* $X_1 = \{\mathbf{x} \in R^n | \mathbf{c}.\mathbf{x} < z\}$ *and* $X_2 = \{\mathbf{x} \in R^n | \mathbf{c}.\mathbf{x} > z\}$ *are called the OPEN HALF-SPACES formed by* $\mathbf{c}.\mathbf{x} = z$.

D.30. *The sets* $X_3 = \{\mathbf{x} \in R^n | \mathbf{c}.\mathbf{x} \leqslant z\}$ *and* $X_4 = \{\mathbf{x} \in R^n | \mathbf{c}.\mathbf{x} \geqslant z\}$ *are called the CLOSED HALF-SPACES formed by* $\mathbf{c}.\mathbf{x} = z$.

These terms are virtually self-explanatory since X_1, X_2 can easily be shown to be open sets, while X_3, X_4 are closed sets. X_1 and X_2 are disjoint, but $X_3 \cap X_4$ is the hyperplane $\boldsymbol{c}.\boldsymbol{x} = z$ itself.

This completes the preliminary concepts needed to discuss convexity, and we can now introduce a special type of set which plays a fundamental role in modern economic analysis.

D.31. *A set X is CONVEX if for any points* $\mathbf{x}_1, \mathbf{x}_2 \in X$, *the line segment joining these points is also in* X.

In other words, X is convex iff $\boldsymbol{x}_1, \boldsymbol{x}_2 \in X$ implies $\lambda \boldsymbol{x}_1 + (1 - \lambda)\boldsymbol{x}_2 \in X$ for all λ satisfying $0 \leqslant \lambda \leqslant 1$. The point $\lambda \boldsymbol{x}_1 + (1 - \lambda)\boldsymbol{x}_2$ is often called a convex linear combination of $\boldsymbol{x}_1$ and $\boldsymbol{x}_2$.

Spheres, rectangles, triangles, parallelograms are all convex sets, as are lines and hyperplanes. On the other hand the surface of a sphere is not a convex set because a convex combination of two points on the sphere's surface gives a point inside the sphere, that is one not in the set. The example of a sphere also illustrates a stronger definition of convexity for sets:

D.32. *A set X is STRICTLY CONVEX if for all* $\mathbf{x}_1, \mathbf{x}_2 \in X$ *and* λ *satisfying* $0 < \lambda < 1$, *the point* $\mathbf{x} = \lambda \mathbf{x}_1 + (1 - \lambda)\mathbf{x}_2$ *is the interior of* X.

Clearly a sphere satisfies this definition, but triangles, squares, cubes are only convex.

D.33. *A point* $\mathbf{x}$ *is an EXTREME POINT of a convex set X if and only if* $\mathbf{x} \in X$ *and there do not exist two points* $\mathbf{x}_1, \mathbf{x}_2 \in X$, $\mathbf{x}_1 \neq \mathbf{x}_2$, *such that for some* λ, $0 < \lambda < 1$, $\mathbf{x} = \lambda \mathbf{x}_1 + (1 - \lambda)\mathbf{x}_2$.

Thus an extreme point is one which cannot be expressed as a convex linear combination of two other distinct points in the set. Clearly an extreme point must be a boundary point of the set, but not all boundary points will be extreme points. The vertices of a triangle, the corners of a rectangle or a cube are extreme points; points on the sides of these figures are boundary points but are not extreme points. However for strictly convex sets every boundary point is also an extreme point – e.g. a hypersphere.

Frequently we will want to combine convex sets in various ways. For example in linear programming each constraint limits the possible solution to a closed half-space in R^n (where n is the number of solution variables). It is left as an exercise for the reader to show that a closed half-space (and an open-half space too) is a convex set. Thus with several constraints the solution must lie in the intersection of the several closed half-spaces. It will be useful to know the character of the set of points which satisfy all the constraints – known as the *set of feasible solutions* or the *feasible set.*

T.1. *The intersection of two convex sets is also convex.*

Proof: Let two sets X_1, X_2 be convex, and $X_3 = X_1 \cap X_2$. Further let $\boldsymbol{x}_1, \boldsymbol{x}_2$ be in X_3. Then $\boldsymbol{x}_1, \boldsymbol{x}_2 \in X_1$ and $\boldsymbol{x}_1, \boldsymbol{x}_2 \in X_2$.

Hence: $$\left.\begin{aligned} &\lambda\boldsymbol{x}_1 + (1-\lambda)\boldsymbol{x}_2 \in X_1 \\ &\lambda\boldsymbol{x}_1 + (1-\lambda)\boldsymbol{x}_2 \in X_2 \end{aligned}\right\} \text{ for all } \lambda \text{ such that } 0 \leqslant \lambda \leqslant 1.$$

So $\lambda\boldsymbol{x}_1 + (1-\lambda)\boldsymbol{x}_2 \in X_3$.

Q.E.D.

By a similar argument one can show that the intersection of any number of convex sets is convex. Thus the feasible set for a linear programming problem must be convex. It should be noted that the union of several convex sets need not be convex.

Another way of combining sets which is useful in economics is to take the sum or difference of them in the sense defined below:

D.34a. *The sum of two sets* X, Y *in* R^n *is defined as:*

$$\mathrm{X} + \mathrm{Y} = \{\mathbf{z} \in \mathrm{R}^n | \mathbf{z} = \mathbf{x} + \mathbf{y} \text{ for } \textit{some } \mathbf{x} \in \mathrm{X} \textit{ and } \mathbf{y} \in \mathrm{Y}\}.$$

D.34b. *The difference of two sets* X, Y *in* R^n *is defined as:*

$$\mathrm{X} - \mathrm{Y} = \{\mathbf{d} \in \mathrm{R}^n | \mathbf{d} = \mathbf{x} - \mathbf{y} \textit{ for some } \mathbf{x} \in \mathrm{X}, \mathbf{y} \in \mathrm{Y}\}.$$

In words the sum of two sets is the set generated by taking a point in one and adding to it every point in the other in turn, and repeating this for all points in the first set. Note that if both sets contain the null vector, then their sum must include their union – i.e. both of the individual sets must be in the sum. Now for convex sets we will prove the following proposition:

T.2. *Both the sum and the difference of two convex sets are convex.*

Proof: (*a*) *Sum.* Suppose that X, Y are convex sets in R^n, and let $Z = X + Y$ with $z_1, z_2 \in Z$. Consider $\lambda z_1 + (1 - \lambda)z_2, 0 \leqslant \lambda \leqslant 1$:

$$\begin{aligned}\lambda z_1 + (1 - \lambda)z_2 &= \lambda(x_1 + y_1) + (1 - \lambda)(x_2 + y_2)\\ &= \lambda x_1 + (1 - \lambda)x_2 + \lambda y_1 + (1 - \lambda)y_2\end{aligned}$$

for $x_1, x_2 \in X, y_1, y_2 \in Y$.

But $\lambda x_1 + (1 - \lambda)x_2 \in X, \lambda y_1 + (1 - \lambda)y_2 \in Y$.

Hence $\lambda z_1 + (1 - \lambda)z_2 \in Z$, and Z is convex.

(*b*) *Difference.* Let $D = X - Y$ and $d_1, d_2 \in D$.

Considering $\lambda d_1 + (1 - \lambda)d_2 = \lambda(x_1 - y_1) + (1 - \lambda)(x_2 - y_2)$ for $0 \leqslant \lambda \leqslant 1$ we can proceed as above.

Q.E.D.

We can easily extend this result to the combination of several sets. It tells us that if the production points attainable by each of two countries give convex production possibility sets for each country, then a world composed of the two countries together will have a convex world production set. Equivalently we might use this for a country with many firms, each of which has a convex production set, so that the country's production set is convex.

2.1 Supporting and Separating Hyperplanes†

In this section we outline some results which provide a basis for much economic theory, as well as decision theory and game theory.

T.3. *Let* X *be a closed convex set. Then a point* **y** *either belongs to* X, *or there exists a hyperplane containing* **y** *such that all of* X *is contained in one open half-space bounded by the hyperplane.*

† The remainder of this chapter is more difficult than most of the material in this book. Further, it covers ground which is largely peripheral to the main line of analysis. Hence it may be safely omitted on first reading.

Proof:

Figure 3 illustrates the proof for R^2. Clearly as $\boldsymbol{y} \notin X$, we can draw a line through $\boldsymbol{y}$ which has X all on one side. A method of doing this

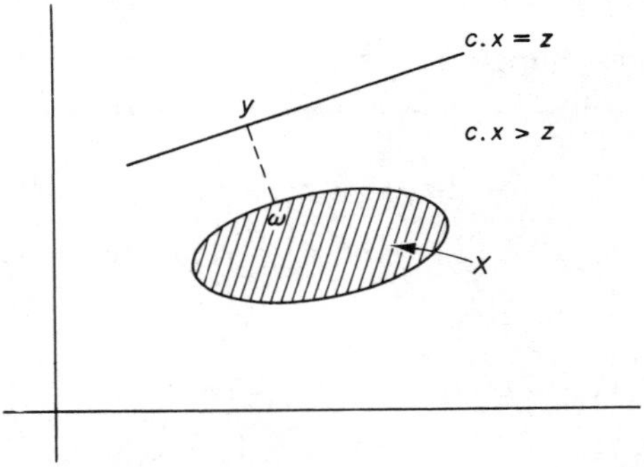

Figure 3

is to draw the shortest line from $\boldsymbol{y}$ to X (shown as $\boldsymbol{yw}$) and then take the perpendicular to this. The following argument does just this for R^n.

Assume $\boldsymbol{y} \notin X$. Choose $\boldsymbol{w} \in X$ such that:

$$|\boldsymbol{y} - \boldsymbol{w}| \leqslant |\boldsymbol{y} - \boldsymbol{x}| \qquad \forall\, \boldsymbol{x} \in X. \tag{2.2}$$

Then $\boldsymbol{w}$ is the 'nearest point of X to $\boldsymbol{y}$' – one can in fact prove rigorously that there is a single nearest point. Now pick $\boldsymbol{u} \in X$.

Clearly: $\lambda \boldsymbol{u} + (1 - \lambda)\boldsymbol{w} \in X$ for $0 \leqslant \lambda \leqslant 1$.

Hence from (2.2):

$$|(\lambda \boldsymbol{u} + (1 - \lambda)\boldsymbol{w}) - \boldsymbol{y}|^2 \geqslant |\boldsymbol{w} - \boldsymbol{y}|^2 \quad \text{for} \quad 0 \leqslant \lambda \leqslant 1. \tag{2.3}$$

Rewriting and expanding (2.3) we get:

$$\sum_{i=1}^{n} |w_i - y_i + \lambda(u_i - w_i)|^2 \geqslant |\boldsymbol{w} - \boldsymbol{y}|^2$$

i.e.

$$\sum_{i=1}^{n} |w_i - y_i|^2 + \lambda^2 . \sum_i |u_i - w_i|^2 + 2\lambda . \sum_i (w_i - y_i)(u_i - w_i)$$
$$\geqslant |\boldsymbol{w} - \boldsymbol{y}|^2$$

i.e.

$$|w - y|^2 + \lambda^2 . |u - w|^2 + 2\lambda(w - y) . (u - w) \geqslant |w - y|^2. \qquad (2.4)$$

Let $\lambda > 0$, divide (2.4) by λ and rearrange to give:

$$\lambda|u - w|^2 + 2(w - y) . (u - w) \geqslant 0. \qquad (2.5)$$

This holds for arbitrarily small $\lambda > 0$, so that by making λ small enough the first term can be made smaller than any preassigned number. Hence it must be the case that:

$$(w - y) . (u - w) \geqslant 0. \qquad (2.6)$$

Now note that $u - w = u - y - (w - y)$, so (2.6) can be rewritten as:

$$(w - y) . (u - y) \geqslant |w - y|^2$$

with $|w - y|^2 > 0$ as $w \in X$, $y \notin X$. Hence

$$(w - y) . u > (w - y) . y. \qquad (2.7)$$

Now define: $c = w - y$

$$z = (w - y) . y = c . y$$

and consider the hyperplane $c . x = z$.

As $c . y = z$, y lies on this hyperplane. But in (2.7) u is any point in X, and

$$c . u > z. \qquad (2.8)$$

Thus all points in X lie in one open half-space created by the hyperplane.

Q.E.D.

D.35. *Given a boundary point* $\mathbf{w}$ *of a convex set* X, *then* $\mathbf{c} . \mathbf{x} = \mathrm{z}$ *is called a SUPPORTING HYPERPLANE at* $\mathbf{w}$ *if* $\mathbf{c} . \mathbf{w} = \mathrm{z}$ *and all of* X *lies in one closed half-space generated by the hyperplane – i.e. if either* $\mathbf{c} . \mathbf{u} \geqslant \mathrm{z}\ \forall\ \mathbf{u} \in \mathrm{X}$, *or* $\mathbf{c} . \mathbf{u} \leqslant \mathrm{z}\ \forall\ \mathbf{u} \in \mathrm{X}$.

T.4. *Supporting Hyperplane Theorem*

If $\mathbf{w}$ *is a boundary point of a closed convex set, then there is at least one supporting hyperplane at* $\mathbf{w}$.

Proof: For R^2 or R^3 this theorem is intuitively appealing from a geometrical point of view, as is illustrated in Figure 4 below. The supporting hyperplane is tangential to the set X at $\boldsymbol{w}$. However to provide a formal proof of the theorem for R^n requires mathematical results beyond the scope of this book. So an outline of the proof will be sketched; those wishing to obtain a full proof should consult an advanced text such as Nikaido (1970).†

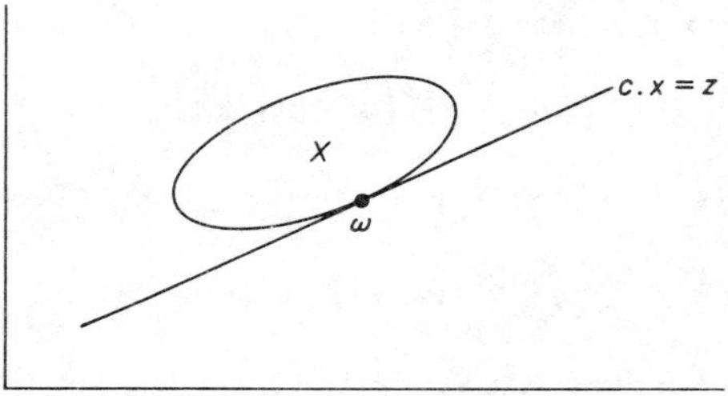

Figure 4

In proving T.3 we did not specifically show that the point $\boldsymbol{w}$ nearest to $\boldsymbol{y}$ was a boundary point of X. Clearly this must be the case. Now from (2.6) we know that: $\boldsymbol{c}\,.\,(\boldsymbol{u} - \boldsymbol{w}) \geqslant 0 \quad \forall \boldsymbol{u} \in X$,

i.e.
$$\boldsymbol{c}\,.\,\boldsymbol{u} \geqslant \boldsymbol{c}\,.\,\boldsymbol{w}. \tag{2.9}$$

Consider the hyperplane:

$$\boldsymbol{c}\,.\,\boldsymbol{x} = \boldsymbol{c}\,.\,\boldsymbol{w} = z, \tag{2.10}$$

$\boldsymbol{w}$ is on it, and by (2.9) every point in X is in the closed half-space $\{\boldsymbol{x} | \boldsymbol{c}\,.\,\boldsymbol{x} \geqslant z\}$. Thus the boundary point $\boldsymbol{w}$ has a supporting hyperplane.

We would expect, and it can be formally shown, that every boundary point has at least one exterior point to which it is closer than is any other point in X. Thus for any boundary point $\boldsymbol{w}$ we can find an exterior point $\boldsymbol{y}$ whose nearest point in X is $\boldsymbol{w}$, and for $\boldsymbol{w}$ the supporting hyperplane will be that in (2.10) with $\boldsymbol{c} = \boldsymbol{w} - \boldsymbol{y}$. In this manner the theorem may be proved.

† See Bibliography, p. 208.

Comments

(i) Even if X is not closed we can show that there is a supporting hyperplane at any boundary point $\boldsymbol{w}$.

(ii) The supporting hyperplane at boundary point $\boldsymbol{w}$ may not be unique; for example there will be an infinite number of supporting hyperplanes at $\boldsymbol{w}$ if $\boldsymbol{w}$ is a vertex of a triangle.

(iii) The idea of a supporting hyperplane may be regarded as formalising the idea of the tangent to the set at $\boldsymbol{w}$. In economic theory results may be formulated in terms of supporting hyperplanes rather than in terms of tangencies and differential calculus.

(iv) The theorem was stated for convex sets. The difference between convex and strictly convex sets here is that convex sets may have flat sections on their boundaries so that a single hyperplane may be the supporting hyperplane at many boundary points. This cannot occur with strictly convex sets.

T.5. *If* X *is a closed convex set bounded either from above or below (or both), then every supporting hyperplane of* X *contains an extreme point.*

Proof: Consider a supporting hyperplane of X at $\boldsymbol{w}$ defined by $\boldsymbol{c} . \boldsymbol{x} = \boldsymbol{c} . \boldsymbol{w}$. Then $\boldsymbol{c} . \boldsymbol{x} \geqslant \boldsymbol{c} . \boldsymbol{w}$ for all $\boldsymbol{x} \in X$. Let T be the intersection of X and the hyperplane; clearly it is a convex subset of X and is bounded in the same way as X. Note also that T is not empty because $\boldsymbol{w} \in T$.

We will first show that any extreme point of T must be an extreme point of X. Suppose that we can express some point $\boldsymbol{t} \in T$ as a strictly convex combination of points $\boldsymbol{x}_1, \boldsymbol{x}_2 \in X$. That is:

$$\boldsymbol{t} = \lambda \boldsymbol{x}_1 + (1 - \lambda)\boldsymbol{x}_2 \qquad (0 < \lambda < 1).$$

Then it must be the case that, if $\boldsymbol{x}_1 \neq \boldsymbol{x}_2$, for $\boldsymbol{x}_1, \boldsymbol{x}_2 \in T$. This follows because we know that $\boldsymbol{c} . \boldsymbol{x}_1 \geqslant z, \boldsymbol{c} . \boldsymbol{x}_2 \geqslant z$ – where $z = \boldsymbol{c} . \boldsymbol{w}$ – and that:

$$\boldsymbol{c} . \boldsymbol{t} = \lambda \boldsymbol{c} . \boldsymbol{x}_1 + (1 - \lambda)\boldsymbol{c} . \boldsymbol{x}_2 = z. \tag{2.11}$$

As λ, $(1 - \lambda) > 0$, (2.11) can only hold if $\boldsymbol{c} . \boldsymbol{x}_1 = z$, $\boldsymbol{c} . \boldsymbol{x}_2 = z$ – i.e. iff $\boldsymbol{x}_1, \boldsymbol{x}_2 \in T$. This says that if any point $\boldsymbol{t}$ in T may be expressed as a strictly convex combination of points in X, then it cannot be an extreme point of T. Thus an extreme point of T cannot be expressed as a strictly convex combination of points in X, and must therefore also be an extreme point of X.

Now we must show that T has an extreme point. Suppose it is bounded below (the argument is symmetrical for a set bounded from above), then there must be a point in T with the smallest first component. If there are several with this value for the first component, choose from these the set of those with the smallest second component, and continue until we have a unique point $\mathbf{t}^*$. Such a point must always exist, and we will show that it is an extreme point of T. If it were not, we could write:

$$\mathbf{t}^* = \lambda \mathbf{t}_1 + (1 - \lambda)\mathbf{t}_2, 0 < \lambda < 1, \mathbf{t}_1 \neq \mathbf{t}_2 \in T. \qquad (2.12)$$

But by the derivation of $\mathbf{t}^*$ this is only possible for $\mathbf{t}_1 = \mathbf{t}_2 = \mathbf{t}^*$. Hence $\mathbf{t}^*$ must be an extreme point.

Q.E.D.

Comment: This theorem is very important when we come to discuss linear programming.

T.6. *Separating Hyperplane Theorems*

If U, V *are two non-empty convex sets in* R^n *with no interior points in common, then there exists a non-zero* n*-vector* **c** *and a scalar* z *such that:*

$$\mathbf{c}.\mathbf{u} \geqslant z \quad \forall \quad \mathbf{u} \in U,$$
$$\mathbf{c}.\mathbf{v} \leqslant z \quad \forall \quad \mathbf{v} \in V.$$

The hyperplane $\mathbf{c}.\mathbf{x} = z$ *is called the separating hyperplane.*

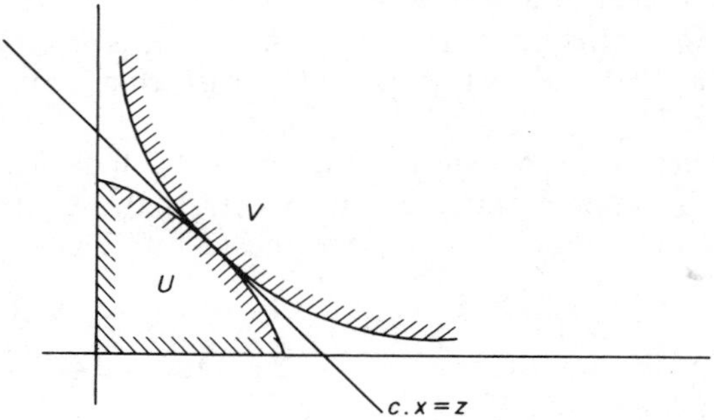

Figure 5

Proof: Figure 5 illustrates the theorem.

Let U, V be two non-empty convex sets in R^n, and $I(U)$, $I(V)$ be the interiors of U, V respectively. By assumption:

$$I(U) \cap I(V) = \varnothing. \qquad (2.13)$$

Clearly $I(U)$, $I(V)$ are convex. Let

$$W = I(U) - I(V). \qquad (2.14)$$

By T.2 W is convex. Suppose that $\mathbf{0} \in W$; then there exist a $\boldsymbol{u} \in I(U)$ and a $\boldsymbol{v} \in I(V)$ such that $\mathbf{0} = \boldsymbol{u} - \boldsymbol{v}$, i.e. $\boldsymbol{u} = \boldsymbol{v}$. Thus $\mathbf{0} \notin W$, and so by T.3 we can find a hyperplane through $\mathbf{0}$ with W contained in one closed half-space. In other words there exists a vector $\boldsymbol{c} \in R^n$ such that:

$$\boldsymbol{c} \,.\, \boldsymbol{w} \leqslant 0 \quad \forall\, \boldsymbol{w} \in W.$$

i.e.
$$\boldsymbol{c} \,.\, (\boldsymbol{u} - \boldsymbol{v}) \leqslant 0 \quad \forall\, \boldsymbol{u} \in U, \boldsymbol{v} \in V.$$

i.e.
$$\boldsymbol{c} \,.\, \boldsymbol{u} \leqslant \boldsymbol{c} \,.\, \boldsymbol{v} \quad \forall\, \boldsymbol{u} \in U, \boldsymbol{v} \in V.$$

Since U, V are non-empty we must therefore be able to find a scalar z such that:

$$\boldsymbol{c} \,.\, \boldsymbol{u} \leqslant z \leqslant \boldsymbol{c} \,.\, \boldsymbol{v} \quad \forall\, \boldsymbol{u} \in U, \boldsymbol{v} \in V.$$

Q.E.D.

Comments: (i) If the sets above share a single boundary point, then the separating hyperplane will be a supporting hyperplane to each set at this boundary point.

(ii) If the sets have many boundary points in common (only possible if they are convex but not strictly convex) then the separating hyperplane must contain all of these common points. Further the hyperplane must contain an extreme point for each set.

At the beginning of this chapter it was noted that the results embodied in T.1–T.6 together with the other properties of convex sets form the analytical basis for much of modern economic theory. To discuss this would take us considerably beyond the scope of this book, but as an illustration a brief example will be discussed. The problem in question is essentially a greatly simplified version of a general equilibrium model for an economy, and the analysis can be generalised and made rigorous for the complete model.

Illustration. Consider a Robinson Crusoe economy endowed with fixed supplies of factors. Goods, indexed by $1, \ldots, n$, may be produced using these factors; we define T, the production set, as the set of output vectors $\boldsymbol{x}$ compatible with the available factor supplies given the economy's technology. We will assume that this set is convex – a sufficient condition for this is that the production function for each good be concave (see Appendix for a definition of this). On the consumption side we assume that Robinson Crusoe has a consistent set of preferences over consumption vectors which may be represented by convex preference sets. A preference set is defined

WHITWORTH COLLEGE LIBRARY
SPOKANE, WASH. 99251

with respect to some consumption vector $\hat{\boldsymbol{x}}$ as the set of all consumption vectors which are either preferred to $\hat{\boldsymbol{x}}$ or are as good as $\hat{\boldsymbol{x}}$. Thus for any $\hat{\boldsymbol{x}}$ we have the set:

$$S(\hat{\boldsymbol{x}}) = \{\boldsymbol{x} \mid \boldsymbol{x} \text{ preferred or indifferent to } \hat{\boldsymbol{x}}\}.$$

and we assume that every $S(\hat{\boldsymbol{x}})$ is convex.†

We assume that Robinson Crusoe wishes to arrange production so that he reaches the highest possible level of utility. Suppose that $\boldsymbol{x}^*$ is the optimal production vector. Then the sets $S(\boldsymbol{x}^*)$ and T will share at least one boundary point – viz. $\boldsymbol{x}^*$, since it will be clear that if $S(\boldsymbol{x}^*)$ and T have interior points in common $\boldsymbol{x}^*$ cannot be optimal. As a result we can apply the separating hyperplane theorem. That is, we can find a vector $\boldsymbol{p}$ such that:

$$\boldsymbol{p} \,.\, \boldsymbol{x} \geqslant \boldsymbol{p} \,.\, \boldsymbol{x}^* \text{ for all } \boldsymbol{x} \in S(\boldsymbol{x}^*),$$

$$\boldsymbol{p} \,.\, \boldsymbol{x} \leqslant \boldsymbol{p} \,.\, \boldsymbol{x}^* \text{ for all } \boldsymbol{x} \in T.$$

In other words we can find a vector of prices for each good such that at these prices the value of production is maximised (i.e. given the production set T we cannot find an $\boldsymbol{x} \in T$ such that $\boldsymbol{p} \,.\, \boldsymbol{x} > \boldsymbol{p} \,.\, \boldsymbol{x}^*$) while the cost of attaining the consumption set $S(\boldsymbol{x}^*)$ is minimised. Thus we say that the optimal vector $\boldsymbol{x}^*$ is *supported* by a price system $\boldsymbol{p}$. From this we can, in the general case, proceed to discuss efficiency, competitive equilibria, and other standard results in economic theory. The use of the theorems established above to demonstrate the existence of supporting price vectors plays a very important part in microeconomic and general equilibrium theory, and also in the modern approach to optimization problems in general.

2.2 Problems

2.1. What are the complements of the following sets? Are the complements open or closed sets, or neither?
(i) $|\boldsymbol{x} - \boldsymbol{a}| < \varepsilon$, (ii) $|\boldsymbol{x} - \boldsymbol{a}| = \varepsilon$, (iii) $\boldsymbol{a} \,.\, \boldsymbol{x} < z$ and
(iv) $X = \{(x_1, x_2) \mid x_1, x_2 \geqslant 0; x_1 + x_2 \leqslant 1\}$.

2.2. Prove that there is no greatest number less than 1.

† A sufficient condition for every $S(\boldsymbol{x})$ to be convex is that Robinson Crusoe has a concave utility function $U(\boldsymbol{x})$.

2.3. Suppose $\boldsymbol{a} . \boldsymbol{x} = 0$ is a hyperplane in R^n. Prove that this is a subspace of R^n.

2.4. Is the union of convex sets $X_1, \ldots, X_n$ itself a convex set? Give an example to demonstrate your result.

2.5. Consider the hyperplane $x_1 - x_2 + 4x_3 - 2x_4 + 6x_5 = 1$. In which half-space does each of the following points lie?

(i) $(1, 1, 1, 1, 1)$; (ii) $(2, 7, -1, 0, -3)$ and (iii) $(0, 1, 1, 4, 1)$.

2.6. Which of the following sets are convex? (i) $X = \{(x_1, x_2)|x_1^2 + 2x_2^2 \leqslant 4\}$; (ii) $X = \{(x_1, x_2)| x_1x_2 \leqslant 1, x_1 \geqslant 0, x_2 \geqslant 0\}$; (iii) $X = \{(x_1, x_2)|x_1 \geqslant 4, x_2 \leqslant 5\}$ and (iv) $X = \{(x_1, x_2)|x_1^2 + x_2 \geqslant 1, x_1 \geqslant 0, x_2 \geqslant 0\}$.

2.7. Does theorem 3 remain unaltered if the convex set is open? Is it true if the set is not closed?

2.8. Given sets X below, find the equation for the supporting hyperplane at any boundary point (α, β). Further, given $\boldsymbol{y}$, find the equation for a hyperplane which contains $\boldsymbol{y}$, and includes X in one half-space.

(i) $X = \{\boldsymbol{x}|x_1^2 + x_2^2 \leqslant 1\}$; $\boldsymbol{y} = (2, 1)$.

(ii) $X = \{\boldsymbol{x}|2x_1 + x_2 \leqslant 3, x_1 - x_2 \geqslant 1\}$; $\boldsymbol{y} = (1, 2)$.

2.9. Determine the separating hyperplanes, if they exist, for the following pairs of sets in R^2: (i) $X = \{\boldsymbol{x}|x_1^2 + x_2^2 + 2x_1 \leqslant 0\}$; $Y = \{\boldsymbol{y}|y_1 \geqslant |y_2|\}$.

(ii) $X = \{\boldsymbol{x}|x_1^2 + x_2^2 \leqslant 8\}$; $Y = \{\boldsymbol{y}|y_1y_2 \geqslant 4, y_1 \geqslant 0\}$. What if the second set were $Y = \{\boldsymbol{y}|y_1 y_2 \geqslant 4\}$?

(iii) $X = \{\boldsymbol{x}|2x_1 + x_2 \leqslant 5, x_1 + 3x_2 \leqslant 10\}$; $Y = \{\boldsymbol{y}|4y_1 + y_2 \geqslant 7, y_1 + y_2 \geqslant 4\}$.

2.10. Prove that the set X of all convex combinations of a finite number of points $\boldsymbol{x}_i (i = 1, \ldots, n)$ is a convex set. Consider a finite number of points in R^2. Taking the points in triples (so that each triple represents the vertices of a triangle), is the set X the smallest convex set which includes all of the triangles?

Appendix Concave and Convex Functions

Definition: (i) *A real-valued function* $f(\mathbf{x})$ *defined on a convex subset* D *of* R^n *is CONCAVE if for any* $\mathbf{x}_1$ *and* $\mathbf{x}_2$ *in* D *and* $0 \leqslant \lambda \leqslant 1$,

$$f[\lambda\mathbf{x}_1 + (1 - \lambda)\mathbf{x}_2] \geqslant \lambda f(\mathbf{x}_1) + (1 - \lambda)f(\mathbf{x}_2);$$

(ii) $f(\mathbf{x})$ *is CONVEX if for* $\mathbf{x}_1, \mathbf{x}_2 \in D$ *and* $0 \leqslant \lambda \leqslant 1$,

$$f[\lambda\mathbf{x}_1 + (1 - \lambda)\mathbf{x}_2] \leqslant \lambda f(\mathbf{x}_1) + (1 - \lambda)f(\mathbf{x}_2).$$

In words a concave function is one for which every chord lies below or on the function itself, while a convex function has every chord above or on the function. In Figure 6 the function $f(x)$ is concave for $x \geqslant 0$, while $g(x)$ is convex. In fact they are strictly concave and convex respectively, where the addition of 'strictly' implies that the inequalities in the definition are strict. Note that a straight line is both a concave function and a convex function, but clearly it is neither strictly concave nor strictly convex.

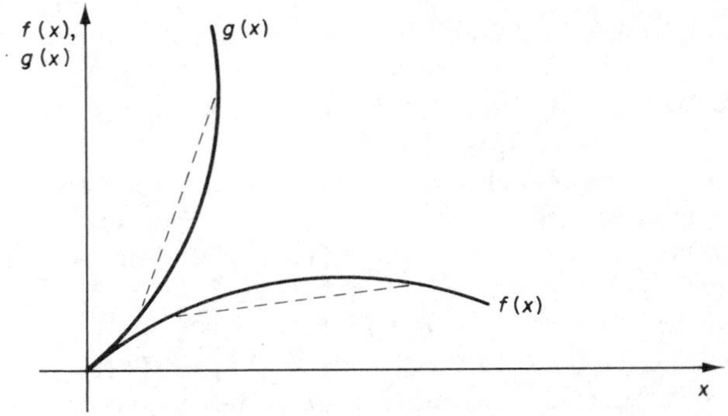

Figure 6

These definitions may be linked to our discussion of convex sets by the following proposition:

Theorem: (i) *The set of points on and below a concave function is convex;* (ii) *The set of points on and above a convex function is also convex.*

Proof: We will prove (i) and leave (ii) for the reader to prove as an exercise. Before proceeding with the proof we must define the set in which we are interested. It is that of all points on or below $f(\boldsymbol{x})$ in the figure. We call this B which is the set of ordered pairs $(\boldsymbol{x}, y)$ given by:

$$B = \{(\boldsymbol{x}, y) | \boldsymbol{x} \in D; y \leqslant f(\boldsymbol{x}), y \in R^1\}.$$

Consider $\boldsymbol{b}_1, \boldsymbol{b}_2 \in B$ where $\boldsymbol{b}_i = (\boldsymbol{x}_i, y_i)$ for $i = 1, 2$. Assuming $0 \leqslant \lambda \leqslant 1$ we have:

$$\lambda \boldsymbol{b}_1 + (1 - \lambda)\boldsymbol{b}_2 = \lambda(\boldsymbol{x}_1, y_1) + (1 - \lambda)(\boldsymbol{x}_2, y_2)$$
$$= (\lambda \boldsymbol{x}_1 + (1 - \lambda)\boldsymbol{x}_2, \lambda y_1 + (1 - \lambda)y_2).$$

But from the definition of a concave function:

$$\lambda f(\boldsymbol{x}_1) + (1 - \lambda)f(\boldsymbol{x}_2) \leqslant f(\lambda\boldsymbol{x}_1 + (1 - \lambda)\boldsymbol{x}_2)$$

and by assumption $y_1 \leqslant f(\boldsymbol{x}_1)$, $y_2 \leqslant f(\boldsymbol{x}_2)$.

So $\lambda y_1 + (1 - \lambda)y_2 \leqslant f(\lambda\boldsymbol{x}_1 + (1 - \lambda)\boldsymbol{x}_2)$.

Hence the pair $(\lambda\boldsymbol{x}_1 + (1 - \lambda)\boldsymbol{x}_2, \lambda y_1 + (1 - \lambda)y_2)$ is in B.

Q.E.D.

3 Linear Dependence and Bases

This chapter will primarily be investigating results obtainable by writing some given vector as a linear combination of vectors from some set. As an example consider the vector $\boldsymbol{x} = (x_1, x_2)$ in R^2. This vector may be written as a linear combination of the two vectors $\boldsymbol{e}_1 = (1, 0), \boldsymbol{e}_2 = (0, 1)$:

$$\boldsymbol{x} = (x_1, x_2) = x_1\boldsymbol{e}_1 + x_2\boldsymbol{e}_2. \tag{3.1}$$

D.36. *In* R^n *the set of* n*-vectors with 1 as their* i*th component* (i = 1, . . . , n) *and zeroes elsewhere is called the set of UNIT VECTORS. The* j*th unit vector—i.e. the member of the set with* 1 *as the* j*th component—is denoted by* $\mathbf{e}_j$.

Obviously any vector in R^n may be written as a linear combination of the n unit vectors for R^n.

There is no reason to confine ourselves to linear combinations of the unit vectors. Figure 7 illustrates the fact that given almost any pair of vectors in R^2 it is possible to write any other vector in R^2 as a linear combination (L.C.) of these. Thus the arbitrary vector $\boldsymbol{p}$ may be written as: $\boldsymbol{p} = \lambda\boldsymbol{x} + \mu\boldsymbol{y}$.

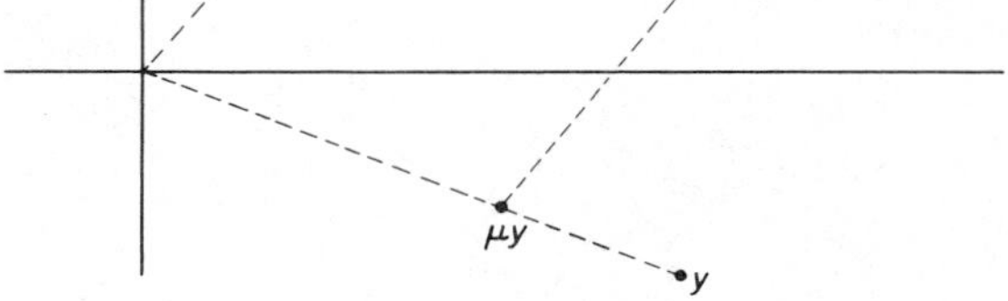

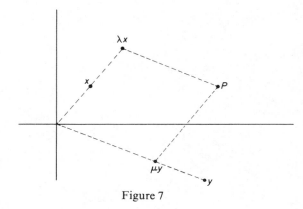

Figure 7

In effect $0X$ and $0Y$ are being used as axes. It will only not be possible to express any vector in R^2 as a L.C. of such a pair of vectors if both $\boldsymbol{x}$ and $\boldsymbol{y}$ lie on the same straight line through the origin, i.e. when $\boldsymbol{x} = \alpha\boldsymbol{y}$ for some scalar α. In that case only vectors lying on the same straight line will be expressible as L.C.s of $\boldsymbol{x}$ and $\boldsymbol{y}$.

These ideas are formalised in the following definitions and theorems.

D.37. *A set of vectors* $\mathbf{x}_1, \mathbf{x}_2, \ldots, \mathbf{x}_m$ *from* R^n *is said to be LINEARLY DEPENDENT if there exist scalars* λ_i *not all zero such that*

$$\lambda_1\mathbf{x}_1 + \lambda_2\mathbf{x}_2 + \ldots + \lambda_m\mathbf{x}_m = \sum_{i=1}^{m} \lambda_i\mathbf{x}_i = \mathbf{0}. \tag{3.2}$$

Otherwise – i.e. if the only set of λ_i *for which* (3.2) *holds is* $\lambda_1 = \lambda_2 = \ldots = \lambda_m = 0$ *– the vectors are said to be LINEARLY INDEPENDENT.*

We can restate the conclusion of the discussion above as: If we have two linearly independent (L.I.) vectors in R^2 then any other vector in R^2 can be expressed as a L.C. of these.

T.7. *The vectors* $\mathbf{x}_1, \mathbf{x}_2, \ldots, \mathbf{x}_m \in \mathrm{R}^n$ *are linearly dependent (L.D.) iff one of the vectors may be written as a L.C. of the others.*

Proof: (*a*) *Sufficiency.* Suppose – without loss of generality – that $\boldsymbol{x}_1$ is a linear combination of the other vectors. Thus

$$\boldsymbol{x}_1 = \lambda_2\boldsymbol{x}_2 + \lambda_3\boldsymbol{x}_3 + \ldots + \lambda_m\boldsymbol{x}_m$$

i.e.
$$(-1)\boldsymbol{x}_1 + \lambda_2\boldsymbol{x}_2 + \ldots + \lambda_m\boldsymbol{x}_m = \mathbf{0}. \tag{3.3}$$

But this satisfies the condition for the vectors to be L.D. since not all the coefficients are zero.

(*b*) *Necessity.* Suppose the vectors are L.D. Then

$$\sum_{i=1}^{m} \lambda_i\boldsymbol{x}_i = \mathbf{0} \text{ for some } \lambda_i \neq 0.$$

Suppose that $\lambda_j \neq 0$. Then:

$$\boldsymbol{x}_j = -\frac{\lambda_1}{\lambda_j}\boldsymbol{x}_1 - \ldots - \frac{\lambda_{j-1}}{\lambda_j}\boldsymbol{x}_{j-1} - \frac{\lambda_{j+1}}{\lambda_j}\boldsymbol{x}_{j+1} - \ldots - \frac{\lambda_m}{\lambda_j}\boldsymbol{x}_m$$

$$= \sum_{\substack{i=1\\ i\neq j}}^{m} \left(-\frac{\lambda_i}{\lambda_j}\right)\boldsymbol{x}_i. \tag{3.4}$$

Hence if the vectors are L.D. one is a L.C. of the others.

Q.E.D.

T.8. *If a set of vectors is L.I., then any subset is also L.I.*

Proof: Let $\boldsymbol{x}_1, \ldots, \boldsymbol{x}_m$ be L.I. Suppose that $\boldsymbol{x}_1, \ldots, \boldsymbol{x}_j$ $(j \leqslant m)$ are L.D., i.e. $\sum_{i=1}^{j} \lambda_i \boldsymbol{x}_i = \mathbf{0}$ for at least one λ_i not zero. Hence if we set $\lambda_{j+1} = \lambda_{j+2} = \ldots = \lambda_m = 0$ we have $\sum_{i=1}^{m} \lambda_i \boldsymbol{x}_i = \mathbf{0}$ for some λ_i (among the first j) not zero. But this contradicts the fact that $\boldsymbol{x}_1, \ldots, \boldsymbol{x}_m$ are L.I.

Q.E.D.

T.9. *If a set of vectors is L.D., then any larger set containing it is L.D.*

Proof: An exercise.

Consider a set of vectors from the space R^n. We shall say that the maximum number of L.I. vectors in this set is k if it contains at least one subset of k L.I. vectors, and there is no subset of more than k L.I. vectors.

T.10. *Suppose that* $\mathrm{k} < \mathrm{m}$ *is the maximum number of L.I. vectors in a subset* $\mathrm{X} = (\mathbf{x}_1, \mathbf{x}_2, \ldots, \mathbf{x}_m)$ *of* R^n. *Then given any L.I. subset of* k *vectors in* X *every other vector in* X *can be written as a L.C. of these.*

Proof: Label the vectors so that $\boldsymbol{x}_1, \ldots, \boldsymbol{x}_k$ are L.I. Then the set $\boldsymbol{x}_1, \ldots, \boldsymbol{x}_k, \boldsymbol{x}_r$ is L.D. for any $r = k+1, \ldots, m$. Hence $\sum_{i=1}^{k} \lambda_i \boldsymbol{x}_i + \lambda_r \boldsymbol{x}_r = \mathbf{0}$ for some λ not zero. But $\lambda_r \neq 0$ since otherwise $\Sigma \lambda_i \boldsymbol{x}_i = \mathbf{0}$ for some λ not zero which would contradict the fact that $\boldsymbol{x}_1, \ldots, \boldsymbol{x}_k$ are L.I. Hence we can write:

$$\boldsymbol{x}_r = -\left[\frac{\lambda_1}{\lambda_r}\boldsymbol{x}_1 + \ \ldots \ + \frac{\lambda_k}{\lambda_r}\boldsymbol{x}_r\right] \tag{3.5}$$

Q.E.D.

We will now generalise the idea that any vector in R^2 can be written as a L.C. of two L.I. vectors in R^2 (i.e. two vectors which are not on the same line through the origin).

D.38. *A set of vectors from* R^n *is said to SPAN* R^n *if every vector in* R^n *can be written as a linear combination of the vectors in this set.*

The same definition can equally be used with reference to any vector space. It will be clear that any set of vectors which contains at least two L.I. vectors will span R^2. However, all elements of the set other than the pair of L.I. vectors are in some sense redundant. This points to the fact that it would be useful to find the set with the smallest number of elements which spans the space under consideration. For R^2 this set will contain two vectors. In general the vectors in the smallest spanning set will be L.I. If they were not L.I., then we know that one or more vectors could be expressed as a L.C. of the others. Using this L.C. in place of the vector we could clearly eliminate it from the set while retaining a set which spans the vector space.

Suppose, on the other hand, that a set of vectors spanning the space is L.I. Then we cannot drop a vector from the set and still span R^n. For if we did this we could no longer express every vector in the space as a L.C. of the vectors left in the set – in particular we could not so express the vector just dropped. Hence in looking for the smallest set spanning the space we are seeking the largest set of L.I. vectors in the space.

D.39. *A BASIS for a vector space is a L.I. set of vectors from the space which spans the entire space.*

It will be clear from our discussion of R^2 that we should not expect a basis for a space to be unique. There will, in general, be infinitely many bases for a particular space.

T.11. *A basis for* R^n *is provided by the* n *unit vectors.*

Proof: Clearly these vectors are L.I. But we have seen that any vector in R^n can be expressed as a L.C. of these; hence they span R^n.

Q.E.D.

T.12. *The representation of any vector in terms of a set of basis vectors is unique; that is, any vector in* R^n *can be written as a L.C. of a set of basis vectors in only one way.*

Proof: Let $\boldsymbol{y} \in R^n$, and $\boldsymbol{x}_1, \ldots, \boldsymbol{x}_n$ be a basis for R^n. Suppose we can write $\boldsymbol{y}$ as a linear combination of the $\boldsymbol{x}_i$ in two ways: i.e.

$$\boldsymbol{y} = \sum_{i=1}^{n} \lambda_i \boldsymbol{x}_i$$

$$\boldsymbol{y} = \sum_{i=1}^{n} \mu_i \boldsymbol{x}_i.$$

Subtracting we get:

$$\Sigma(\lambda_i - \mu_i)\boldsymbol{x}_i = \mathbf{0} \tag{3.6}$$

But the $\boldsymbol{x}_i$ are L.I., so this implies that $\lambda_i - \mu_i = 0$ for all i. Thus

$\lambda_i = \mu_i$, and the representation of $\boldsymbol{y}$ with respect to any given basis is unique.

Q.E.D.

We now introduce the following important concept:

D.40. *The DIMENSION of a vector space is the maximum number of L.I. vectors which can be found in that space.*

This links up with the usual idea of dimension if we note that R^n is of dimension n. The n unit vectors in R^n are L.I., while any other vector in R^n can be expressed as a L.C. of these. This shows that the dimension of R^n cannot exceed n. It is more difficult to prove that the dimension of R^n cannot be less than n, i.e. that it is not possible to span R^n with less than n vectors. However, formally we will state the theorem:

T.13. *The vector space* R^n *– i.e. the set of all* n*-component vectors – has dimension* n. *Any set of* $(\mathrm{n} + 1)$ *vectors from* R^n *must be L.D.*

In general it will be clear that any set of n L.I. vectors from a space of dimension n spans that space since any other vector in the space can be written as a L.C. of the n vectors. Formally:

T.14. *Any L.I. set of* n *vectors in an* n*-dimensional vector space forms a basis for that space.*

A further result which follows naturally from the above ideas is:

T.15. *All bases for a space have the same number of elements.*

Proof: The proof proceeds by replacing vectors in a basis. We consider two bases for the space:

$$\left.\begin{matrix}\boldsymbol{x}_1, \ldots, \boldsymbol{x}_m \\ \boldsymbol{y}_1, \ldots, \boldsymbol{y}_n\end{matrix}\right\} \qquad (m \neq n)$$

Then $\boldsymbol{y}_1 = \sum_{i=1}^{m} \lambda_i \boldsymbol{x}_i$ with at least one $\lambda_i \neq 0$. Suppose, without loss of generality, $\lambda_m \neq 0$. Then:

$$\boldsymbol{x}_m = \frac{1}{\lambda_m}\left[\boldsymbol{y}_1 - \sum_{i=1}^{m-1} \lambda_i \boldsymbol{x}_i\right]. \tag{3.7}$$

This implies that the first basis set may be written as:

$$\boldsymbol{x}_1, \ldots, \boldsymbol{x}_{m-1}, \frac{1}{\lambda_m}\left[\boldsymbol{y}_1 - \sum_1^{m-1} \lambda_i \boldsymbol{x}_i\right].$$

In effect this implies that a new basis would be:

$$\boldsymbol{x}_1, \ldots, \boldsymbol{x}_{m-1}, \boldsymbol{y}_1.$$

Then:

$$\boldsymbol{y}_2 = \sum_1^{m-1} \mu_i \boldsymbol{x}_i + \mu \boldsymbol{y}_1 \tag{3.8}$$

where some $\mu_i \neq 0$ $(i = 1, \ldots, m-1)$, since otherwise the $\boldsymbol{y}$'s would be L.D. Thus we can gradually replace $\boldsymbol{x}$'s in the basis by $\boldsymbol{y}$'s to give a final basis set of the following possible forms:

(i) $\boldsymbol{x}_1, \ldots, \boldsymbol{x}_{m-n}, \boldsymbol{y}_1, \ldots, \boldsymbol{y}_n$ for $m > n$;
(ii) $\boldsymbol{y}_1, \ldots, \boldsymbol{y}_n$ for $m = n$;
(iii) $\boldsymbol{y}_1, \ldots, \boldsymbol{y}_{n-m}$ for $m < n$.

But (i) is not possible because the set $\boldsymbol{y}_1, \ldots, \boldsymbol{y}_n$ is a basis, so that the $\boldsymbol{x}$'s are linear combinations of vectors in this basis. In other words the set of vectors in (i) is not L.I. On the other hand (iii) contradicts our assumption that $\boldsymbol{y}_1, \ldots, \boldsymbol{y}_n$ is a basis. Hence (ii) must hold.

Q.E.D.

It is frequently convenient to use special sets of basis vectors. Two of these are:

(*a*) *Orthogonal basis* – a set of basis vectors for a space such that any pair of vectors in the set are orthogonal. In other words, if the set is $\boldsymbol{x}_1, \ldots, \boldsymbol{x}_n$, then

$$\boldsymbol{x}_i \cdot \boldsymbol{x}_j = 0 \qquad (\text{all } i, j, i \neq j).$$

(b) *Orthonormal basis* – an orthogonal basis satisfying the requirement that:

$$\boldsymbol{x}_i \cdot \boldsymbol{x}_i = 1 \text{ for all } i.$$

The set of unit vectors $\boldsymbol{e}_1, \ldots, \boldsymbol{e}_n$ is an example of an orthonormal basis for R^n.

An alternative way of writing the conditions satisfied by the vectors in an orthonormal basis is:

$$\boldsymbol{x}_i \cdot \boldsymbol{x}_j = \delta_{ij} \text{ all } i, j$$

where $\delta_{ij} = 1$ if $i = j$, $\delta_{ij} = 0$ if $i \neq j$. In this δ_{ij} is known as the *Kronecker* δ; it is an extremely useful piece of notation.

Finally we return to the idea of a subspace to show that the set of all vectors which can be written as linear combinations of some given vectors forms a subspace. Suppose we are given $\boldsymbol{x}_1, \ldots, \boldsymbol{x}_r \in R^n$, and let

$$\boldsymbol{z}_1 = \sum_{i=1}^{r} \lambda_i \boldsymbol{x}_i, \quad \boldsymbol{z}_2 = \sum_{i=1}^{r} \mu_i \boldsymbol{x}_i.$$

Then

$$\alpha_1 \boldsymbol{z}_1 + \alpha_2 \boldsymbol{z}_2 = \sum_{i=1}^{r} (\alpha_1 \lambda_i + \alpha_2 \mu_i) \boldsymbol{x}_i, \tag{3.9}$$

so that the set of $\boldsymbol{z}$'s is closed under linear combinations and thus forms a subspace spanned by the vectors $\boldsymbol{x}_i$ $(i = 1, \ldots, r)$.

3.1 Problems

3.1. Prove that any set of vectors containing the null vector $(0, 0, \ldots, 0)$ cannot form a basis for a vector space. Can such a set span the space?

3.2. Prove that any two n-vectors are linearly dependent if and only if one of the vectors is a scalar multiple of the other.

3.3. Prove that the m unit n-vectors $\boldsymbol{e}_1, \ldots, \boldsymbol{e}_m$ form a basis for a subspace of R^n $(n > m)$.

3.4. Consider three linearly independent vectors $\boldsymbol{a}$, $\boldsymbol{b}$ and $\boldsymbol{c}$. Are the three vectors $\boldsymbol{a} + \boldsymbol{b}$, $\boldsymbol{b} + \boldsymbol{c}$, and $\boldsymbol{a} + \boldsymbol{c}$ linearly independent?

3.5. Is the dimension of a vector space unique?

3.6. Prove that any linearly independent set of m n-vectors can be supplemented by additional vectors to form a basis for R^n $(n > m)$.

3.7. Are the following sets of vectors linearly dependent or independent?

(i) (1, 2, 0, 0), (0, 1, 3, 0), (0, 0, 5, 0), (0, 1, 4, 2);

(ii) (4, 3, 2, 1), (0, −1, −2, −3), (8, 3, −2, −7);

(iii) (3, 4), (2, 3);

(iv) (1, −1, −1), (4, 3, 1), (−1, 1, 1);

(v) (3, 4), (2, 3), (3, 3).

Which of these sets span either R^2, R^3 or R^4? Which of these sets forms a basis for either R^2, R^3, R^4?

3.8. Let $\boldsymbol{a}, \boldsymbol{b}, \boldsymbol{c}, \boldsymbol{d}$ be vectors such that $a_i = 1, b_i = i, c_i = i^2, d_i = 1 + i + i^2$ for $i = 1, \ldots, n$. Prove that the set of $\boldsymbol{a}, \boldsymbol{b}, \boldsymbol{c}, \boldsymbol{d}$ is linearly dependent but that any three of the vectors form a linearly independent set.

3.9. Show that a set of m vectors forms a basis for R^n if and only if they are linearly independent and $m = n$.

3.10. Find a basis for the vector space V for which $\boldsymbol{x} \in V$ if $\boldsymbol{x} = (x_1, x_2, \ldots, x_{n-1}, \sum_{j=1}^{n-1} a_j x_j)$. What is the dimension of V?

3.11. Prove that a set of mutually orthogonal non-zero vectors $(\boldsymbol{x}_i \cdot \boldsymbol{x}_j = 0 \;\; \forall\, i \neq j)$ is linearly independent. Why is it important that $\boldsymbol{x}_i \cdot \boldsymbol{x}_j = 0$ for all i *not equal* to j?

3.12. How would you convert a set of n linearly independent vectors which forms a basis for a vector space V into an orthonormal basis for V? Find an orthonormal basis (i) for R^3, (ii) for the space spanned by (1, −1, 2), (5, 0, 3).

3.13. Find a basis for the vector space $V = \{\boldsymbol{x} \in V \mid \boldsymbol{x} = (x_1, \ldots, x_m, x_{m+1}, \ldots, x_n)\}$ where $x_{m+i} = \sum_{j=1}^{m} a_{ij} x_j$, $i = 1, \ldots, n-m$. Consider the two vector spaces $U = \{\boldsymbol{u} \in U \mid \boldsymbol{u} = \sum_{k=1}^{m-1} b_k \boldsymbol{x}_k \text{ where } \boldsymbol{x}_k \in V\}$ and $W = \{\boldsymbol{z} \in W \mid \boldsymbol{z} = (\boldsymbol{x} \cdot \boldsymbol{u}, -\boldsymbol{x} \cdot \boldsymbol{u})\}$. Show that the basis for V also spans U, and write down a basis for W.

4 Matrices

D.41. *A MATRIX is a rectangular array of numbers arranged in rows and columns. More particularly an* m × n *matrix is a set of* m . n *elements arranged in* m *rows and* n *columns.*

Thus $\begin{bmatrix} 1 & 1 \\ 0 & 1 \end{bmatrix}$ is a 2 × 2 matrix,

while [1 2 3] is a 1 × 3 matrix – alternatively, of course, it is a 3-component row vector. The general matrix is written:

$$A = \|a_{ij}\| = \begin{bmatrix} a_{11} & a_{12} & a_{13} \cdots & a_{1n} \\ a_{21} & a_{22} & \cdots & a_{2n} \\ \vdots & & & \\ a_{m1} & a_{m2} & \cdots & a_{mn} \end{bmatrix}$$

where a_{ij} refers to the element in the ith row and the jth column.

Notice that we may regard a matrix as an ordered set of vectors.

Thus $A = [\boldsymbol{a}_1 \ \ \boldsymbol{a}_2 \ \ \ldots \ \ \boldsymbol{a}_n]$ where $\boldsymbol{a}_j$ is the column vector $\begin{bmatrix} a_{1j} \\ \vdots \\ a_{mj} \end{bmatrix}$. Similarly we could write A as a column of row vectors. This will be useful in due course, and also links matrix operations to similar vector operations.

4.1 Matrix Operations

D.42. *EQUALITY. Two matrices* **A** *and* **B** *are defined to be equal,* **A** = **B**, *if and only if they are identical, i.e. if the corresponding elements are equal.*

Thus, $A = B$ iff $a_{ij} = b_{ij}$ for all i, j, and hence matrix equality is only defined for matrices of the same order. Note that by extension we may define matrix inequalities in precisely the same way as we did vector inequalities. Thus:

$$A > B \text{ iff } a_{ij} > b_{ij} \qquad \text{all } i, j.$$

$$A \geqslant B \text{ iff } a_{ij} \geqq b_{ij} \qquad \text{all } i, j.$$

D.43. *MULTIPLICATION BY A SCALAR. Given a matrix* **A** *and a scalar λ, the product of the two – written* **A**λ *or* λ**A** *– is:*

$$\lambda \mathbf{A} = ||\lambda a_{ij}|| = \begin{bmatrix} \lambda a_{11} & \cdots & \lambda a_{1n} \\ \vdots & & \vdots \\ \lambda a_{m1} & & \lambda a_{mn} \end{bmatrix}$$

D.44. *ADDITION. The sum* **C** *of two* m × n *matrices* **A** *and* **B** *is an* m × n *matrix whose elements are given by:* $c_{ij} = a_{ij} + b_{ij}$.

Thus two matrices are added by adding corresponding elements. Clearly addition is only defined for matrices with the same numbers of rows and columns. Further, it may be shown that the associative, commutative, and distributive rules apply for these last two operations.

Matrix Multiplication

In discussing the product of two matrices or of a vector and a matrix we have to distinguish between the result of pre-multiplying ***A*** by ***B*** – written ***BA*** – and that of post-multiplying ***A*** by ***B*** – written ***AB***. As a preliminary to defining the product of two matrices it is helpful to start by defining the product of a vector and a matrix.

D.45A. *The result of post-multiplying an* m × n *matrix* **A** *by a column* n*-vector* **x**, *written* **Ax**, *is defined to be the column* m*-vector whose* i*th component is* $\sum_{j=1}^{n} a_{ij}x_j$.

Note: This multiplication is only defined if the number of columns of ***A*** equals the number of rows of ***x*** (i.e. the number of elements).

D.45B. *The result of pre-multiplying an* m × n *matrix* **A** *by a row* m*-vector* **y**, *written* **yA**, is *defined to be the row* n*-vector whose* j*th component is* $\sum_{i=1}^{m} y_i a_{ij}$.

Note: In this case the product is only defined if the number of rows of ***A*** equals the number of columns of ***y*** (i.e. the number of elements of ***y***).

Clearly only if $\boldsymbol{A}$ is $n \times n$ and the vector has n components is it possible to pre-and post-multiply $\boldsymbol{A}$ by the same vector in row and column form. $\boldsymbol{A}$ is then called an nth order square matrix.

If we consider these definitions we note that the products may be restated in terms of vector products. For instance:

$$\sum_{i=1}^{m} y_i a_{ij} = \boldsymbol{y}. \begin{bmatrix} a_{1j} \\ \vdots \\ a_{mj} \end{bmatrix} = \boldsymbol{y} \,.\, \boldsymbol{a}_j \tag{4.1}$$

where $\boldsymbol{a}_j$ is the vector forming the jth column in the matrix $\boldsymbol{A}$. Hence it follows that:

$$\boldsymbol{y} \,.\, \boldsymbol{A} = [\boldsymbol{y} \,.\, \boldsymbol{a}_1, \boldsymbol{y} \,.\, \boldsymbol{a}_2, \ldots, \boldsymbol{y} \,.\, \boldsymbol{a}_n]. \tag{4.2}$$

Similarly

$$\boldsymbol{A}\boldsymbol{x} = \begin{bmatrix} \boldsymbol{a}^1 \,.\, \boldsymbol{x} \\ \boldsymbol{a}^2 \,.\, \boldsymbol{x} \\ \vdots \\ \boldsymbol{a}^m \,.\, \boldsymbol{x} \end{bmatrix} \tag{4.3}$$

where $\boldsymbol{a}^i$ is the vector forming the ith row in the matrix $\boldsymbol{A}$.

Now suppose that we wish to obtain the product $\boldsymbol{C} = \boldsymbol{AB}$ of two matrices $\boldsymbol{A}$, which is $m \times n$, and $\boldsymbol{B}$, which is $n \times r$. Write $\boldsymbol{A}$ as a column of row vectors and $\boldsymbol{B}$ as a row of column vectors. Thus we have:

$$\boldsymbol{C} = \begin{bmatrix} \boldsymbol{a}^1 \\ \boldsymbol{a}^2 \\ \vdots \\ \boldsymbol{a}^m \end{bmatrix} [\boldsymbol{b}_1 \; \ldots \; \boldsymbol{b}_r]. \tag{4.4}$$

Then so long as each of these vectors has the same number of elements – implying that the number of columns in $\boldsymbol{A}$ must equal the number of rows in $\boldsymbol{B}$ – we can perform the multiplication either by post-multiplying each vector $\boldsymbol{a}^i$ by $\boldsymbol{B}$ or pre-multiplying each vector $\boldsymbol{b}_j$ by $\boldsymbol{A}$. If we arrange the result in the appropriate order by rows i or columns j we get:

$$\boldsymbol{C} = \begin{bmatrix} \boldsymbol{a}^1 \boldsymbol{B} \\ \boldsymbol{a}^2 \boldsymbol{B} \\ \vdots \\ \boldsymbol{a}^m \boldsymbol{B} \end{bmatrix} = [\boldsymbol{A}\boldsymbol{b}_1 \; \boldsymbol{A}\boldsymbol{b}_2 \; \ldots \; \boldsymbol{A}\boldsymbol{b}_r]. \tag{4.5}$$

Expanding these gives us:

$$\boldsymbol{C} = \begin{bmatrix} \boldsymbol{a}^1 \,.\, \boldsymbol{b}_1 & \ldots & \boldsymbol{a}^1 \,.\, \boldsymbol{b}_r \\ \vdots & & \\ \boldsymbol{a}^m \,.\, \boldsymbol{b}_1 & & \boldsymbol{a}^m \,.\, \boldsymbol{b}_r \end{bmatrix} \tag{4.6}$$

Thus the typical element c_{ik} of $\boldsymbol{C}$ is given by

$$c_{ik} = \boldsymbol{a}^i \cdot \boldsymbol{b}_k = \sum_{j=1}^{n} a_{ij} b_{jk}. \tag{4.7}$$

Note that the result of post-multiplying an $m \times n$ matrix by an $n \times r$ matrix is an $m \times r$ matrix.

These ideas can now be expressed formally:

D.46. *Two matrices* **A** *and* **B** *are said to be CONFORMABLE for multiplication to yield the product* **AB** *iff the number of columns in* **A** *equals the number of rows in* **B**.

D.47. *The operation of multiplication is defined only for matrices which are conformable for multiplication. Given an* $\mathrm{m} \times \mathrm{n}$ *matrix* **A** *and an* $\mathrm{n} \times \mathrm{r}$ *matrix* **B**, *the product* **AB** *is defined to be the* $(\mathrm{m} \times \mathrm{r})$ *matrix* **C** *whose elements are computed from those of* **A** *and* **B** *according to:*

$$\mathrm{c}_{\mathrm{ik}} = \sum_{\mathrm{j}=1}^{\mathrm{n}} \mathrm{a}_{\mathrm{ij}} \mathrm{b}_{\mathrm{jk}} \qquad (\mathrm{i} = 1, \ldots, \mathrm{m};\ \mathrm{k} = 1, \ldots, \mathrm{r}).$$

Note: It is very important to remember that matrix multiplication is *not commutative.* In general $\boldsymbol{AB} \neq \boldsymbol{BA}$ just as $\boldsymbol{Ax} \neq \boldsymbol{x}'\boldsymbol{A}$. In many cases if $\boldsymbol{A}$ and $\boldsymbol{B}$ are conformable to yield $\boldsymbol{AB}$, they are not conformable to yield $\boldsymbol{BA}$. In fact they would only be conformable for both products either if one is $m \times n$ and the other $n \times m$ or if, as a special case, both are square of the same order. Only in the latter case can the two product matrices be compared, since only then do they have the same numbers of rows and columns. Even then:

$$\boldsymbol{AB} = \left\| \sum_{j=1}^{n} a_{ij} b_{jk} \right\| \text{ while } \boldsymbol{BA} = \left\| \sum_{j=1}^{n} b_{ij} a_{jk} \right\|$$

so that the two will not in general be the same.

Examples:

(1)
$$\boldsymbol{A} = \begin{bmatrix} 2 & 1 \\ 3 & 1 \end{bmatrix}, \boldsymbol{B} = \begin{bmatrix} 2 \\ 1 \end{bmatrix}$$

$\boldsymbol{AB} = \begin{bmatrix} 5 \\ 7 \end{bmatrix}$, but $\boldsymbol{BA}$ does not exist.

(2)
$$\boldsymbol{A} = \begin{bmatrix} 1 \\ 2 \\ 0 \end{bmatrix}, \boldsymbol{B} = [3 \ \ 4 \ \ 1]$$

$$\boldsymbol{AB} = \begin{bmatrix} 1 \\ 2 \\ 0 \end{bmatrix} [3 \; 4 \; 1] = \begin{bmatrix} 3 & 4 & 1 \\ 6 & 8 & 2 \\ 0 & 0 & 0 \end{bmatrix}$$

$$\boldsymbol{BA} = [3 \; 4 \; 1] \begin{bmatrix} 1 \\ 2 \\ 0 \end{bmatrix} = 11.$$

This demonstrates the point that the scalar product of two vectors is equivalent to post-multiplying a row vector by a column vector with the same number of components.

(3)
$$\boldsymbol{A} = \begin{bmatrix} 2 & 1 \\ 0 & 3 \end{bmatrix}, \quad \boldsymbol{B} = \begin{bmatrix} 4 & 0 \\ 1 & 3 \end{bmatrix}$$

$$\boldsymbol{AB} = \begin{bmatrix} 9 & 3 \\ 3 & 9 \end{bmatrix}, \quad \boldsymbol{BA} = \begin{bmatrix} 8 & 4 \\ 2 & 10 \end{bmatrix}$$

$$\boldsymbol{AB} \neq \boldsymbol{BA}.$$

Though matrix multiplication is not commutative it is possible to show that it follows the associative and distributive rules: i.e.

$$(\boldsymbol{AB})\boldsymbol{C} = \boldsymbol{A}(\boldsymbol{BC}) = \boldsymbol{ABC} \qquad (4.8)$$

$$\boldsymbol{A}(\boldsymbol{B} + \boldsymbol{C}) = \boldsymbol{AB} + \boldsymbol{AC}. \qquad (4.9)$$

The demonstration of these is left as an exercise.

4.2 Matrix Concepts

There are a number of special matrices and other concepts which need to be defined.

D.48. *A matrix all of whose elements are zero is called a NULL or ZERO MATRIX and is denoted by* $\boldsymbol{0}$.

D.49. *The IDENTITY MATRIX of order* n, *denoted by* $\mathbf{I}$ *or* $\mathbf{I}_n$, *is an* nth *order square matrix with 1's along the main diagonal and zeroes elsewhere*

$$\mathbf{I} = \begin{bmatrix} 1 & 0 & & 0 \\ 0 & 1 & & \vdots \\ 0 & 0 & \ddots & \\ \vdots & \vdots & & 0 \\ 0 & & & 1 \end{bmatrix}$$

Using the Kronecker δ, we may write: $\boldsymbol{I} = \|\delta_{ij}\|$.

Examining the identity matrix it should be clear that if A is an nth order square matrix

$$AI_n = I_nA = A \tag{4.10}$$

while if A is $m \times n$, then

$$I_mA = A = AI_n. \tag{4.11}$$

In other words I is the matrix equivalent to 1 in the real number system. Note also that the identity matrix can be written as: $I = [e_1 \; e_2 \; \ldots \; e_n]$.

D.50. *For any scalar* λ *the square matrix* $\mathbf{S} = ||\lambda\delta_{ij}|| = \lambda\mathrm{I}$ *is called a SCALAR MATRIX.*

D.51. *For scalars* λ_i, *a square matrix* $\mathbf{D} = ||\lambda_i\delta_{ij}||$ *is called a DIAGONAL MATRIX.*

On some occasions it is of interest to interchange rows and columns in a matrix. The new form is defined by:

D.52. *The TRANSPOSE of a matrix* $\mathbf{A} = ||\mathrm{a}_{ij}||$ *is a matrix formed from* $\mathbf{A}$ *by interchanging rows and columns so that row* i *of* A *becomes column* i *of the transposed matrix. The transpose is denoted by* $\mathbf{A}'$ *and*

$$\mathbf{A}' = ||\mathrm{a}_{ji}||$$

i.e. if a'_{ij} *is the* ij*th element of* $\mathbf{A}'$, *then* $\mathrm{a}'_{ij} = \mathrm{a}_{ji}$.

Examples:

(i) $$A = \begin{bmatrix} 1 & 3 \\ 2 & 5 \end{bmatrix}, \quad A' = \begin{bmatrix} 1 & 2 \\ 3 & 5 \end{bmatrix}$$

(ii) $$A = \begin{bmatrix} 1 & 3 & 4 \\ 0 & 1 & 0 \end{bmatrix}, \quad A' = \begin{bmatrix} 1 & 0 \\ 3 & 1 \\ 4 & 0 \end{bmatrix}$$

Note that if A is $m \times n$, A' is $n \times m$, and that: $I' = I, (A')' = A$. Further it can be shown that if $C = A + B$ is defined, then

$$C' = A' + B'$$

while if $D = AB$ exists then

$$D' = (AB)' = B'A'.$$

This last result can be generalised so that:

$$(A_1A_2 \; \ldots \; A_n)' = A'_nA'_{n-1} \; \ldots \; A'_1. \tag{4.12}$$

All these results are left as exercises for the reader.

It will now be clear why we used x' to denote a row vector when assuming that x was a column vector. Treating x as a $n \times 1$ matrix its transpose x' is an $1 \times n$ matrix – that is a row vector. In a similar manner we see that many of the definitions of operations on vectors may be expressed in terms of matrix operations. In particular, if x, y are column vectors their scalar product $x \cdot y$ may be written as the result of post-multiplying an $1 \times n$ matrix by a $n \times 1$ matrix. Thus:

$$x \cdot y = \sum_{i=1}^{n} x_i y_i = x'y. \tag{4.13}$$

The transpose enables us to define a very important type of matrix:

D.53. *A SYMMETRIC MATRIX is a matrix* $\mathbf{A}$ *for which:* $\mathbf{A} = \mathbf{A}'$.

Note: A symmetric matrix must be square and its elements satisfy: $a_{ij} = a_{ji}$,

e.g. $$\begin{bmatrix} 2 & 0 & 7 \\ 0 & 3 & 5 \\ 7 & 5 & 1 \end{bmatrix} \text{ is symmetric.}$$

D.54. *A SKEW-SYMMETRIC MATRIX is a matrix* $\mathbf{A}$ *for which:* $\mathbf{A} = -\mathbf{A}'$.

Note: The diagonal elements of a skew-symmetric matrix must be all zero.

4.3 Elementary Operations

We will examine certain operations on the columns (or rows) of a matrix which can be used to simplify a matrix while leaving it unaltered in certain fundamental respects. The discussion will refer only to operations on columns; however, every statement can be rephrased in terms of operations on rows.

D.55. *There are three types of ELEMENTARY OPERATION which may be carried out on the columns of a matrix. They are:*

(i) *the interchange of two columns,*

(ii) *the multiplication of each element in a column by any scalar* $\lambda \neq 0$,

(iii) *the addition, to each element of the* j*th column, of* λ *times the corresponding element of the* i*th column.*

Suppose that we have any $m \times n$ matrix, then we can use these operations to reduce the matrix to one of two forms: either (*a*)

$$\begin{bmatrix}
a_{11} & 0 & 0 & \dots & & 0 & 0\dots 0 \\
a_{21} & a_{22} & 0 & 0 & & 0 & 0 \\
a_{31} & a_{32} & a_{33} & 0 & & 0 & 0 \\
 & & & a_{44} & \dots & 0 & 0 \\
 & & & & \ddots & 0 & 0 \\
a_{k1} & a_{k2} & \dots & & \ddots & a_{kk} & 0 \\
 & & & & & a_{k+1,k} & 0 \\
 & & & & & \vdots & \\
a_{m1} & & & & & a_{mk} & 0 \quad 0
\end{bmatrix}$$

or (*b*)

$$\begin{bmatrix}
a_{11} & 0 & 0 \dots 0 \\
a_{21} & a_{22} & 0 \\
a_{31} & & a_{33} \\
 & & \ddots \quad 0 \\
 & & \ddots \quad a_{nn} \\
 & & \quad\; a_{n+1,n} \\
 & & \quad\; \vdots \\
a_{m1} & \dots & \quad\; a_{mn}
\end{bmatrix}$$

In general: $a_{ii} \neq 0 \qquad i = 1, \dots, k, \qquad k \leqslant n.$
$a_{i,i+j} = 0 \qquad \text{for } j > 0.$
$a_{i,i-j}$ may have any value for $j > 0$.

Thus we generate a matrix whose first k columns ($k \leqslant n$) are non-zero, and the first non-zero element in the ith column lies in the ith row ($i \leqslant k$). This type of matrix is called an *echelon matrix*.

We will examine how to perform such a transformation. If the original matrix consists entirely of zeroes, the result is trivial. Otherwise, assume the matrix contains a non-zero element. By interchanging (permuting) the rows and columns we can bring this to the upper left-hand corner. Then, by subtracting from every column the first column multiplied by some suitable coefficient, we can make all the other elements of the first row vanish. If there are no non-zero elements among the remaining elements – i.e. among those outside the 1st row and 1st column – we stop. Otherwise if there is a non-zero element among these, then by suitably rearranging rows and columns we bring this to the (2, 2) position and make all the elements in the 2nd row following it vanish. These operations do not affect the first row and column. Continuing in this fashion we reduce the matrix to one of the forms illustrated above.

Example:

$$\text{Reduce} \quad \begin{bmatrix} 1 & 2 & 3 \\ 4 & 5 & 6 \\ 7 & 8 & 9 \end{bmatrix} \quad \text{to an echelon matrix.}$$

Subtract 2 × the 1st column from the second, and 3 × the 1st from the 3rd. This gives

$$\begin{bmatrix} 1 & 0 & 0 \\ 4 & -3 & -6 \\ 7 & -6 & -12 \end{bmatrix}$$

Now subtract 2 × the 2nd column from the 3rd which gives the echelon matrix:

$$\begin{bmatrix} 1 & 0 & 0 \\ 4 & -3 & 0 \\ 7 & -6 & 0 \end{bmatrix}$$

Clearly this procedure is quite general and can be used to transform any matrix into an echelon matrix.

Now it can be shown that the elementary column operations discussed above can be performed by post-multiplying the matrix by an appropriate matrix $\boldsymbol{F}$ which will be of a very simple type. For instance, if we consider the matrix in the above example, then post-multiplying it by

$$\begin{bmatrix} 0 & 1 & 0 \\ 1 & 0 & 0 \\ 0 & 0 & 1 \end{bmatrix}$$

would interchange the first two columns, while post-multiplication by

$$\begin{bmatrix} 1 & 0 & 0 \\ 0 & 2 & 0 \\ 0 & 0 & 1 \end{bmatrix}$$

would multiply the second column by 2. Finally post-multiplication by

$$\begin{bmatrix} 1 & 2 & 0 \\ 0 & 1 & 0 \\ 0 & 0 & 1 \end{bmatrix}$$

will add 2 times the first column to the second. For:

$$\begin{bmatrix} 1 & 2 & 3 \\ 4 & 5 & 6 \\ 7 & 8 & 9 \end{bmatrix} \begin{bmatrix} 1 & 2 & 0 \\ 0 & 1 & 0 \\ 0 & 0 & 1 \end{bmatrix} = \begin{bmatrix} 1 & 2+2 & 3 \\ 4 & 8+5 & 6 \\ 7 & 14+8 & 9 \end{bmatrix}$$

In fact the matrix $\boldsymbol{F}$ which performs these operations is found by performing on the identity matrix the appropriate elementary operation.

For elementary row operations on a matrix we pre-multiply it by a matrix $\boldsymbol{E}$ obtained by elementary row operations on the identity matrix of the appropriate order. Thus by a combination of pre-multiplication by matrices $\boldsymbol{E}_i$ and post-multiplication by matrices $\boldsymbol{F}_i$ any matrix can be transformed into an echelon matrix.

4.4 The Rank of a Matrix

D.56A. *The column rank of a matrix is defined as the maximum number of L.I. columns in the matrix.*

D.56B. *The row rank of a matrix is defined as the maximum number of L.I. rows in the matrix.*

These definitions treat the columns and rows of a matrix as vectors and use the concepts of linear dependence and independence developed earlier. To find the maximum number of L.I. vectors one could solve sets of simultaneous equations to determine the existence of a set of scalars giving a L.C. of the vectors equal to zero. However, this is laborious, and we must seek quicker ways of establishing L.D. or L.I.

We can show that the elementary operations defined in D.55 do not affect the appropriate rank – column rank for column operations, row rank for row operations. This follows because:

(*a*) Neither interchanging vectors in the matrix nor multiplying them by a non-zero scalar affects the L.D. or L.I. of a set of vectors.

(*b*) If the set of vectors is L.D., then replacing the system $\boldsymbol{x}_1, \ldots, \boldsymbol{x}_n$ for which $\Sigma\mu_i\boldsymbol{x}_i = \boldsymbol{0}$ by $\boldsymbol{x}_1, \ldots, \boldsymbol{x}_k + \lambda\boldsymbol{x}_j, \ldots, \boldsymbol{x}_n$ must imply that

$$\sum_{i \neq k} \mu_i \boldsymbol{x}_i + \mu_k \hat{\boldsymbol{x}}_k - \mu_k \lambda \boldsymbol{x}_j = \boldsymbol{0} \tag{4.14}$$

where $\hat{\boldsymbol{x}}_k$ is the new kth vector $(= \boldsymbol{x}_k + \lambda\boldsymbol{x}_j)$ in place of $\boldsymbol{x}_k$. Hence the set remains L.D. Similarly it can be shown that if the new set is

L.D., then the original set must have been L.D. Thus a L.I. set of vectors remains L.I. after a series of elementary operations.

Alternatively the proposition may be demonstrated by noting that we are in effect obtaining the dimension of the subspace spanned by the rows/columns of the matrix. This subspace is the set of all L.C.'s of these vectors. Let the subspace spanned by the original columns be L_1 and that spanned by the new columns be L_2. All L.C.'s of vectors in the new set are also L.C.'s of the vectors in the old set; hence $L_2 \subset L_1$. But note that: $\boldsymbol{x}_k' = (\boldsymbol{x}_k + \lambda \boldsymbol{x}_j) - \lambda \boldsymbol{x}_j$ so that all vectors in the old set can be written as L.C.'s of the new set; this implies $L_1 \subset L_2$. Thus $L_1 = L_2$; so the spaces spanned are the same, and the dimension is unaffected by elementary operations. It is also straightforward to show that row operations leave the column rank unaffected and vice-versa. This is left as an exercise.

If we now examine the echelon matrix produced by elementary operations on the original matrix, it is clear that all the non-zero columns are L.I. Hence the column rank of the original matrix may be read off. In the general case it will be $k(\leqslant n)$ where k is the number of non-zero columns.

T.16. *The row rank of any matrix* **A** *is equal to the column rank of the matrix. Thus the number of L.I. rows in the matrix equals the number of L.I. columns.*

Proof: Consider the echelon matrix derived by elementary operations on $\boldsymbol{A}$. The rows are n-vectors in which all but the first k components of the vectors are zero. They, therefore, span a vector space whose dimension is at most k. But the first k rows are clearly L.I., and so the dimension of the vector space spanned by the rows is at least k. Hence the row rank of the matrix must be k – that is it is equal to the column rank.

Q.E.D.

Note: By a series of row operations on the echelon matrix it would be possible to reduce the last $(m - k)$ rows to all zeroes.

Now that we know that the row rank must equal the column rank we will refer only to the rank of a matrix – written $r(\boldsymbol{A})$.

T.17. *If* **A** *is an* m × n *matrix,* r(**A**) *cannot exceed the smaller of* m *or* n.

Proof: Suppose $m \leqslant n$; then the maximum number of L.I. rows cannot exceed m, i.e. $r(\boldsymbol{A}) \leqslant m$. Similarly for $n \leqslant m$.

Q.E.D.

For square matrices the following definition is used:

D.57. *A square matrix of order* n *is said to be SINGULAR if the rank is less than* n, *and to be NON-SINGULAR if the rank equals* n.

The following results about ranks are useful:

T.18. *If two matrices* **A**, **B** *are such that their product* **AB** *is defined, then the rank of* **AB** *satisfies:*

$$\mathrm{r}(\boldsymbol{AB}) \leqslant \min\,[\mathrm{r}(\boldsymbol{A}), \mathrm{r}(\boldsymbol{B})].$$

Proof: Suppose that $\boldsymbol{A}$ is $m \times p$, $\boldsymbol{B}$ is $p \times n$. Let $\boldsymbol{C} = \boldsymbol{AB} =$

$$\begin{bmatrix} \boldsymbol{a}^1 . \boldsymbol{b}_1 & \dots & \boldsymbol{a}^1 . \boldsymbol{b}_n \\ \boldsymbol{a}^m . \boldsymbol{b}_1 & \dots & \boldsymbol{a}^m . \boldsymbol{b}_n \end{bmatrix}$$

as in (4.6). We first show that $r(\boldsymbol{C}) \leqslant r(\boldsymbol{B})$. If $r(\boldsymbol{B}) = n$, this follows from T.17. If $r(\boldsymbol{B}) < n$, we consider any set of k columns from $\boldsymbol{C}$ where $r(\boldsymbol{B}) < k \leqslant n$. Without loss of generality suppose these are the first k columns in $\boldsymbol{C}$. The corresponding set of k column vectors in $\boldsymbol{B}$ must be L.D. (since $r(\boldsymbol{B}) < k$), so that there exist scalars λ_i – not all zero – such that:

$$\lambda_1\boldsymbol{b}_1 + \lambda_2\boldsymbol{b}_2 \dots + \lambda_k\boldsymbol{b}_k = \boldsymbol{0}. \tag{4.15}$$

Now form a system of equations by pre-multiplying this equation in turn by each $\boldsymbol{a}^i$ $\quad (i = 1, \dots, m)$

$$\begin{aligned} &\lambda_1\boldsymbol{a}^1 . \boldsymbol{b}_1 + \lambda_2\boldsymbol{a}^1 . \boldsymbol{b}_2 \dots + \lambda_k\boldsymbol{a}^1 . \boldsymbol{b}_k = 0 \\ &\lambda_1\boldsymbol{a}^m . \boldsymbol{b}_1 + \dots + \lambda_k\boldsymbol{a}^m . \boldsymbol{b}_k = 0. \end{aligned} \tag{4.16}$$

This system may be written as:

$$\lambda_1 \begin{bmatrix} \boldsymbol{a}^1 . \boldsymbol{b}_1 \\ \boldsymbol{a}^m . \boldsymbol{b}_1 \end{bmatrix} + \dots + \lambda_k \begin{bmatrix} \boldsymbol{a}^1 . \boldsymbol{b}_k \\ \boldsymbol{a}^m . \boldsymbol{b}_k \end{bmatrix} = \boldsymbol{0}.$$

But these k column vectors are the first k columns of $\boldsymbol{C}$. Since at least one $\lambda_i \neq 0$ these must be L.D.; hence any k columns from $\boldsymbol{C}$ are L.D. if $k > r(\boldsymbol{B})$. Thus $r(\boldsymbol{C}) \leqslant r(\boldsymbol{B})$.

Similarly by regarding $\boldsymbol{C}$ as a column of row vectors and using the same approach – post-multiplying the rows of $\boldsymbol{A}$ by columns of $\boldsymbol{B}$ – we see that $r(\boldsymbol{C}) \leqslant r(\boldsymbol{A})$.

Q.E.D.

T.19. *If a matrix of rank* k *is pre-multiplied (or post-multiplied) by a non-singular matrix, the rank of the product matrix is* k.

Proof: This is a special case of T.18, in which the equality sign holds. It will be later proved when certain other concepts have been introduced.

T.20. *The matrix representing any sequence of elementary operations is non-singular.*

Proof: Such a matrix is obtained by performing the appropriate operations on the identity matrix. But the identity matrix $\boldsymbol{I}_n$ has rank n, while the elementary operations do not alter rank.

Q.E.D.

4.5 Problems

4.1. Let $\boldsymbol{A} = \begin{bmatrix} 5 & 2 & 1 \\ 3 & 1 & 1 \\ 6 & 3 & 1 \end{bmatrix}$ and $\boldsymbol{B} = \begin{bmatrix} 5 & 3 & 6 \\ 2 & 1 & 3 \\ 1 & 1 & 1 \end{bmatrix}$

(a) compute $(\boldsymbol{A} + \boldsymbol{B})$, $\boldsymbol{AB}$ and $\boldsymbol{BA}$;
(b) is there any relationship between $\boldsymbol{A}$ and $\boldsymbol{B}$?

4.2. For an $(m \times n)$ matrix $\boldsymbol{A} = \|a_{ij}\|$ and a $(p \times m)$ matrix $\boldsymbol{B} = \|b_{ij}\|$, decide in what sense $\boldsymbol{A}$ and $\boldsymbol{B}$ are conformable and write out the i, jth element of any product that exists. What is the order of any such product?

4.3. Let $\boldsymbol{A}$ be an $(m \times n)$ matrix $(m > n)$. What is the rank of $\boldsymbol{A}$ when
(i) the columns of $\boldsymbol{A}$ are linearly independent;
(ii) the rows of $\boldsymbol{A}$ are linearly independent?
Check first that the question is sensible.

4.4 Find the rank of $\mathbf{A} = \begin{bmatrix} 1 & 2 & 1 \\ 1 & 0 & 3 \\ 4 & 8 & 6 \end{bmatrix}$

and the rank of $\boldsymbol{B} = \begin{bmatrix} 2 & -3 \\ 3 & 1 \\ 11 & 0 \end{bmatrix}$.

What is the rank of $\boldsymbol{AB}$?

4.5. (a) Prove that $(\boldsymbol{A}_1 + \boldsymbol{A}_2 + \ldots + \boldsymbol{A}_n)' = \boldsymbol{A}_1' + \boldsymbol{A}_2' + \ldots + \boldsymbol{A}_n'$.
(b) Prove by induction that $(\boldsymbol{A}_1\boldsymbol{A}_2 \ldots \boldsymbol{A}_n)' = \boldsymbol{A}_n'\boldsymbol{A}_{n-1}' \ldots \boldsymbol{A}_2'\boldsymbol{A}_1'$.

4.6. Let $\boldsymbol{A} = \|a_i\delta_{ij}\|$ and $\boldsymbol{B} = \|b_i\delta_{ij}\|$ be two diagonal matrices.

Compute $\boldsymbol{AB}$ and $\boldsymbol{BA}$ and state the relationship between them.

4.7. Let A be an $n \times n$ matrix. The nullity of $\boldsymbol{A} = n(\boldsymbol{A})$ is defined as $n - r(\boldsymbol{A})$, where $r(\boldsymbol{A}) =$ rank of $\boldsymbol{A}$. Prove that $r(\boldsymbol{A}) + r(\boldsymbol{B}) - n \leqslant r(\boldsymbol{AB})$ for any conformable matrix $\boldsymbol{B}$. Does this result conflict with Theorem 19?

4.8. Prove that the set of all 2×2 matrices is a vector space. Consider two matrices $\boldsymbol{A} = \begin{bmatrix} 0 & 0 \\ 1 & 0 \end{bmatrix}$ and $\boldsymbol{B} = \begin{bmatrix} 0 & 1 \\ 0 & 0 \end{bmatrix}$. Show that the four matrices $\boldsymbol{A}$, $\boldsymbol{B}$, $\boldsymbol{I}$ and $\boldsymbol{AB}$ form a basis for this vector space.

4.9. Let $\boldsymbol{A}$ be an $n \times n$ matrix and $\boldsymbol{x}$ a $(n \times 1)$ column vector. Is it true that there is a vector $\boldsymbol{x} \neq \boldsymbol{0}$ such that $\boldsymbol{Ax} = \boldsymbol{0}$ if

(i) $r(\boldsymbol{A}) < n$;

(ii) $\boldsymbol{A}$ is non-singular?

4.10. Reduce the following matrices to echelon form

(i) $\boldsymbol{A} = \begin{bmatrix} 1 & 3 & 0 & 1 \\ 2 & -5 & 7 & 2 \\ 0 & -3 & -2 & 5 \\ 4 & 1 & 2 & 3 \end{bmatrix}$ (ii) $\boldsymbol{B} = \begin{bmatrix} a & b & c & d \\ a^2 & b^2 & c^2 & d^2 \\ a^3 & b^3 & c^3 & d^3 \end{bmatrix}$

(iii) $\boldsymbol{C} = \begin{bmatrix} 1 & 3 & 6 + 2k \\ 3 & 10 & 17 + 6k \\ 1 & 4 & 7 + 3k \end{bmatrix}$.

For what values of k will the rank of $\boldsymbol{C}$ be 1, 2 or 3?

4.11. Do matrices satisfy the rule that the product of two numbers a and b can only be zero if one of them is zero?

4.12. Prove that any matrix $\boldsymbol{A}$ may be written as the sum of a symmetric matrix and a skew-symmetric matrix.

Appendix Partitioning of Matrices

It is often useful to study or manipulate a matrix in terms of subsets of elements in it. To do this we can form a *submatrix* of some matrix $\boldsymbol{A}$ by omitting all but k rows and s columns of $\boldsymbol{A}$ to give a $k \times s$ matrix. A matrix may be *partitioned* into submatrices if the submatrices are formed by taking the first f rows, the next g rows, and so on until all the rows are exhausted and also the first p columns, the next q columns, etc. In this way each submatrix formed by a set of rows and columns will be an element in the partitioned matrix.

Suppose $\boldsymbol{A}$ is $m \times n$; it may be partitioned as follows

$$\boldsymbol{A} = \left[\begin{array}{c:c:c} \boldsymbol{A}_{11} & \boldsymbol{A}_{12} & \boldsymbol{A}_{13} \\ \hdashline \boldsymbol{A}_{21} & \boldsymbol{A}_{22} & \boldsymbol{A}_{23} \end{array}\right] \begin{array}{l} g \text{ rows} \\ (m-g) \text{ rows} \end{array}$$
$$p \text{ cols} \quad q \text{ cols} \quad (n-p-q) \text{ cols}$$

Clearly $\boldsymbol{A}$ could be partitioned in many ways; familiar alternatives are to partition $\boldsymbol{A}$ into a column of row vectors, that is each submatrix is a $1 \times n$ matrix, or into a row of column vectors.

We will want to be able to perform the standard operations on partitioned matrices. To do this it is clear that the rules of conformability must be observed since the elements of a partitioned matrix are themselves matrices.

(*a*) *Addition.* Suppose we have another $m \times n$ matrix $\boldsymbol{B}$ partitioned in the same way as $\boldsymbol{A}$ so that $\boldsymbol{A}_{11}, \boldsymbol{B}_{11}$ are of the same order as are $\boldsymbol{A}_{12}, \boldsymbol{B}_{12}$, and so on. Then it follows directly from the definition of matrix addition that:

$$\boldsymbol{A} + \boldsymbol{B} = \left[\begin{array}{c:c:c} \boldsymbol{A}_{11} + \boldsymbol{B}_{11} & \boldsymbol{A}_{12} + \boldsymbol{B}_{12} & \boldsymbol{A}_{13} + \boldsymbol{B}_{13} \\ \hdashline \boldsymbol{A}_{21} + \boldsymbol{B}_{21} & \boldsymbol{A}_{22} + \boldsymbol{B}_{22} & \boldsymbol{A}_{23} + \boldsymbol{B}_{23} \end{array}\right]$$

We may that $\boldsymbol{A}$ and $\boldsymbol{B}$ are *conformably partitioned* for the operation of addition.

(*b*) *Scalar Multiplication.* This is trivial since directly from the rule for scalar multiplication we see that for any scalar λ;

$$\lambda \boldsymbol{A} = \left[\begin{array}{c:c:c} \lambda \boldsymbol{A}_{11} & \lambda \boldsymbol{A}_{12} & \lambda \boldsymbol{A}_{13} \\ \hdashline \lambda \boldsymbol{A}_{21} & \lambda \boldsymbol{A}_{22} & \lambda \boldsymbol{A}_{23} \end{array}\right]$$

(*c*) *Matrix Multiplication.* We have already examined the special case of multiplying matrices partitioned into vectors. Reconsidering the procedure giving (4.6) we note that not only must the two matrices be conformable for multiplication, but also that the submatrices (vectors) to be multiplied must be conformable for multiplication. In addition it is clear that regarding the matrix as a collection of single elements is but a special case of partitioning where each submatrix is 1×1. Thus the nature of the multiplication rule must be the same for matrices in normal or partitioned form. Hence, if $\boldsymbol{C} = \boldsymbol{B}\boldsymbol{A}$, we must have

$$\boldsymbol{C}_{ij} = \sum_k \boldsymbol{B}_{ik} \boldsymbol{A}_{kj}.$$

This requires that every product $\boldsymbol{B}_{ik}\boldsymbol{A}_{kj}$ must exist, i.e. that the number of columns in submatrix $\boldsymbol{B}_{ik}$ must equal the number of rows in $\boldsymbol{A}_{kj}$ for every i and j. This can only be true if, given that $\boldsymbol{B}$ is $m \times k$ and $\boldsymbol{A}$ is $k \times n$, the columns of $\boldsymbol{B}$ are partitioned in the same way as the rows of $\boldsymbol{A}$. Suppose this is the case, i.e. that:

$$\boldsymbol{B} = \left[\begin{array}{c:c} \boldsymbol{B}_{11} & \boldsymbol{B}_{12} \\ \hdashline \boldsymbol{B}_{21} & \boldsymbol{B}_{22} \end{array}\right] \begin{array}{l} f \text{ rows} \\ (m-f) \text{ rows} \end{array} \qquad \boldsymbol{A} = \left[\begin{array}{c:c} \boldsymbol{A}_{11} & \boldsymbol{A}_{12} \\ \hdashline \boldsymbol{A}_{21} & \boldsymbol{A}_{22} \end{array}\right] \begin{array}{l} g \text{ rows} \\ (k-g) \text{ rows} \end{array}$$

$$\quad g \text{ cols} \quad (k-g) \text{ cols} \qquad\qquad\qquad h \text{ cols} \quad (n-h) \text{ cols}$$

then

$$\boldsymbol{C} = \left[\begin{array}{c:c} \boldsymbol{B}_{11}\boldsymbol{A}_{11} + \boldsymbol{B}_{12}\boldsymbol{A}_{21} & \boldsymbol{B}_{11}\boldsymbol{A}_{12} + \boldsymbol{B}_{12}\boldsymbol{A}_{22} \\ \hdashline \boldsymbol{B}_{21}\boldsymbol{A}_{11} + \boldsymbol{B}_{22}\boldsymbol{A}_{21} & \boldsymbol{B}_{21}\boldsymbol{A}_{12} + \boldsymbol{B}_{22}\boldsymbol{A}_{22} \end{array}\right] \begin{array}{l} f \text{ rows} \\ (m-f) \text{ rows} \end{array}$$

$$h \text{ cols} \qquad\qquad (n-h) \text{ cols}$$

This result may be confirmed by direct multiplication of the matrices.

Thus we have seen that, if properly partitioned, submatrices may be treated as if they were ordinary elements of the matrix. This can be very useful in computational or analytical work when matrices of large order or of a special structure are being handled. For instance various standard computer programs for handling matrices rely on partitioning. Alternatively the interpretation of input–output tables or of certain types of social survey material rely on partitioning via the grouping of industries or interrelated variables. However, in all cases the importance of properly partitioning the original matrix before performing any operations must be emphasised.

5 Linear Equations

5.1 The Leontief System

Consider an economy composed of a number of interlinked industries; each produces one good only using one process to do so. Label industries by i where $i = 1, \ldots, n$. Industry i produces an output x_i of the ith good using inputs from the other industries. We assume that the input requirements are directly proportional to the amount of the output produced; specifically, to produce one unit of the ith output a_{ji} units of the jth good are required as an input so that if x_i units are produced the input demand for good j will be $a_{ji}x_i$. Summing over all industries we thus get the input demand for the j th good. In addition we assume that there is a final demand (for consumption, export, etc.) of f_j. Now if the system is to be in equilibrium the demand for and supply of each good must be equal. So for the typical ith industry we must have:

$$x_i = a_{i1}x_1 + a_{i2}x_2 + \ldots + a_{in}x_n + f_i$$

or

$$-a_{i1}x_1 - a_{i2}x_2 \ldots + (1 - a_{ii})\,x_i \ldots - a_{in}x_n = f_i \tag{5.1}$$

There will be n such equations and the whole system can be expressed in matrix form as:

$$\begin{bmatrix} 1 - a_{11} & -a_{12} \ldots & -a_{1n} \\ -a_{21} & 1 - a_{22} \ldots & -a_{2n} \\ & & \\ -a_{n1} & & 1 - a_{nn} \end{bmatrix} \begin{bmatrix} x_1 \\ x_2 \\ \vdots \\ x_n \end{bmatrix} = \begin{bmatrix} f_1 \\ f_2 \\ \vdots \\ f_n \end{bmatrix}$$

Notice that if we write the matrix of technical or input–output coefficients as $\boldsymbol{A}$, i.e. $\boldsymbol{A} = \|a_{ij}\|$, then this equation system may be written as:

$$[\boldsymbol{I} - \boldsymbol{A}]\boldsymbol{x} = \boldsymbol{f} \tag{5.2}$$

where $\boldsymbol{x}$ and $\boldsymbol{f}$ are the column vectors of output and final demand.

A vector $\boldsymbol{x}$ satisfying these equations will give the outputs for each industry such that interindustry and final demands can just be fulfilled. A search for such a set of outputs is therefore one for a solution vector to the matrix equation stated above. If we now write $[\boldsymbol{I} - \boldsymbol{A}]$ as a row of column vectors $\hat{\boldsymbol{a}}_i$ where:

$$\hat{\boldsymbol{a}}_i = \begin{bmatrix} -a_{1i} \\ \vdots \\ 1 - a_{ii} \\ \vdots \\ -a_{ni} \end{bmatrix}$$

then it is possible to write the equation system as:

$$x_1\hat{\boldsymbol{a}}_1 + x_2\hat{\boldsymbol{a}}_2 + \dots + x_n\hat{\boldsymbol{a}}_n = \boldsymbol{f}. \tag{5.3}$$

In other words the problem becomes one of finding scalars x_i making the linear combination of the columns of $[\boldsymbol{I} - \boldsymbol{A}]$ equal to the final demand vector.

We know that this will always be possible if the vector $\boldsymbol{f}$ lies in the subspace spanned by the column vectors $\hat{\boldsymbol{a}}_1, \dots, \hat{\boldsymbol{a}}_n$. In general, that is for any $\boldsymbol{f}$, there will always be a solution if the $\hat{\boldsymbol{a}}_i$ form a basis for R^n, since then any other vector in R^n can be expressed as a linear combination of them.

There is one economic complication: only non-negative values for the x_i make sense. We will return to this later. For the moment we will pursue the general problem of finding an $\boldsymbol{x}$ satisfying the system of m equations in n variables

$$\boldsymbol{A}\boldsymbol{x} = \boldsymbol{b}$$

where $\boldsymbol{A}$ is $m \times n$, and $\boldsymbol{x}$ is an n-vector, $\boldsymbol{b}$ is an m-vector.

5.2 Systems of Linear Equations

D.58. *A LINEAR EQUATION is one involving only the first powers of the unknown variables.*

It derives its name from the fact that the set of points satisfying a linear equation in two variables is a straight line in R^2. For a linear equation in n variables this set will be a hyperplane in R^n. A system of linear equations is a set of equations involving a given set of variables. The Leontief system discussed in the previous section is an example of a system of equations. In that case, as in general, we want to find a solution vector for the system. Suppose that we have a general system of m equations in n variables. Then by a solution vector we mean an n-vector $\boldsymbol{c} = (c_1, c_2, \ldots, c_n)$ which, if $c_1, \ldots, c_n$ are substituted for the unknowns $x_1, , , , , x_n$, will turn each equation into an identity. There may be zero, one, or many solutions (or solution vectors) to a particular system of equations.

Noting the geometrical interpretation of linear equations given above the solution to a system of equations in two variables will be the point(s) where the lines given by each equation intersect. This case shows that it is a simple matter to find systems of equations with no solutions and many solutions (e.g. two parallel lines and two identical lines) as well as systems with a single solution. In the general case of R^n the solution to a system will be the intersection of the hyperplanes associated with each equation.

D.59. *A system of equations with at least one solution is called COMPATIBLE. If it has no solutions it is INCOMPATIBLE.*

D.60. *If a compatible system of equations has only one solution it is said to be DETERMINATE; otherwise it is INDETERMINATE.*

T.21. *The set of solution vectors to a system of linear equations is convex.*

Proof: By definition a unique solution vector forms a convex set of one element only. If the system is indeterminate consider two solution vectors $\boldsymbol{x}_1$ and $\boldsymbol{x}_2$. Let

$$\boldsymbol{y} = \lambda \boldsymbol{x}_1 + (1 - \lambda)\boldsymbol{x}_2 \qquad (0 \leqslant \lambda \leqslant 1)$$

Then:

$$\begin{aligned} \boldsymbol{A}\boldsymbol{y} &= \lambda \boldsymbol{A}\boldsymbol{x}_1 + (1 - \lambda)\boldsymbol{A}\boldsymbol{x}_2 \\ &= \boldsymbol{b}. \end{aligned}$$

Hence any convex combination of two solution vectors is also a solution, and is thus a member of the set.

Q.E.D.

In order to apply the point developed in the previous section, that a solution vector is a set of scalars which when used to make an L.C. of the column vectors of $\boldsymbol{A}$ gives $\boldsymbol{b}$, we divide systems of linear equations into two types.

D.61. *The system of simultaneous linear equations:* **Ax** = **b** *is said to be HOMOGENEOUS if* **b** = *0. Otherwise the system is NON-HOMOGENEOUS.*

A. *Homogeneous Systems*

Every homogeneous system $\boldsymbol{Ax} = \mathbf{0}$ has at least one solution, namely the trivial possibility $\boldsymbol{x} = \mathbf{0}$. For a non-trivial solution it is necessary that the columns of $\boldsymbol{A}$ be L.D., since only then will it be possible to form a non-trivial L.C. of the $\boldsymbol{a}_i$ equal to $\mathbf{0}$. Hence:

T.22. *The homogeneous system* $\mathbf{Ax} = \mathbf{0}$ *will have a non-trivial solution iff*

$$\mathrm{r}(\mathbf{A}) < \mathrm{n}.$$

This suggests a number of possible cases:

(i) $n > m$ – i.e. more unknowns than equations. The columns of $\boldsymbol{A}$ are thus n m-vectors, and, since n exceeds m, they must be L.D. Hence there is always a non-trivial solution in this case. This may alternatively be seen from:

$$\begin{aligned} r(A) &\leqslant \min(m, n) \\ &\leqslant m < n. \end{aligned}$$

(ii) $n = m$ }
(iii) $n < m$ } In both of these cases the n column vectors of $\boldsymbol{A}$ may be L.I., in which case there is no non-trivial solution. For instance if the vectors form a basis for R^m when $n = m$ then this will be true.

T.23. *The set of all solutions to a system of homogeneous equations forms a vector space.*

Proof: left as an example.

If we consider this vector space it may be shown that its dimension is $n - k$ where $k = r(A)$. This follows from the fact that we can arbitrarily assign values to $n - k$ of the x_n. Suppose, without loss of generality, that the first k columns of $\boldsymbol{A}$ are L.I., and that we assign arbitrary values $c_{k+1}, \ldots, c_n$ to the variables $x_{k+1}, \ldots, x_n$. Now we know that:

$$\boldsymbol{a}_j = \sum_{i=1}^{k} \mu_{ji}\boldsymbol{a}_i \qquad (j = k + 1, \ldots, n). \tag{5.4}$$

Thus

$$\sum_{j=k+1}^{n} x_j\boldsymbol{a}_j = \sum_{j=k+1}^{n} c_j\boldsymbol{a}_j = \sum_{j=k+1}^{n} c_j \sum_{i=1}^{k} \mu_{ji}\boldsymbol{a}_i. \tag{5.5}$$

In other words the homogeneous system in n variables has been transformed into a non-homogeneous system in k variables $x_1,\ldots,x_k$, for which the constant vector can be expressed as a L.C. of the k L.I. columns of $\boldsymbol{A}$. Hence we can find a solution vector for this system which, completed by the assumed values $c_{k+1}, \ldots, c_n$, is also a solution of $\boldsymbol{Ax} = \boldsymbol{0}$.

D.62. *A set of basis vectors spanning the subspace of* R^n *generated by the solutions to* $\mathbf{Ax} = \mathbf{0}$ *is called a FUNDAMENTAL SYSTEM for* $\mathbf{Ax} = \mathbf{0}$.

Example: Consider the equation system

$$\begin{bmatrix} 1 & 0 & 1 \\ 0 & 1 & 1 \end{bmatrix} \begin{bmatrix} x_1 \\ x_2 \\ x_3 \end{bmatrix} = \begin{bmatrix} 0 \\ 0 \end{bmatrix}.$$

For this $r(A) = 2$, so that all the solution vectors form a 1-dimensional vector subspace of R^3. They will be of the form $(a, a, -a)$ since the equations require $x_1 = x_2 = -x_3$. A fundamental system for the system of equations is the single vector $(1, 1, -1)$. Note that this is only one of infinitely many possible fundamental systems. A further point is that the set of all solutions gives a line through the origin in R^3. In general all homogeneous systems have solution sets which are hyperplanes through the origin.

B. *Non-Homogeneous Systems*

We now consider the system $\boldsymbol{Ax} = \boldsymbol{b}$, with which we may associate the *augmented matrix*, $\boldsymbol{A}_b$, where:

$$\boldsymbol{A}_b = [\boldsymbol{A}, \boldsymbol{b}] \tag{5.6}$$

i.e. the matrix $\boldsymbol{A}$ with an extra column composed of the elements of $\boldsymbol{b}$. Using this we can state the basic theorem for the compatibility of the system.

T.24. *The system* $\mathbf{Ax} = \mathbf{b}$ *is compatible iff the rank of the augmented matrix* $\mathbf{A}_b$ *equals that of* $\mathbf{A}$.

Proof: If the system has a solution, then $\boldsymbol{b}$ is a L.C. of the columns of $\boldsymbol{A}$. Hence adding the column $\boldsymbol{b}$ to $\boldsymbol{A}$ does not change its rank and $r(\boldsymbol{A}_b) = r(\boldsymbol{A})$.

Suppose $r(\boldsymbol{A}_b) = r(\boldsymbol{A}) = k$. Then the maximum number of L.I. columns in $\boldsymbol{A}$ is k; let these be $\boldsymbol{a}_1, \ldots, \boldsymbol{a}_k$. Now the maximum number of L.I. columns in $\boldsymbol{A}_b$ is also k, and $\boldsymbol{a}_1, \ldots, \boldsymbol{a}_k$ forms a set of L.I. columns in $\boldsymbol{A}_b$. Thus any other column in $\boldsymbol{A}_b$ may be expressed as a

L.C. of $\boldsymbol{a}_1, \ldots, \boldsymbol{a}_k$; i.e. there exists a set of λ_i such that

$$\boldsymbol{b} = \sum_{i=1}^{k} \lambda_i \boldsymbol{a}_i.$$

Q.E.D.

Now we consider the determinateness of the system, assuming that solutions do exist.

T.25. *A compatible system is determinate iff* $\mathrm{r}(\mathbf{A}) = \mathrm{r}(\mathbf{A}_b) = \mathrm{n}$ *where* n *is the number of variables.*

Proof: Let $r(A) = n$, but suppose that there are two solutions $\boldsymbol{c} = (c_1, \ldots, c_n)$ and $\boldsymbol{d} = (d_1, \ldots, d_n), \boldsymbol{c} \neq \boldsymbol{d}$. Then $\boldsymbol{b} = \sum_i c_i \boldsymbol{a}_i$ and $\boldsymbol{b} = \sum_i d_i \boldsymbol{a}_i$, so that $\sum_i (c_i - d_i)\boldsymbol{a}_i = \mathbf{0}$ where $(c_i - d_i) \neq 0$ for some i. This contradicts the assumption that $r(A) = n$, i.e. that the $\boldsymbol{a}_i$ are L.I.

Now suppose $r(A) = r(A_b) = k < n$. Then by the same argument leading to (5.5) it is possible to assign arbitrary values to $n - k$ variables and find a solution for the remaining x_i, provided that the appropriate columns form a L.I. set of vectors. Hence there must be an infinitely large number of solutions to such a system.

Q.E.D.

Note that if $r(A) = r(A_b) < m$, where m is the number of equations, then $m - k$ of the equations are redundant. Only k of the rows of $\boldsymbol{A}$ and of $\boldsymbol{A}_b$ are L.I., so that the remaining rows (and thus the associated equations) may be expressed as L.C.'s of these k rows/equations. They may thus be dispensed with, as they add no more constraints on the values of the x_i. Clearly this will always be the case if we have more equations than variables – provided that the equations are not inconsistent.

We will now discuss the relationship between sets of solutions to equivalent systems of homogeneous and non-homogeneous equations, i.e. to $\boldsymbol{Ax} = \mathbf{0}$ and $\boldsymbol{Ax} = \boldsymbol{b}$. Put:

$$H = \{\boldsymbol{x} \mid \boldsymbol{Ax} = \mathbf{0}\},$$

and

$$N.H = \{\boldsymbol{x} \mid \boldsymbol{Ax} = \boldsymbol{b}\}.$$

Lemma: $\boldsymbol{x} \in N.H$ implies that $\boldsymbol{x}$ can be expressed as: $\boldsymbol{x} = \hat{\boldsymbol{x}} + \bar{\boldsymbol{x}}$, where $\hat{\boldsymbol{x}} \in N.H$ and $\bar{\boldsymbol{x}} \in H$. This is trivial because $\mathbf{0} \in H$.

Lemma: If $\hat{x} \in N.H$ and $\bar{x} \in H$, then $x = \hat{x} + \bar{x} \in N.H$.

Proof:

$$\begin{aligned} Ax &= A\hat{x} + A\bar{x} \\ &= b + 0 \\ &= b \end{aligned}$$

Q.E.D.

Together these results imply:

T.26. *A vector* $\mathbf{x} \in N.H$ *iff* $\mathbf{x} = \hat{\mathbf{x}} + \bar{\mathbf{x}}$ *where* $\hat{\mathbf{x}} \in N.H, \bar{\mathbf{x}} \in H$.

Thus any vector which is the sum of a solution to the H system and a solution to the $N.H$ system is itself a solution to the $N.H$ system. This point is clear if we remember that when $r(A) = n$ there is no non-trivial solution to H while $N.H$ has a unique solution. Alternatively if $r(A) < n$ then H has many non-trivial solutions and $N.H$ also has many solutions.

T.27. *Suppose we have one solution* $\hat{\mathbf{x}}$ *to the N.H system. Then any other solution* $\mathbf{x}$ *can be written:* $\mathbf{x} = \hat{\mathbf{x}} + \mathbf{y}$ *when* $\mathbf{y} \in H$.

Proof: We can write $x = \hat{x} + (x - \hat{x})$. Put $y - (x - \hat{x})$ and examine Ay:

$$Ay = Ax - A\hat{x} = 0.$$

Q.E.D.

Thus if we know the set H and one member of $N.H$ we can find all elements of $N.H$.

Example: To extend the earlier example we will examine the equation system:

$$\begin{bmatrix} 1 & 0 & 1 \\ 0 & 1 & 1 \end{bmatrix} \begin{bmatrix} x_1 \\ x_2 \\ x_3 \end{bmatrix} = \begin{bmatrix} 1 \\ 1 \end{bmatrix}.$$

We know that the general solution to the homogeneous system is $x = (a, a, -a)$. Clearly $x = (0, 0, 1)$ is a solution to the non-homogeneous problem. Thus the general solution for the non-homogeneous problem is $x = (a, a, 1 - a)$.

5.3 Gaussian Elimination

In this section we discuss elimination methods for solving systems of equations. The object of these methods is to reduce the original system to a system of equations with the same solutions, but which is in an easily soluble form. Note first that the solutions of a system are not altered if we perform the following elementary row operations on it:

(i) multiplying an equation by a scalar;

(ii) adding an arbitrary multiple of one equation to another.

For example the solution of:

$$a_{11}x_1 + a_{12}x_2 = b_1$$
$$a_{21}x_1 + a_{22}x_2 = b_2$$

is the same as:

$$\lambda_1 a_{11}x_1 + \lambda_1 a_{12}x_2 = \lambda_1 b_1$$
$$\lambda_2 a_{21}x_1 + \lambda_2 a_{22}x_2 = \lambda_2 b_2$$

and also the same as:

$$a_{11}x_1 + a_{12}x_2 = b_1$$
$$(a_{21} + \lambda_1 a_{11})x_1 + (a_{22} + \lambda_1 a_{12})x_2 = (b_2 + \lambda_1 b_1)$$

The demonstration of this is left as an exercise.

D.63. *Two systems of equations which have the same solution sets and which can be obtained from each other by means of elementary row operations are said to be EQUIVALENT.*

Given this point the elimination procedure is obvious. In the same way as we reduced a matrix to echelon form in order to determine its rank, so to solve $\boldsymbol{Ax} = \boldsymbol{b}$ we perform the appropriate row operations on the whole system until $\boldsymbol{A}$ is reduced to an echelon matrix $\hat{\boldsymbol{A}}$ so that $\hat{\boldsymbol{A}}\boldsymbol{x} = \hat{\boldsymbol{b}}$. Thus if $r(\boldsymbol{A}) = k$ the equivalent system will have the form:

$$\begin{aligned} \hat{a}_{11}x_1 + \hat{a}_{12}x_2 + \ldots + \hat{a}_{1n}x_n &= \hat{b}_1 \\ \hat{a}_{22}x_2 + \ldots + \hat{a}_{2n}x_n &= \hat{b}_2 \\ \hat{a}_{kk}x_k + \ldots + \hat{a}_{kn}x_n &= \hat{b}_k. \end{aligned} \tag{5.7}$$

If $k < m$ the naining equations are redundant and will have disappeared. We know that $n - k$ variables – $x_{k+1}, \ldots, x_n$ – can be given arbitrary values. If we assign values to these variables, we can substitute them into the k equations. Immediately from the kth equation the value of x_k can be read off; by substituting this in the $(k - 1)$th we can get x_{k-1} and so on.

In fact this whole procedure can be simplified by reducing the system further so that the equivalent system is:

$$\bar{A}x = \bar{b}$$

where $\bar{A}$ is the canonical form of A.

D.64. *A system of* m *equations in* n *unknowns is said to be in CANONICAL FORM if the coefficient of the* i*th* (i = *1*, . . . , k) *non-arbitrary variable is 1 in the* i*th equation and zero elsewhere.*

We can reduce the system in (5.7) to canonical form: divide the kth equation by $\hat{a}_{kk}$; then divide the $(k-1)$th equation by $\hat{a}_{k-1,k-1}$ and add to it the appropriate multiple of the kth equation so as to eliminate the coefficient $\hat{a}_{k-1,k}/\hat{a}_{k-1,k-1}$; and so on. In effect we are substituting in each equation for x_k, then $x_{k-1}, \ldots$ and dividing through by $\hat{a}_{ii}$ in order to reduce the system to the form:

$$\begin{array}{llll} x_1 & & + \bar{a}_{1,k+1}x_{k+1} + \ldots \bar{a}_{1n}x_n = \bar{b}_1. \\ & \ddots & & \\ & x_k & + \bar{a}_{k,k+1}x_{k+1} + \ldots \bar{a}_{kn}x_n = \bar{b}_k. \end{array} \tag{5.8}$$

Now by assigning the arbitrary values to $x_{k+1}, \ldots, x_n$ as necessary, we can immediately read off the solutions for $x_1, \ldots, x_k$.

In many cases we will want to set each of the arbitrary variables equal to zero. This leads to

D.65. *In the general* m × n *equation system some of the variables have to be given arbitrary values. These are referred to as INDEPENDENT variables; the others are DEPENDENT or BASIC variables. A solution to the system in which all the independent variables are set equal to zero is called a BASIC SOLUTION.*

Clearly the number of non-zero elements in a basic solution will be at most k where $k = r(A)$.

D.66. *A basic solution to* **Ax** = **b** *is said to be DEGENERATE if one or more of the basic variables is zero.*

Note: There may be several basic solutions to $Ax = b$, each having a different set of k basic variables out of $x_1, \ldots, x_n$, provided that the columns associated with these variables are L.I. Thus the number of basic solutions is equal to the maximum number of ways k L.I. vectors may be chosen from the columns of A.

5.4 Problems

5.1. Let $\boldsymbol{A}$ be an $n \times m$ matrix and $\boldsymbol{x}$ an $m \times 1$ column vector. If the homogeneous system of equations $\boldsymbol{Ax} = \boldsymbol{0}$ has no non-trivial solution, what can you say about solutions to the non-homogneous system: $\boldsymbol{y}'\boldsymbol{A} = \boldsymbol{b}$?

5.2. Solve the following systems of equations by Gaussian Elimination

(i)
$$\begin{aligned} 2x_1 + x_2 - x_3 &= -1 \\ -x_1 + 2x_2 - 3x_4 &= 6 \\ 6x_1 + 3x_3 + x_4 &= 9 \\ -x_2 + 2x_3 - x_4 &= 8 \end{aligned}$$

(ii)
$$\begin{aligned} 15x_1 - x_2 + 4x_3 &= 22 \\ -2x_1 + x_2 + 3x_3 &= -10 \\ -x_1 + 7x_2 - 2x_3 &= 2 \end{aligned}$$

5.3. By considering the rank of $\boldsymbol{A}$ and the rank of the augmented matrix $[\boldsymbol{A}, \boldsymbol{b}]$, determine the values of α and β for which the system of equations $\boldsymbol{Ax} = \boldsymbol{b}$ has

(*a*) no non-trivial solution;

(*b*) a unique non-trivial solution;

(*c*) an infinite number of solutions when

$$\text{(i) } \boldsymbol{A} = \begin{bmatrix} \alpha & 1 & 1 \\ 1 & 0 & 2 \\ 1 & 2 & 1 \end{bmatrix}; \boldsymbol{b} = \boldsymbol{0}$$

$$\text{(ii) } \boldsymbol{A} = \begin{bmatrix} 2 & -1 & 2 \\ 3 & 1 & 2 \\ \alpha & \alpha & 1 \end{bmatrix}; \boldsymbol{b} = \begin{bmatrix} 3 \\ 2 \\ \beta \end{bmatrix}.$$

5.4. Consider the system of equations

$$\begin{aligned} 2x_1 + x_2 + x_3 \qquad &= -1 \\ x_1 + 2x_2 \qquad + x_4 &= 1 \\ 5x_1 + 4x_2 + 3x_3 + 2x_4 &= -1 \end{aligned}$$

(i) Find the basic solution for the system in terms of x_1, x_3 and x_4.

(ii) Find the general solution for the system, treating x_4 as the arbitrary variable.

(iii) Are there any solutions for which $\boldsymbol{x} > \boldsymbol{0}$, $\boldsymbol{x} = \boldsymbol{0}$ or $\boldsymbol{x} < \boldsymbol{0}$?

5.5. Prove that, if a system of equations has two distinct solutions, it has an infinite number of solutions.

5.6. Consider the system of equations:

$$\begin{aligned} 2x_1 - x_2 + x_3 + 2x_4 &= 6 \\ 6x_1 + 3x_2 - 3x_3 + x_4 &= 3 \end{aligned}$$

Do all of the possible basic solutions exist? Find the basic solutions that do exist. Are any of them degenerate?

5.7. Prove that a system of homogeneous equations has a non-trivial solution if the number of unknowns exceeds the number of equations.

5.8. Prove that the number of solution vectors to the homogeneous system $\boldsymbol{Ax} = \boldsymbol{0}$ which form a basis for the set of all solutions is $n - r$, where $\boldsymbol{A}$ is an $m \times n$ matrix of rank r.

5.9. Explain how you would reduce any matrix (of any order) to echelon form. Hence establish a general method for obtaining a solution to a set of equations.

5.10. Prove that all of the possible basic solutions of the system $\boldsymbol{Ax} = \boldsymbol{b}$ of m equations in n unknowns ($m < n$) exist and are not degenerate if and only if every set of m columns of the augmented matrix $[\boldsymbol{A}, \boldsymbol{b}]$ is a linearly independent set.

5.11. Show that the two systems of equations

$$\begin{aligned} x_1 + x_2 + 2x_3 &= 9 \\ 4x_1 + 4x_2 + 3x_3 &= 21 \\ 2x_2 + x_3 &= 7 \end{aligned} \quad \text{and} \quad \begin{aligned} 3x_1 - x_2 + 4x_3 &= 13 \\ 3x_1 + 5x_2 + 2x_3 &= 19 \\ x_1 + 3x_2 + 3x_3 &= 16 \end{aligned}$$

are equivalent in that they have the same solution.

5.12. In a basic solution for k variables, we equate the independent variables to zero. Suppose that the system of equations $\boldsymbol{Ax} = \boldsymbol{b}$ with m equations and n unknowns ($n > m > 1$) has a degenerate basic solution in $x_1, \ldots, x_k$ ($k < m$) with $x_k = 0$. Explain in what sense this solution differs from the basic solution in $x_1, \ldots, x_{k-1}, x_{k+1}$ when this solution is degenerate with $x_{k+1} = 0$.

5.13. Suppose that the homogeneous system of equations $\boldsymbol{Ax} = \boldsymbol{0}$ has a non-trivial solution. What can you infer about any solutions to the non-homogeneous system $\boldsymbol{Ax} = \boldsymbol{b}$?

6 Linear Transformations

In economics it is common to say that one variable is a function of another – e.g. consumption C is a function of income Y. This means that corresponding to any value of Y there is some value of C, which we can calculate if we know the functional form. In other words the function provides a rule for transforming a given Y into the corresponding C. Put more generally:

D.67. *A rule associating members of one set with members of another is called a MAPPING.*

The consumption–income relationship may be written:

$$C = \alpha Y + \beta,$$

where α, β are known constants. This equation indicates the rule for mapping Y- values into C-values. In general if x is a function of y this is written $x = f(y)$; x need not depend on a single variable y – there may be a vector $\boldsymbol{y}$ of variables which determine it. Equally the object x need not be a number; it could be a vector. If both $\boldsymbol{x}$ and $\boldsymbol{y}$ are vectors then we would have: $\boldsymbol{x} = f(\boldsymbol{y})$. For example, we say that an individual's consumption vector $\boldsymbol{C}$ is a function of the vector of prices $\boldsymbol{p}$ and his income Y, i.e. $\boldsymbol{C} = f(\boldsymbol{p}, Y)$.

D.68. *If* $\mathbf{x} = \mathrm{f}(\mathbf{y})$, *we say that* $\mathbf{x}$ *is the IMAGE of* $\mathbf{y}$ *under* f.

D.69. *The DOMAIN* D(f) *of a mapping is the set of all values upon which it operates.*

D.70. *The RANGE* R(f) *of a mapping is the set of all points that are images of some point in* D(f).

A mapping is the general term for the operations we are considering. Special types of mappings are given other names:

(*a*) A *transformation* or a *function* associates each point in the domain of the mapping with a single point in the range. We say that these are single-valued mappings. Thus if f is a single-valued mapping, and if $\boldsymbol{x} \in D(f)$, $\boldsymbol{y}, \hat{\boldsymbol{y}} \in R(f)$ with $\boldsymbol{y} = f(\boldsymbol{x})$, $\hat{\boldsymbol{y}} = f(\boldsymbol{x})$ then we must have $\boldsymbol{y} = \hat{\boldsymbol{y}}$. Note that this does not rule out the possibility that two points $\boldsymbol{x}$, $\hat{\boldsymbol{x}}$ in the domain might both be mapped by f into the point $\boldsymbol{y}$ in the range.

(*b*) A *correspondence* associates a point in the domain with a set of points in the range. Thus consider the relationship $Y = \boldsymbol{p} \cdot \boldsymbol{x}$. If Y is varied over some set $Y(i)$ then each value of Y is associated with a set of possible vectors $\boldsymbol{x}$ given the mapping vector $\boldsymbol{p}$.

Correspondences present a number of special problems. We will in this book only consider single-valued mappings, that is transformations or functions. On a point of notation, if a mapping f transforms an n-vector into an m-vector we will write this as: $f: R^n \to R^m$. This does not imply that R^n is necessarily the domain nor that R^m is the range of f.

Of course there is the reverse question of whether a given point in the range is the image of only one point or of a set of points in the domain. Thus:

D.71. *A transformation is ONE-TO-ONE (1–1) if each point in* R(f) *is the image of only one point in* D(f).

We will investigate whether certain transformations satisfy this definition in due course. We will focus on a special type of transformation.

D.72. f *is a LINEAR TRANSFORMATION (L.T.) if*:

(i) *For* $\mathbf{x} \in \mathrm{D(f)}$ *and* λ *any scalar*,

$$\mathrm{f}(\lambda \mathbf{x}) = \lambda \mathrm{f}(\mathbf{x}).$$

(ii) *For* $\mathbf{x}_1, \mathbf{x}_2 \in \mathrm{D(f)}$

$$\mathrm{f}(\mathbf{x}_1 + \mathbf{x}_2) = \mathrm{f}(\mathbf{x}_1) + \mathrm{f}(\mathbf{x}_2).$$

It clearly follows that for any L.T. f, if $\boldsymbol{y}_i \in D(f)$ $(i = 1, \ldots, n)$ and λ_i are scalars, then:

$$f\left(\sum_{i=1}^{n} \lambda_i \boldsymbol{y}_i\right) = \sum_{i=1}^{n} \lambda_i f(\boldsymbol{y}_i).$$

Now consider an $m \times n$ matrix $\boldsymbol{A}$ and let $\boldsymbol{x} \in R^n$. Define $\boldsymbol{y} \in R^m$ by $\boldsymbol{y} = \boldsymbol{A}\boldsymbol{x}$. Then $\boldsymbol{A}$ may be said to transform $\boldsymbol{x}$ into $\boldsymbol{y}$; this transformation, achieved by pre-multiplying $\boldsymbol{x}$ by $\boldsymbol{A}$, is obviously a L.T. since:

$$\boldsymbol{A} \cdot (\lambda \boldsymbol{x}) = \lambda \boldsymbol{A}\boldsymbol{x}$$

and

$$A(x_1 + x_2) = Ax_1 + Ax_2.$$

In this case the domain is R^n as A operates on any vector in R^n. The image y of x is always an m-vector so the range must be a subset of R^m. Further, y is a L.C. of the columns of A, the coefficients of the L.C. being the elements of x. If x may be any vector in R^n these coefficients take on all values. Hence the set of all possible images y of some point x consists of the set of all L.C.s of the columns of A. In other words the columns of A span the range of the transformation. Thus the dimension of the range will be equal to the maximum number of L.I. columns in A, that is it equals the rank of A. Stated formally:

T.28. *The transformation* $\mathrm{y} = \mathrm{T}(\mathrm{x})$ *represented by* $\mathrm{y} = \mathrm{Ax}$ *is a linear transformation. If* A *is an* $\mathrm{m} \times \mathrm{n}$ *matrix of rank* k*, then* $\mathrm{D(T)} = \mathrm{R^n}$, $\mathrm{R(T)} \subset \mathrm{R^m}$ *and* $\mathrm{R(T)}$ *is of dimension* k.

Example: The projection matrix $\begin{bmatrix} 1 & 0 \\ 0 & 0 \end{bmatrix}$ transforms any vector $(x_1, x_2) \in R^2$ into its horizontal projection $(x_1, 0)$. The range of this L.T. is the x_1–axis, a subset of R^2 of dimension 1.

T.29. *Every L.T.,* $\mathrm{T} : \mathrm{R^n} \to \mathrm{R^m}$*, can be represented by an* $\mathrm{m} \times \mathrm{n}$ *matrix.*

Proof: Let T be a L.T. with $D(T) \subset R^n$ and $R(T) \subset R^m$, and suppose that $g_i (i = 1, \ldots, n)$ and $f_j (j = 1, \ldots, m)$ are bases for R^n and R^m respectively. First examine the effect of T on the elements of a basis for R^n. The vector g_i is transformed into $T(g_i) \in R^m$, which may be written as a L.C. of the vectors f_j. Suppose:

$$T(g_i) = \sum_{j=1}^{m} a_{ji} f_j \tag{6.1}$$

writing this out for each of the g_i:

$$\begin{aligned} T(g_1) &= a_{11}f_1 + a_{21}f_2 + \ldots + a_{m1}f_m. \\ T(g_2) &= a_{12}f_1 + a_{22}f_2 + \ldots + a_{m2}f_m. \\ T(g_n) &= a_{1n}f_1 + \ldots \qquad\qquad + a_{mn}f_m. \end{aligned} \tag{6.2}$$

Denote by A the transposed matrix of coefficients:

$$A = \begin{bmatrix} a_{11} & a_{22} \ldots a_{1n} \\ a_{21} & a_{22} \ldots a_{2n} \\ a_{m1} & a_{m2} \ldots a_{mn} \end{bmatrix}.$$

We call this the matrix of the L.T. *with respect to the bases* g_i and f_j.

It is important to note that if different bases has been used for the two spaces, a different matrix would have resulted.

Now look at the effects of the transformation T on any arbitrary vector $\boldsymbol{x} \in R^n$. In terms of the assumed basis $\boldsymbol{x} = \sum_{i=1}^{n} x_i \boldsymbol{g}_i$, so that

$$T(\boldsymbol{x}) = T\left(\sum_{i=1}^{n} x_i \boldsymbol{g}_i\right) = \sum_{1}^{n} x_i T(\boldsymbol{g}_i) \tag{6.3}$$

by the definition of a L.T. Thus

$$\begin{aligned} T(\boldsymbol{x}) &= \sum_{i=1}^{n} x_i \left\{\sum_{j=1}^{m} a_{ji} \boldsymbol{f}_j\right\} \\ &= \sum_{j=1}^{m} \left\{\sum_{i=1}^{n} x_i a_{ji}\right\} \boldsymbol{f}_j. \end{aligned} \tag{6.4}$$

So the components of $T(\boldsymbol{x})$ with respect to the basis $\boldsymbol{f}_j$ of R^m are $\sum_{i=1}^{n} x_i a_{ji}$, $j = 1, \ldots, m$. But these numbers are precisely the components of the vector $\boldsymbol{Ax}$. Thus if we express vectors with respect to the bases $\boldsymbol{g}_i (i = 1, \ldots, n)$ and $\boldsymbol{f}_j (j = 1, \ldots, m)$

$$T(\boldsymbol{x}) = \boldsymbol{Ax}. \tag{6.5}$$

The L.T., $T: R^n \to R^m$, has been represented by an $m \times n$ matrix.

Q.E.D.

This relationship between L.T.s and matrices illuminates many of the operations and results which we have obtained earlier. For example, consider the product matrix $\boldsymbol{AB}$ where $\boldsymbol{A}$ is $m \times n$ and $\boldsymbol{B}$ is $n \times r$, and suppose we have some $\boldsymbol{x} \in R^r$. Now $\boldsymbol{C} = \boldsymbol{AB}$ represents a transformation from $R^r \to R^m$. But

$$\boldsymbol{z} = (\boldsymbol{AB})\boldsymbol{x} = \boldsymbol{A}(\boldsymbol{Bx}) = \boldsymbol{Ay} \tag{6.6}$$

i.e. the transformation from $R^r \to R^m$ is equivalent to the successive transformations $R^r \to R^n$ and $R^n \to R^m$. This underlines the need for conformability of the matrices for multiplication to be defined. The range of the transformation $\boldsymbol{B}$ is a subset of R^n; therefore for a further transformation the domain of $\boldsymbol{A}$ must be R^n. Hence the condition on the numbers of columns in $\boldsymbol{A}$ and of rows in $\boldsymbol{B}$. Furthermore, for consistency of the alternative ways of transforming $\boldsymbol{x}$ into $\boldsymbol{z}$ the result of multiplying $\boldsymbol{A}$ by $\boldsymbol{B}$ must be as we have defined.

Now let us re-examine the problem of solving the equation system

$\boldsymbol{Ax} = \boldsymbol{b}$. We see that to solve this we must find a point – or set of points – in the domain of the transformation represented by $\boldsymbol{A}$ whose image is $\boldsymbol{b}$. When $\boldsymbol{b} = \boldsymbol{0}$, we are looking for points which are mapped into the null vector. For this we have the special definition:

D.73. *The NULL SPACE of a transformation* T, *written* N(T), *is the set of all vectors* **x** *satisfying the condition* T(**x**) = ***0***. *The dimension of the null space is called the NULLITY, written* n(T).

Note that we have already proved that the set of all vectors satisfying $T(\boldsymbol{x}) = \boldsymbol{0}$ forms a vector space.

T.30. *If the transformation* T *is a linear transformation mapping* V → W then:

$$\mathrm{r}(\mathbf{A}) + \mathrm{n}(\mathrm{T}) = \textit{dimension of } \mathrm{V}$$

where **A** *is the matrix representing* T.

Proof: Let $(\boldsymbol{v}_1, \boldsymbol{v}_2, \ldots, \boldsymbol{v}_m, \boldsymbol{v}_{m+1}, \ldots, \boldsymbol{v}_n)$ be a basis for the domain, assuming that the dimension of V is n, and let $(\boldsymbol{v}_1, \ldots, \boldsymbol{v}_m)$ be a basis for $N(T)$. Then every $\boldsymbol{x} \in \boldsymbol{V}$ may be written:

$$\boldsymbol{x} = \sum_{i=1}^{m} \lambda_i \boldsymbol{v}_i + \sum_{i=m+1}^{n} \lambda_i \boldsymbol{v}_i. \tag{6.7}$$

So

$$T(x) = \sum_{1}^{m} \lambda_i \boldsymbol{A}\boldsymbol{v}_i + \sum_{m+1}^{n} \lambda_i \boldsymbol{A}\boldsymbol{v}_i$$

$$= \sum_{m+1}^{n} \lambda_i \boldsymbol{A}\boldsymbol{v}_i \tag{6.8}$$

since any point in the space spanned by $(\boldsymbol{v}_1, \ldots, \boldsymbol{v}_m)$ is mapped by T into the null vector. Now we show that $(\boldsymbol{A}\boldsymbol{v}_{m+1}, \ldots, \boldsymbol{A}\boldsymbol{v}_n)$ is a basis for the range. From the above we know that these vectors span $R(T)$. Suppose that they are not L.I.; then there exist some μ_i, not all zero, such that

$$\sum_{i=m+1}^{n} \mu_i \,.\, \boldsymbol{A}\boldsymbol{v}_i = \boldsymbol{A} \,.\, \sum_{m+1}^{n} \mu_i \boldsymbol{v}_i = \boldsymbol{0}. \tag{6.9}$$

This means that $\boldsymbol{y} = \sum_{m+1}^{n} \hat{\mu}_i \boldsymbol{v}_i \in N(T)$, so that we can write: $\boldsymbol{y} = \sum_{i=1}^{m} \hat{\mu}_i \boldsymbol{v}_i$. In other words $\boldsymbol{y}$ has two different representations in terms of the same basis $(\boldsymbol{v}_1, \ldots, \boldsymbol{v}_n)$, which is not possible. Hence

$(\boldsymbol{Av}_{m+1}, \ldots, \boldsymbol{Av}_n)$ must be a basis for $R(T)$ and the result follows immediately.

Q.E.D.

Returning to our homogeneous equation system it follows that:

(i) If there are no non-trivial solutions then $n(T) = 0$. In other words, if $\boldsymbol{x} \in R^n$, the system $\boldsymbol{Ax} = \boldsymbol{0}$ can have non-trivial solutions if and only if $r(\boldsymbol{A}) < n$.

(ii) Suppose $r(\boldsymbol{A}) = k < n$. Then we have $n(T) = n - k$ and the set of possible solutions can be generated by any basis for $N(T)$. A set of $n - k$ basis vectors for $N(T)$ is, as in D.62, a fundamental system for the equations.

Using theorems T.26 and T.27 on the relationship between the solutions to equivalent systems of homogeneous and non-homogeneous equations we can apply these results to the system $\boldsymbol{Ax} = \boldsymbol{b}$. Given one solution $\hat{\boldsymbol{x}}$ to this we can generate all solutions by adding to $\hat{\boldsymbol{x}}$ any $\boldsymbol{y} \in N(\boldsymbol{A})$. Thus the solution will be unique if and only if $r(\boldsymbol{A}) = n$, when $\boldsymbol{y} \in N(\boldsymbol{A})$ implies $\boldsymbol{y} = \boldsymbol{0}$. This, of course, raises the question of whether even one solution exists to the problem of finding a vector $\boldsymbol{x}$ in the domain of the transformation which is mapped into the vector $\boldsymbol{b}$. For there to be any solutions $\boldsymbol{b}$ must be in the range of the transformation. But $R(T)$ is spanned by the columns of $\boldsymbol{A}$. Thus immediately we get the condition for compatibility that $r(\boldsymbol{A}) = r(\boldsymbol{A}_b)$, and we now have all the results deduced earlier.

Note that we have also shown that:

T.31. *The transformation* T *from* $\mathrm{R^n} \rightarrow \mathrm{R^m}$ *(represented by the matrix* A*) is one-to-one if and only if* r(A) = n.

D.74. *A transformation* $\mathrm{T{:}R^n} \rightarrow \mathrm{R^m}$ *is said to be ONTO if* $\mathrm{R(T) = R^m}$.

For example a transformation which maps from R^n to R^n with range the whole of R^n is onto. We will be particularly concerned with mappings which are one-to-one and onto.

T.32. *A transformation T is 1–1 and onto iff its matrix is a square matrix of maximal rank.*

Proof: (i) *Sufficiency*. Let $\boldsymbol{A}$ be the matrix of T and suppose that $\boldsymbol{A}$ is $n \times n$, $r(\boldsymbol{A}) = n$. Then $D(T) = R^n$, $R(T) = R^n$. Hence T is onto. Suppose that T is not 1-1 – i.e. there exist $\boldsymbol{x}, \hat{\boldsymbol{x}} \in R^n$ such that $T(\boldsymbol{x}) = T(\hat{\boldsymbol{x}})$, $\boldsymbol{x} \neq \hat{\boldsymbol{x}}$. Now

$$T(\boldsymbol{x}) = \sum_{i=1}^{n} x_i \boldsymbol{a}_i$$

$$T(\hat{\boldsymbol{x}}) = \sum_{i=1}^{n} \hat{x}_i \boldsymbol{a}_i \tag{6.10}$$

where $\boldsymbol{a}_i$ are the columns of $\boldsymbol{A}$. Hence $T(\boldsymbol{x}) = T(\hat{\boldsymbol{x}})$ implies $\sum_{i=1}^{n} (x_i - \hat{x}_i) \boldsymbol{a}_i = \boldsymbol{0}$ for some $x_i - \hat{x}_i \neq 0$. This contradicts $r(\boldsymbol{A}) = n$. Thus T is 1-1.

(ii) *Necessity*. Let T be 1-1 and onto, and suppose that $T{:}R^n \to R^m$. Then $\boldsymbol{A}$ is $m \times n$. Now, if T is onto it follows that $r(\boldsymbol{A}) = m$, for dimension of $R(T) = r(\boldsymbol{A})$. Thus $n \geqslant m$.

Let the columns of $\boldsymbol{A}$ be $\boldsymbol{a}_1, \ldots, \boldsymbol{a}_n$. Any $\boldsymbol{x} \in R^n$ gives:

$$\boldsymbol{y} = T(\boldsymbol{x}) = \sum_{i=1}^{n} x_i \boldsymbol{a}_i.$$

Consider $\boldsymbol{x}$, $\hat{\boldsymbol{x}}$; as long as $\boldsymbol{x} \neq \hat{\boldsymbol{x}}$, $T(\boldsymbol{x}) \neq T(\hat{\boldsymbol{x}})$. Thus for $\boldsymbol{x} \neq \hat{\boldsymbol{x}}$, i.e. some $x_i \neq \hat{x}_i$

$$\sum_{i=1}^{n} (\hat{x}_i - x_i)\boldsymbol{a}_i \neq \boldsymbol{0} \tag{6.11}$$

so that the $\boldsymbol{a}_i$ are L.I. Hence $r(\boldsymbol{A}) = n$. Thus $n = m$, and necessity follows.

Q.E.D.

Note that the matrix $\boldsymbol{A}$ is non-singular. Any linear transformation with an associated matrix which is non-singular must be 1-1 and onto. Thus such transformations are said to be non-singular. The next chapter focuses on their properties.

6.1 Problems

6.1. Suppose L_1 and L_2 are linear transformations such that $L_1 : U \to V$, $L_2 : V \to W$. Show that the product of these transformations $L_3 = L_2 L_1$ is linear and has domain U and range W.

6.2. Consider a linear transformation T with domain R^n and range in R^m. If $m > n$, prove that the dimension of the range is less than m.

6.3. Write down the matrix representation of the transformation that takes row vectors in R^2, (x_1, x_2), into the subspace of R^4 composed of row vectors of the form

(i) $(x_1, -x_1, x_2, -x_2)$;

(ii) $(x_1 + x_2, 0, x_1 - x_2, 0)$.

6.4. Show, for both cases in problem 3, that the dimension of the range equals the rank of the matrix.

6.5. Determine which of the following transformations on column vectors are (*a*) 1-1 and (*b*) 1-1 and onto; and write down the nullity of each transformation;

(i) $\begin{bmatrix} 4 & 3 & 2 \\ 1 & 2 & 3 \\ 2 & -1 & -4 \end{bmatrix}$ (ii) $\begin{bmatrix} 1 & 0 & 0 \\ 0 & 1 & 0 \\ 0 & 0 & 1 \end{bmatrix}$

(iii) $\begin{bmatrix} 3 & 0 & 1 \\ 1 & 2 & 3 \end{bmatrix}$ (iv) $\begin{bmatrix} 2 & 1 \\ 1 & 2 \\ -1 & 1 \end{bmatrix}$

(v) $\begin{bmatrix} 6 & -2 & 7 \\ 5 & 3 & -1 \\ 2 & 1 & 0 \end{bmatrix}$

6.6. Prove that a linear transformation T is 1-1 and onto if and only if there is a linear transformation L such that

$$TL = LT = I.$$

6.7. Let T be a 1-1 and onto transformation for $R^2 \to R^2$. The matrix representation with respect to the unit vectors as bases is $\begin{bmatrix} 1 & -1 \\ 3 & 1 \end{bmatrix}$. By using steps in the proof of T.29, find the matrix representation of T when vectors (2, 1) and (1, 2) are used as a basis for the domain of T.

6.8. Prove that, if T is a linear transformation with rank $\leqslant 1$, then the matrix representation of this transformation $A = \|a_{ij}\|$ has elements of the form $a_{ij} = a_i a_j$ with respect to any basis.

6.9. Prove that, if T is a linear transformation of rank r, then T may be written as the sum of r transformations of rank 1.

6.10. Show, by example, that the range and null space of a linear transformation need not be disjoint.

6.11. Are the following transformations linear:

(i) the differential operator; $T(y) = d/dx(y)$;

(ii) the logarithmic operator; $T(y) = \log(y)$;
(iii) the difference operator; $T(y_t) = \Delta y_t = y_t - y_{t-1}$;
(iv) a polynomial operator; $T(x) = \sum_{i=0}^{n} a_i x^i$?

7 Inverse Mappings and the Inverse Matrix

Suppose that a L.T. $T: R^n \to R^n$ and is onto. Then given any $\boldsymbol{y} \in R^n$ we may ask 'of what point is this the image under T?' In other words we have $\boldsymbol{y}$, and know that $\boldsymbol{y} = T(\boldsymbol{x})$ for some $\boldsymbol{x}$; the problem is to find this $\boldsymbol{x}$. Given that T is a L.T. this is the same basic problem as that of finding a solution to a system of linear equations. Here, however, we take a different approach by focusing on the mapping aspect of the problem. Essentially it requires that we reverse T; T sends us from $\boldsymbol{x} \to \boldsymbol{y}$, and we wish to go the opposite way. Specifically we wish to find another transformation such that the image of any point $\boldsymbol{x}$ under the reverse transformation would be the point that T would map into $\boldsymbol{x}$. If such a transformation exists we call it the inverse of T. It is defined as follows:

D.75. *Let* T *be any L.T. Then if there exists another transformation, denoted by* T^{-1}, *satisfying:*

(*i*) $\mathrm{D}(\mathrm{T}^{-1}) = \mathrm{R}(\mathrm{T})$.

(ii) $\mathrm{R}(\mathrm{T}^{-1}) = \mathrm{D}(\mathrm{T})$.

(iii) $\forall\, \mathbf{x} \in \mathrm{D}(\mathrm{T}), \mathrm{T}(\mathbf{x}) = \mathbf{y} \Rightarrow \mathrm{T}^{-1}(\mathbf{y}) = \mathbf{x}$, i.e. $\forall\, \mathbf{x} \in \mathrm{D}(\mathrm{T}), \mathrm{T}^{-1}[\mathrm{T}(\mathbf{x})] = \mathbf{x}$,

we call T^{-1} *the INVERSE of* T.

T.33. *The inverse of a linear transformation, if it exists, is also a linear transformation.*

Proof: Let $(\boldsymbol{x}_1 + \boldsymbol{x}_2) \in D(T^{-1})$, and consider $\boldsymbol{y} = T^{-1}(\boldsymbol{x}_1 + \boldsymbol{x}_2) \in D(T)$. Clearly $T(\boldsymbol{y}) = \boldsymbol{x}_1 + \boldsymbol{x}_2$. Now choose $\boldsymbol{y}_1, \boldsymbol{y}_2 \in D(T)$ such that:

$$T(\boldsymbol{y}_1) = \boldsymbol{x}_1, \text{ i.e. } T^{-1}(\boldsymbol{x}_1) = \boldsymbol{y}_1$$

$$T(\boldsymbol{y}_2) = \boldsymbol{x}_2, \text{ i.e. } T^{-1}(\boldsymbol{x}_2) = \boldsymbol{y}_2$$

Then

$$T(\boldsymbol{y}_1 + \boldsymbol{y}_2) = T(\boldsymbol{y}_1) + T(\boldsymbol{y}_2) = \boldsymbol{x}_1 + \boldsymbol{x}_2.$$

Hence

$$\begin{aligned} T^{-1}(\boldsymbol{x}_1 + \boldsymbol{x}_2) &= \boldsymbol{y}_1 + \boldsymbol{y}_2 \\ &= T^{-1}(\boldsymbol{x}_1) + T^{-1}(\boldsymbol{x}_2). \end{aligned}$$

We now consider $T^{-1}(\lambda x)$. This is a point $y \in D(T)$ such that $T(y) = \lambda x$. Let $\hat{y} \in D(T)$ be such that $T(\hat{y}) = x$, i.e. $T^{-1}(x) = \hat{y}$. Then

$$T(\lambda \hat{y}) = \lambda T(\hat{y}) = \lambda x$$

So

$$T^{-1}(\lambda x) = \lambda \hat{y} = \lambda T^{-1}(x).$$

Q.E.D.

T.34. *A L.T. T has an inverse if and only if it is 1–1 and onto, that is iff its matrix is non-singular.*

Proof: (*a*) We first prove that if T is 1-1 and onto, T^{-1} exists.

Let us set up a mapping between each point $\in R(T)$ and the point or points in $D(T)$ from which it came. Call this mapping H. We have to show that H satisfies the definition of T^{-1}. Consider $y, \hat{y} \in R(H)$. To prove that H is a single-valued mapping, we require that if:

$$y = H(x), \hat{y} = H(x), \quad \text{then } y = \hat{y}.$$

But $$T(y) = x, T(\hat{y}) = x \text{ implies } y = \hat{y}$$

as T is 1-1. Hence H is single-valued.

By construction H satisfies (i) and (ii) of the definition of T^{-1} since T is onto. Also

$$H(x) = \{y \in D(T) | T(y) = x\}.$$

But we have shown that $H(x)$ is a single point. Hence:

$$H(x) = y \in D(T) \text{ such that } T(y) = x.$$

So $T(y) = x$ implies $H(x) = y \; \forall \; x \in D(T)$. Thus H satisfies point (iii) of the definition of T^{-1}.

(*b*) We now show that if T^{-1} exists, T is 1-1 and onto. We are given that T is a L.T. Suppose $T(x) = T(y) = z$, say, then $T^{-1}(z) = x$ and $T^{-1}(z) = y$ which implies that $x = y$, as T^{-1} is a transformation. So T is 1-1.

Further $R(T) = D(T^{-1})$. But as T^{-1} is a L.T. it follows that $D(T^{-1})$ is a whole vector space. Hence T must be onto.

Q.E.D.

T.35. *If* T *is 1–1 and onto, then* T^{-1} *is 1–1 and onto.*

Proof: Let $x, \hat{x} \in D(T^{-1})$. We wish to show that $T^{-1}(x) = y$, $T^{-1}(\hat{x}) = y$ implies that $\hat{x} = x$. But $T(y) = x$, and $T(y) = \hat{x}$. Since T is a transformation, $x = \hat{x}$, and so T^{-1} is 1-1.

Now we show that T^{-1} is onto. $R(T^{-1}) = D(T)$. But T is a L.T. so its domain is a whole vector space, and T^{-1} is onto.

Q.E.D.

This theorem implies that the matrix of the inverse transformation T^{-1} is non-singular. Hence T^{-1} itself has an inverse. This is the original transformation – that is:

$$(T^{-1})^{-1} = T. \tag{7.1}$$

D.76. *Suppose* **A** *is the matrix of the transformation* T; *then we denote the matrix of* T^{-1} *by* $\mathbf{A}^{-1}$. *This is called the INVERSE MATRIX of* **A**.

If $T: R^n \to R^n$, A is $n \times n$. But then $T^{-1}: R^n \to R^n$, so that A^{-1} is also $n \times n$. Now $T^{-1}(T(x)) = x$ for $x \in D(T)$.

So
$$A^{-1}Ax = Ix$$

or
$$A^{-1}A = I. \tag{7.2}$$

T is also the inverse of T^{-1}, i.e.

$$T(T^{-1}(y)) = y \text{ for } y \in D(T^{-1}) \text{ so } AA^{-1}y = y \text{ or } AA^{-1} = I$$

i.e.

$$AA^{-1} = I = A^{-1}A. \tag{7.3}$$

By the previous theorems we know that A^{-1} exists iff A is non-singular, and that A^{-1} is non-singular. Pre- or post-multiplying a matrix by its inverse leads to the unit matrix.

We can return to the equation system $Ax = b$; provided that A is non-singular we may pre-multiply both sides by A^{-1}. Hence

$$A^{-1}Ax = A^{-1}b, \quad \text{i.e. } x = A^{-1}b \tag{7.4}$$

In this case the solution is unique (and trivial if $b = 0$); this reinforces our previous conclusions.

Suppose that S, T are two transformations, both 1-1 and onto and mapping $R^n \to R^n$, so that S^{-1} and T^{-1} exist. Further we suppose that:

$$x_2 = T(x_1), x_3 = S(x_2) = (ST)(x_1).$$

The transformation ST, the product of two L.T.'s which are 1-1 and onto, is also a L.T. which is 1-1 and onto. Hence (ST) has an inverse $(ST)^{-1}$. It is interesting to know the relationship between this inverse and the inverses S^{-1} and T^{-1}. Consider returning from $\boldsymbol{x}_3$ to $\boldsymbol{x}_1$. We go from $\boldsymbol{x}_3$ to $\boldsymbol{x}_2$ by applying S^{-1}:

$$\boldsymbol{x}_2 = S^{-1}(\boldsymbol{x}_3)$$

and

$$\boldsymbol{x}_1 = T^{-1}(\boldsymbol{x}_2)$$

i.e.

$$\boldsymbol{x}_1 = (ST)^{-1}(\boldsymbol{x}_3) = T^{-1}(S^{-1}(\boldsymbol{x}_3))$$

so that $(ST)^{-1} = T^{-1}S^{-1}$. Thus the inverse of the product is the product of the inverses in reverse order. Hence if the matrices of S and T are $\boldsymbol{A}$ and $\boldsymbol{B}$ respectively,

$$(\boldsymbol{AB})^{-1} = \boldsymbol{B}^{-1}\boldsymbol{A}^{-1}. \tag{7.5}$$

A further implication of this discussion is that the product of two non-singular matrices is a non-singular matrix. This is a special case of T.19 which states that the result of multiplying a matrix of rank k by a non-singular matrix of rank m, $m \geqslant k$, is a matrix of rank k. We will now prove this for pre-multiplication; the proof for post-multiplication is similar.

Proof of T.19: Suppose that $\boldsymbol{B}$ is an $m \times n$ matrix of rank k, and let $\boldsymbol{A}$ be an mth order non-singular matrix. Put $r = r(\boldsymbol{AB})$. Then $r \leqslant \min(m, k) \leqslant k$ since $k \leqslant m$. Now we may write:

$$\boldsymbol{B} = \boldsymbol{A}^{-1}(\boldsymbol{AB}).$$

Thus $k \leqslant min\,[r(\boldsymbol{A}^{-1}), r] \leqslant r$. Hence we must have $r(\boldsymbol{AB}) = k$.

Q.E.D.

Two further results may be stated with the proofs left as exercises.

T.36. *If* **A** *is a non-singular matrix then*

$$(\mathbf{A}')^{-1} = (\mathbf{A}^{-1})'. \tag{7.6}$$

T.37. *If* **A** *and* **B** *are two matrices such that* **AB** $= \boldsymbol{0}$, *and if* **A** *is non-singular, then* **B** *is the null matrix.*

7.1 Calculating the inverse of a matrix

We have discussed the conditions under which an inverse transformation, and the matrix corresponding to it, will exist. In addition we have seen some of the properties of these inverses. It is sometimes useful to be able to calculate the inverse matrix; this is straightforward, though time-consuming. We know that we can perform elementary row or column operations on a matrix by pre- or post-multiplying the matrix by a series of non-singular elementary matrices. Suppose that by performing the row operations represented by $\boldsymbol{E}_1, \ldots, \boldsymbol{E}_p$ we reduce the non-singular matrix $\boldsymbol{A}$ to the identity matrix $\boldsymbol{I}$. Then:

$$\boldsymbol{E}_p\boldsymbol{E}_{p-1}\ldots\boldsymbol{E}_2\boldsymbol{E}_1\boldsymbol{A} = \boldsymbol{I}$$

i.e.

$$\boldsymbol{A}^{-1} = \boldsymbol{E}_p\boldsymbol{E}_{p-1}\ldots\boldsymbol{E}_2\boldsymbol{E}_1\boldsymbol{I}.$$

In other words by performing these same operations on the identity matrix we will obtain the inverse of $\boldsymbol{A}$.

The computations can be conveniently performed by writing $\boldsymbol{I}$ alongside $\boldsymbol{A}$ to form an $n \times 2n$ matrix $[\boldsymbol{I}|\boldsymbol{A}]$. Perform the row operations on this matrix to reduce $\boldsymbol{A}$ to $\boldsymbol{I}$ obtaining $[\boldsymbol{B}|\boldsymbol{I}]$. Then $\boldsymbol{B} = \boldsymbol{A}^{-1}$. For example, we will find the inverse of

$$\boldsymbol{A} = \begin{bmatrix} 1 & 2 & 2 \\ 3 & 2 & 1 \\ 2 & 3 & 2 \end{bmatrix}.$$

The steps are:

(i) $$\left[\begin{array}{ccc|ccc} 1 & 0 & 0 & 1 & 2 & 2 \\ 0 & 1 & 0 & 3 & 2 & 1 \\ 0 & 0 & 1 & 2 & 3 & 2 \end{array}\right]$$

(ii) $$\left[\begin{array}{ccc|ccc} 1 & 0 & 0 & 1 & 2 & 2 \\ -3 & 1 & 0 & 0 & -4 & -5 \\ -2 & 0 & 1 & 0 & -1 & -2 \end{array}\right]$$

(iii) $$\left[\begin{array}{ccc|ccc} -3 & 0 & 2 & 1 & 0 & -2 \\ 5 & 1 & -4 & 0 & 0 & 3 \\ -2 & 0 & 1 & 0 & -1 & -2 \end{array}\right]$$

(iv) $$\left[\begin{array}{ccc|ccc} -3 & 0 & 2 & 1 & 0 & -2 \\ 2 & 0 & -1 & 0 & 1 & 2 \\ \frac{5}{3} & \frac{1}{3} & -\frac{4}{3} & 0 & 0 & 1 \end{array}\right]$$

so that $A^{-1} = \begin{bmatrix} \frac{1}{3} & \frac{2}{3} & -\frac{2}{3} \\ -\frac{4}{3} & -\frac{2}{3} & \frac{5}{3} \\ \frac{5}{3} & \frac{1}{3} & -\frac{4}{3} \end{bmatrix}$.

There are other procedures useful for finding the inverse of a matrix which depend upon partitioning the matrix and working with the submatrices. These are important when large matrices are involved only for matrices with special structures.

7.2 Other Special Linear Transformations

There are a number of linear transformations with special properties. This chapter has principally focused on non-singular transformations. In this section we will discuss certain special non-singular transformations and other linear transformations of particular interest in various contexts.

(*a*) *Orthogonal transformations* are L.T.'s which map R^n into itself in such a way that the Euclidean norm of a vector is unchanged by the transformation. In other words T is an orthogonal transformation if it maps the vector $\boldsymbol{x} \in D(T)$ into $\boldsymbol{y} \in R(T)$ such that $\boldsymbol{y}'\boldsymbol{y} = \boldsymbol{x}'\boldsymbol{x}$. It may be proved that an orthogonal transformation preserves the scalar product of vectors: i.e.

$$T(\boldsymbol{x}) \,.\, T(\hat{\boldsymbol{x}}) = \boldsymbol{x} \,.\, \hat{\boldsymbol{x}} \text{ for } \boldsymbol{x}, \hat{\boldsymbol{x}} \in D(T). \tag{7.7}$$

T.38. T *is an orthogonal linear transformation which maps* R^n *onto itself. Let* **A** *be the matrix of T with respect to some set of basis vectors for* R^n. *Then* **A** *is non-singular and* $\mathbf{A}'\mathbf{A} = \mathbf{I}_n$.

Proof: Suppose $\boldsymbol{x} \in D(T), \boldsymbol{y} \in R(T)$ such that: $\boldsymbol{y} = A\boldsymbol{x}$. Then

$$\begin{aligned} \boldsymbol{y}' \,.\, \boldsymbol{y} &= (A\boldsymbol{x})'(A\boldsymbol{x}) \\ &= \boldsymbol{x}'A'A\boldsymbol{x} \end{aligned}$$

But as T is orthogonal:

$$\boldsymbol{y}'\boldsymbol{y} = \boldsymbol{x}'\boldsymbol{x}$$

Thus

$$A'A = I_n. \tag{7.8}$$

We will now show that A is non-singular. We know that T is onto, so let us suppose that it is not 1-1. Then there exist vectors $\boldsymbol{x}, \hat{\boldsymbol{x}} \in D(T)$

such that for some $\boldsymbol{y} \in R(T)$

$$\boldsymbol{y} = \boldsymbol{A}\boldsymbol{x}, \boldsymbol{y} = \boldsymbol{A}\hat{\boldsymbol{x}}$$

i.e.

$$\boldsymbol{A}(\boldsymbol{x} - \hat{\boldsymbol{x}}) = \boldsymbol{0}.$$

Thus T transforms $(\boldsymbol{x} - \hat{\boldsymbol{x}})$ into the null vector, and so by the orthogonality of T: $(\boldsymbol{x} - \hat{\boldsymbol{x}})' (\boldsymbol{x} - \hat{\boldsymbol{x}}) = \boldsymbol{0}$.

But a vector can only be orthogonal to itself if it is the null vector. Hence we must have $\boldsymbol{x} = \hat{\boldsymbol{x}}$, and $\boldsymbol{A}$ is non-singular.

Q.E.D.

The matrix of an orthogonal transformation is called an orthogonal matrix. The theorem just proved shows that any matrix $\boldsymbol{A}$ which is non-singular with its inverse such that $\boldsymbol{A}^{-1} = \boldsymbol{A}'$ is an orthogonal matrix. The name orthogonal matrix is derived from the fact that since $\boldsymbol{A}'\boldsymbol{A} = \boldsymbol{I} = \boldsymbol{A}\boldsymbol{A}'$, we must have:

$$\boldsymbol{a}_i'\boldsymbol{a}_j = \delta_{ij}$$

where $\boldsymbol{a}_i$ is the ith column of $\boldsymbol{A}$. In other words the columns of $\boldsymbol{A}$ are mutually orthogonal. It is worth noting that if $\boldsymbol{A}_1$ and $\boldsymbol{A}_2$ are orthogonal nth order matrices, then their products will also be orthogonal since $(\boldsymbol{A}_1\boldsymbol{A}_2)'(\boldsymbol{A}_1\boldsymbol{A}_2) = \boldsymbol{A}_2'\boldsymbol{A}_1'\boldsymbol{A}_1\boldsymbol{A}_2 = \boldsymbol{I}_n$. As an example let us consider the matrix

$$\boldsymbol{A} = \begin{bmatrix} 0 & -1 \\ 1 & 0 \end{bmatrix}$$

which is easily seen to be orthogonal. This transforms any vector (x_1, x_2) in R^2 into the vector $(-x_2, x_1)$. In other words the transformation has rotated the original vector through 90° anti-clockwise to give the new vector. Another orthogonal matrix is:

$$\boldsymbol{B} = \begin{bmatrix} 1 & 0 \\ 0 & -1 \end{bmatrix}.$$

This transforms the vector (x_1, x_2) into $(x_1, -x_2)$; in other words the matrix represents a reflection of the x_2-axis in the origin. In general, all rotations and reflections of R^n may be represented by orthogonal matrices. This explains why the product of several orthogonal matrices should be orthogonal, since clearly several rotations applied in succession to R^n may be represented by a single rotation.

(*b*) *Idempotent transformations* are L.T.'s which satisfy the condition:

$$T(T(\boldsymbol{x})) = T(\boldsymbol{x}) \text{ for } \boldsymbol{x} \in D(T) \tag{7.9}$$

i.e.

$$T^2(\boldsymbol{x}) = T(\boldsymbol{x}).$$

Thus for the matrix $\boldsymbol{A}$ associated with an idempotent transformation we have:

$$\boldsymbol{A}^2 = \boldsymbol{A}. \tag{7.10}$$

The identity matrix represents an idempotent transformation. In fact it is a quite special one since it is the only non-singular idempotent transformation. This follows if we assume that the matrix $\boldsymbol{A}$ is non-singular and pre- or post-multiply both sides of (7.10) by $\boldsymbol{A}^{-1}$, obtaining:

$$\boldsymbol{A} = \boldsymbol{I}.$$

Idempotent matrices – i.e. the matrices of idempotent transformations – are rather useful in econometrics. Note that as $\boldsymbol{A}^2 = \boldsymbol{A}$ for an idempotent matrix, it follows that $\boldsymbol{A}^n = \boldsymbol{A}$ for any $n > 0$.

7.3 Equivalence and Similarity Transformations

It has already been stressed that the matrix representing a linear transformation depends upon the bases chosen for the domain and range of the transformation. Thus we should investigate the effect of altering either basis on the matrix representation of a transformation.

We will consider the transformation $T: R^n \to R^m$ represented by the matrix $\boldsymbol{A}$ with respect to the n basis vectors $\boldsymbol{c}_1, \ldots, \boldsymbol{c}_n$ for R^n and the m basis vectors $\boldsymbol{d}_1, \ldots, \boldsymbol{d}_m$ for R^m. We wish to discover the effect of altering the bases to $\boldsymbol{g}_1, \ldots, \boldsymbol{g}_n$ for R^n and $\boldsymbol{h}_1, \ldots, \boldsymbol{h}_m$ for R^m. Expressing the new basis vectors in terms of the old ones we have:

$$\boldsymbol{g}_i = \sum_{j=1}^{n} g_{ji}\boldsymbol{c}_j \tag{7.11}$$

$$\boldsymbol{h}_i = \sum_{k=1}^{m} h_{ki}\boldsymbol{d}_k. \tag{7.12}$$

Consider any vector $\chi \in R^n$ represented by $\boldsymbol{x} = (x_1, x_2, \ldots, x_n)$ in

terms of the basis $\boldsymbol{c}_1, \ldots, \boldsymbol{c}_n$ and by $\hat{\boldsymbol{x}} = (\hat{x}_1, \hat{x}_2, \ldots, \hat{x}_n)$ in terms of the basis $\boldsymbol{g}_1, \ldots, \boldsymbol{g}_n$.
Then:

$$\chi = \sum_{i=1}^{n} \hat{x}_i \boldsymbol{g}_i$$

$$= \sum_{i=1}^{n} \hat{x}_i \left(\sum_{j=1}^{n} g_{ji} \boldsymbol{c}_j \right)$$

$$= \sum_{j=1}^{n} \left(\sum_{i=1}^{n} \hat{x}_i g_{ji} \right) \boldsymbol{c}_j.$$

But

$$\chi = \sum_{j=1}^{n} x_j \boldsymbol{c}_j,$$

so that

$$x_j = \sum_{i=1}^{n} \hat{x}_i g_{ji}$$

i.e.

$$\boldsymbol{x} = \boldsymbol{G}\hat{\boldsymbol{x}} \tag{7.13}$$

where $\boldsymbol{G} = \|g_{ij}\|$. Note that $\boldsymbol{G}$ is an nth order square matrix; further, it is non-singular because the vectors $\boldsymbol{g}_1, \ldots, \boldsymbol{g}_n$ are L.I. Thus to re-express a vector in terms of the new basis we pre-multiply it by the inverse of $\boldsymbol{G}$, since

$$\hat{\boldsymbol{x}} = \boldsymbol{G}^{-1}\boldsymbol{x}.$$

Similarly, for any vector $\gamma \in R^m$ with representations $\boldsymbol{y}$, $\hat{\boldsymbol{y}}$ in terms of the two bases we have:

$$\hat{\boldsymbol{y}} = \boldsymbol{H}^{-1}\boldsymbol{y} \tag{7.14}$$

where $\boldsymbol{H} = \|h_{ij}\|$.

Now suppose that γ is the image of χ under T, so that:

$$\boldsymbol{y} = \boldsymbol{A}\boldsymbol{x}$$

i.e.

$$\boldsymbol{H}\hat{\boldsymbol{y}} = \boldsymbol{A}\boldsymbol{G}\hat{\boldsymbol{x}}$$

or

$$\hat{\boldsymbol{y}} = \boldsymbol{H}^{-1}\boldsymbol{A}\boldsymbol{G}\hat{\boldsymbol{x}}. \tag{7.15}$$

Thus the matrix representing T with respect to the new bases is given by $\boldsymbol{H}^{-1}\boldsymbol{A}\boldsymbol{G}$. This is still $m \times n$, since $\boldsymbol{H}$ is $m \times m$ and $\boldsymbol{G}$ is $n \times n$.

The transformation of a matrix due to the change in bases is a particular example of a general type of transformation.

D.77. *The transformation of* **A**:

$$\mathbf{B} = \mathbf{EAF}$$

where **E** *and* **F** *are non-singular matrices is called an EQUIVALENCE TRANSFORMATION.* **A** *and* **B** *are said to be equivalent.*

It immediately follows from the argument in the previous paragraph that any two matrices which are equivalent represent the same linear transformation with respect to different sets of basis vectors. Formally:

T.39. *Two* m × n *matrices are equivalent if and only if they represent the same linear mapping from* R^n *to* R^m *relative to two suitably chosen pairs of bases.*

The idea of equivalence may be used to illuminate various results derived earlier. First we note that elementary operations on the rows or columns of a matrix are special types of equivalence transformations. Since matrices which are equivalent represent the same linear transformation, they must have the same rank. Thus elementary operations do not affect the rank of the matrix and, as we have seen, they simplify the computation of the rank by allowing us to reduce the matrix to echelon form. Secondly, any multiplication of a matrix A by a non-singular matrix may be regarded as an equivalence transformation. Hence we see that the rank of the product matrix must be equal to $r(A)$. In a similar manner we can re-interpret all of the results about matrices in terms of equivalence. This illustrates the fundamental point that there is a complete duality between matrices and linear transformations. Thus, instead of defining and establishing the properties of matrices before introducing linear transformations, we could have started with linear transformations and derived many results before introducing matrices.

For square matrices two special kinds of equivalence transformations will be useful.

D.78. *A CONGRUENCE TRANSFORMATION on a square matrix* **A** *is one such that:*

$$\mathbf{B} = \mathbf{R}'\mathbf{AR}$$

where **R** *is non-singular.* **A** *and* **B** *are said to be congruent.*

Note that if $\boldsymbol{A}$ is symmetric, then $\boldsymbol{B}$ will also be symmetric.

D.79. *A SIMILARITY TRANSFORMATION on a square matrix* **A** *is one such that:*

$$\mathbf{B} = \mathbf{S}^{-1}\mathbf{A}\mathbf{S}.$$

A *and* **B** *are said to be similar.*

If $\boldsymbol{A}$ is $n \times n$, then it represents a mapping of R^n into itself. Thus if in the discussion of change of bases we had had $\boldsymbol{G} = \boldsymbol{H}$, the new matrix representation obtained in (7.15) would be similar to the original one. In other words the matrix $\boldsymbol{A}$ represents a transformation $T: R^n \to R^n$ with respect to a given basis for R^n, and any matrix $\boldsymbol{B}$ similar to $\boldsymbol{A}$ represents the same transformation with respect to some other basis for R^n. Hence:

T.40. *Two* $\mathrm{n} \times \mathrm{n}$ *matrices* **A** *and* **B** *are similar if and only if they represent the same linear transformation of* $\mathrm{R^n}$ *into itself, each with respect to a suitably chosen basis for* $\mathrm{R^n}$.

Notice that if $\boldsymbol{B} = \boldsymbol{S}^{-1}\boldsymbol{A}\boldsymbol{S}$ and the matrix $\boldsymbol{S}$ is orthogonal, then $\boldsymbol{A}$ and $\boldsymbol{B}$ must be congruent as well as similar.

7.4 Problems

7.1. Explain why a linear transformation $T: U \to V$ does not have an inverse if the rank of the transformation is not maximal, and the vector spaces U and V have the same dimension.

7.2. Compute the inverses of the following matrices and show in each case that $\boldsymbol{A}^{-1}\boldsymbol{A} = \boldsymbol{A}\boldsymbol{A}^{-1} = \boldsymbol{I}$;

$$\text{(i)} \begin{bmatrix} 1 & 1 & -1 \\ 1 & 2 & 3 \\ 3 & 2 & 1 \end{bmatrix} \qquad \text{(ii)} \begin{bmatrix} 1 & -1 & 1 & -1 & 1 \\ 0 & 1 & 0 & 1 & 0 \\ -2 & 0 & 2 & 0 & -2 \\ 0 & -2 & 0 & 2 & 0 \\ 1 & 2 & 1 & 2 & 3 \end{bmatrix}.$$

7.3. Prove by induction or otherwise that

$$(\boldsymbol{A}_1\boldsymbol{A}_2\boldsymbol{A}_3 \ldots \boldsymbol{A}_{n-1}\boldsymbol{A}_n)^{-1} = (\boldsymbol{A}_n^{-1}\boldsymbol{A}_{n-1}^{-1} \ldots \boldsymbol{A}_3^{-1}\boldsymbol{A}_2^{-1}\boldsymbol{A}_1^{-1}).$$

7.4. Show that elementary matrices – i.e. those representing elementary operations – have inverses of the same form as themselves.

7.5. Prove that, for a square matrix A, the following statements are equivalent:

(i) A is non-singular;

(ii) A has an inverse;

(iii) A is a product of elementary matrices.

7.6. Explain why the following two properties of a linear transformation $T: U \to V$ are necessary and sufficient for the transformation to have an inverse:

(i) for all $x_1, x_2 \in U$ such that $x_1 \neq x_2$, $T(x_1) \neq T(x_2)$;

(ii) for every $y \in V$, there exists at least one vector $x \in U$ such that $T(x) = y$?

7.7. Prove that, if L and T are two transformations on a finite-dimensional vector space such that $LT(x) = x$ then both L^{-1} and T^{-1} exist.

7.8. Prove that the inverse of a non-singular symmetric matrix is itself symmetric. Hence show, for any matrix X for which $X'X$ is non-singular, that $[X'X]^{-1}$ is symmetric.

7.9. Let A have an inverse A^{-1}. Show that the inverse of B, where B is the result of a sequence of elementary operations on A, can be obtained from A^{-1} by applying the same sequence of elementary operations to A^{-1}, but at each state using the inverse operation and post-multiplying. Show the result holds for

$$A = \begin{bmatrix} 3 & 2 & 1 \\ 0 & 1 & 2 \\ 6 & 4 & 6 \end{bmatrix} \text{ and } B = \begin{bmatrix} 0 & 1 & 2 \\ 6 & 4 & 2 \\ 0 & 0 & 4 \end{bmatrix}.$$

7.10. Determine which of the following matrices have inverses and find them if they exist:

$$\text{(i)} \begin{bmatrix} 3 & 20 & -10 \\ 4 & 5 & 6 \\ -2 & -2 & -2 \end{bmatrix} \quad \text{(ii)} \begin{bmatrix} 11 & 11 & 17 & 23 \\ 5 & 3 & 7 & 11 \\ 1 & 2 & 3 & 4 \\ 5 & 6 & 7 & 8 \end{bmatrix} \quad \text{(iii)} \begin{bmatrix} 2 & -1 & 5 \\ 6 & -7 & 3 \\ 14 & -19 & -1 \end{bmatrix}$$

7.11. Prove that $A^{-1} = A'$ for $A = \begin{bmatrix} \cos\theta & \sin\theta \\ -\sin\theta & \cos\theta \end{bmatrix}$.

Give a geometrical interpretation of this transformation A and show what the inverse does.

7.12. Prove that, if L and T are linear transformations on the same vector space, L and T are equivalent if and only if they have the same rank.

7.13. Show that, if $\boldsymbol{A}$ and $\boldsymbol{B}$ are similar matrices, then so are $\boldsymbol{A}^2$, $\boldsymbol{B}^2$ and $\boldsymbol{A}'$, $\boldsymbol{B}'$. If $\boldsymbol{A}$ and $\boldsymbol{B}$ are non-singular, are their inverses $\boldsymbol{A}^{-1}$, $\boldsymbol{B}^{-1}$ also similar?

7.14. If two $n \times n$ matrices are similar, show that they are also equivalent. Is the converse of this true?

7.15. Let

$$\boldsymbol{A} = \begin{bmatrix} 1 & 2 & 1 \\ 5 & -2 & 1 \\ 2 & 1 & 0 \end{bmatrix}$$

be the matrix representation of $T: R^3 \to R^3$ with respect to the unit vectors as a basis for R^3. What is the matrix representation when the vectors (2, 0, 1), (0, 1, 1,), (1, 1, 1) are chosen as a basis for R^3? Are $\boldsymbol{A}$ and $\boldsymbol{B}$ similar and/or equivalent?

7.16. Let T be a linear transformation with domain R^3 and range R^2. Suppose that the matrix representation of T is

$$\boldsymbol{A}' = \begin{bmatrix} 2 & 1 \\ -1 & 3 \\ 2 & 2 \end{bmatrix}$$

when the vectors (1, 1), (1, 0) are used as a basis for the range and (0, 1, 1), (1, 1, 1), (1, 1, 0) are used as a basis for the domain. What is the matrix representation of T when the unit vectors are used as bases for the domain and the range?

8 Determinants

Determinants are frequently used in some treatments of linear algebra and in the classical optimisation approach to micro-economy theory. In this book we have made little use of them, except where they are unavoidable, because the manipulation of determinants is a rather inelegant and unilluminating method of deriving results. However, their use cannot be avoided in the discussion of eigenvalues and quadratic forms contained in the next chapter. Thus the present chapter provides a definition of determinants and some fundamental properties which may be deduced quite easily from this definition. These will be quite sufficient for almost all problems in which determinants arise. For a fuller treatment of them Aitken (1956) or Mirsky (1955) are recommended.

We shall have to deal with submatrices derived from a given matrix by deletion of some of its rows and columns. We denote the submatrix obtained by deleting from the matrix $\boldsymbol{A}$ the ith row and the jth column by $\boldsymbol{A}(i|j)$; e.g. if

$$\boldsymbol{A} = \begin{bmatrix} 1 & 2 & 1 \\ 4 & 6 & 3 \\ 2 & 1 & 5 \end{bmatrix}, \quad \boldsymbol{A}(2|3) = \begin{bmatrix} 1 & 2 \\ 2 & 1 \end{bmatrix}.$$

A determinant is a number associated with a square matrix. The following definition of a determinant gives a rule which when applied iteratively tells us how to compute the determinant of a matrix $\boldsymbol{A}$, written as det $\boldsymbol{A}$ or $|\boldsymbol{A}|$.

D.80. *The DETERMINANT of an* $n \times n$ *matrix is defined as follows:*
(*i*) *for* $n = 1$, *det* $\mathbf{A} = a_{11}$ (*i.e. det* $\mathbf{A}$ *equals the single element of* $\mathbf{A}$);
(ii) *for* $n > 1$, *we assume that the determinant of an* $(n - 1) \times (n - 1)$ *matrix has been defined and then:*

$$\det \mathbf{A} = \sum_{v=1}^{n} a_{iv} (-1)^{i+v} \det \mathbf{A}(i|v), \quad \text{any } i.$$

Usually it will be easiest to take $i = 1$.

Clearly by applying this definition we evaluate the determinant of any $n \times n$ matrix by a series of steps reducing it to the sum of lower order determinants. Given the definition for $n = 1$ we can calculate the determinant of a 2×2 matrix, and hence that of a 3×3 matrix and so on. For example:

$$A = [a_{11}], \quad \det A = a_{11}.$$

$$A = \begin{bmatrix} a_{11} & a_{12} \\ a_{21} & a_{22} \end{bmatrix}, \quad \det A = a_{11} \det A(1|1) + (-1)^3 a_{12} \det A(1|2)$$

$$= a_{11} \det [a_{22}] - a_{12} \det [a_{21}]$$

$$= a_{11}a_{22} - a_{12}a_{21}.$$

Now if

$$A = \begin{bmatrix} a_{11} & a_{12} & a_{13} \\ a_{21} & a_{22} & a_{23} \\ a_{31} & a_{32} & a_{33} \end{bmatrix}$$

$$\det A = a_{11} \det A(1|1) - a_{12} \det A(1|2) + a_{13} \det A(1|3)$$

$$= a_{11} \begin{vmatrix} a_{22} & a_{23} \\ a_{32} & a_{33} \end{vmatrix} - a_{12} \begin{vmatrix} a_{21} & a_{23} \\ a_{31} & a_{33} \end{vmatrix} + a_{13} \begin{vmatrix} a_{21} & a_{22} \\ a_{31} & a_{32} \end{vmatrix}$$

$$= a_{12}(a_{22}a_{33} - a_{32}a_{23}) - a_{12}(a_{21}a_{33} - a_{31}a_{23})$$
$$+ a_{13}(a_{21}a_{32} - a_{22}a_{31}).$$

In like manner the determinant of any square matrix can be calculated, though clearly for large sizes it is a long process.

D.81. *The term* $(-1)^{i+j}$ *det* $\mathbf{A}(i|j)$ *is referred to as the COFACTOR of the element* a_{ij}*; it is written as* A_{ij}*. Thus we have what is called expansion by cofactors:* $|\mathbf{A}| = \sum_{j=1}^{n} a_{ij}A_{ij}$.

In fact there is no reason to restrict ourselves to expanding the determinant using only a row. We could equally expand using a column so that we have:

$$|A| = \sum_{j=1}^{n} a_{ij}A_{ij} = \sum_{i=1}^{n} a_{ij}A_{ij}. \tag{8.1}$$

Using the definition of a determinant it is possible to deduce a number of results on the manipulation and properties of determinants. These are outlined below:

1. If matrix $\boldsymbol{B}$ is derived from the square matrix $\boldsymbol{A}$ by interchanging two rows or by interchanging two columns, then

$$|\boldsymbol{B}| = -|\boldsymbol{A}|. \tag{8.2}$$

Proof: This is a little lengthy, but it can be demonstrated by expanding $\boldsymbol{B}$ by one of the interchanged rows/columns and then expanding the cofactors by the other interchanged row or column. The result can be seen to be the same as expanding $\boldsymbol{A}$ in the same manner but with a change in sign.

2. If $\boldsymbol{A}$ is any square matrix, $|\boldsymbol{A}| = |\boldsymbol{A}'|$.

Proof: This is a matter of expanding one determinant by a row and the other by the equivalent column.

3. If $\boldsymbol{A}$ is any square matrix, and $\boldsymbol{B}$ is derived from it by multiplying the ith row/column by a scalar λ, then:

$$|\boldsymbol{B}| = \lambda|\boldsymbol{A}|.$$

Proof: Simply expand by the row/column in question.

4. If $\boldsymbol{A}$ is a square matrix with two identical rows/columns, then $|\boldsymbol{A}| = 0$.

Proof: Suppose that $\boldsymbol{A}$ has two identical rows. Form $\boldsymbol{B}$ by interchanging these two rows; then $|\boldsymbol{B}| = -|\boldsymbol{A}|$, but $\boldsymbol{B} = \boldsymbol{A} \Rightarrow |\boldsymbol{A}| = -|\boldsymbol{A}|$, i.e. $|\boldsymbol{A}| = 0$.

An immediate extension of this is to a matrix for which one row/column is equal to λ times another row/column, where λ is any scalar.

5. If $\boldsymbol{A}$ is any square matrix and if $\boldsymbol{B}$ is obtained from it by replacing row i of $\boldsymbol{A}$ with row i itself plus λ times row k, then $|\boldsymbol{B}| = |\boldsymbol{A}|$. The same is true for column operations.

Proof: Expand $|\boldsymbol{B}|$ by the ith row. Then:

$$|\boldsymbol{B}| = \sum_{j=1}^{n} (a_{ij} + \lambda a_{kj})B_{ij}$$

$$= \sum_{j=1}^{n} (a_{ij} + \lambda a_{kj})A_{ij}$$

$$= \sum_{1}^{n}(a_{ij}A_{ij} + \lambda a_{kj}A_{ij})$$

$$= |A| + \lambda|\hat{A}|$$

where $\hat{A}$ is the matrix obtained from A by substituting a_{kj} for a_{ij} $(j = 1, \ldots, n)$. Thus $\hat{A}$ has two identical rows.

Q.E.D.

Note: this is an application of another result which states that the expansion by a row or column i in terms of the cofactors of row or column k is equal to zero when $i \neq k$ and is equal to $|A|$ when $i = k$.

6. The square matrix A is singular (i.e. of less than maximal rank) iff $|A| = 0$.

Proof: If $|A| = 0$ then it must be possible by the row or column operations outlined in 5 to transform A to a matrix in which one row/column is a scalar multiple of another. Thus the appropriate row/column vectors are L.D. and so A singular.

If A is singular then at least one row may be written as a linear combination of the others. Hence by appropriate row operations we can transform A to a matrix with two identical rows.

Q.E.D.

A corollary of this is that we can discover the rank of any matrix A by finding the largest square submatrix of A with a non-zero determinant. If this is of order p, then $r(A) = p$. In fact this is generally not a good way to compute the rank of a matrix unless it is relatively small – say 3×3 or less. The determinant of a kth order square submatrix of A is called a kth *order minor* of A. If A is an $n \times n$ square matrix, the minor formed by deleting the last d rows and columns of A is called a *principal leading minor* of A. Thus if $k = n - d$ the submatrix formed in this way will be the kth order principal leading minor.

7. If the square matrix A is non-singular we define A^+, called the adjoint matrix, as:

$$A^+ = \begin{vmatrix} A_{11} & A_{21} & \cdots & A_{n1} \\ A_{12} & A_{22} & & A_{n2} \\ \vdots & & & \\ A_{1n} & A_{2n} & & A_{nn} \end{vmatrix}$$

i.e. if $A^+ = \|a_{ij}^+\|$, $a_{ij}^+ = A_{ji}$.

Then the inverse of A is given by

$$A^{-1} = \frac{1}{|A|} A^+.$$

Proof: Consider the product matrix $\boldsymbol{AA}^+$; let this be the matrix $\boldsymbol{B} = \|b_{ij}\|$. Then:

$$b_{ij} = \sum_{k=1}^{n} a_{ik}A_{jk} = \delta_{ij} \cdot |\boldsymbol{A}|$$

since this is an expansion of A by the ith row and its cofactors if $i = j$, and by the ith row but the cofactors of row j which thus vanishes for $i \neq j$. Hence

$$\boldsymbol{A} \frac{1}{|\boldsymbol{A}|} \boldsymbol{A}^+ = \boldsymbol{I}.$$

Similarly we can show:

$$\frac{1}{|\boldsymbol{A}|} \boldsymbol{A}^+ . \boldsymbol{A} = \boldsymbol{I}.$$

Q.E.D.

This result makes it clear why $|\boldsymbol{A}|$ cannot be zero if an inverse is to exist.

8. *Cramer's Rule* for solving the equation system $\boldsymbol{Ax} = \boldsymbol{b}$. Provided that $\boldsymbol{A}$ is non-singular – i.e. $|\boldsymbol{A}| \neq 0$ – the unique solution to this system is given by:

$$x_k = \frac{1}{|\boldsymbol{A}|} \sum_{i=1}^{n} b_i A_{ik} \qquad (k = 1, \ldots, n).$$

Note that:

$$\sum_{i=1}^{n} b_i A_{ik} = \det [\boldsymbol{a}_1 \boldsymbol{a}_2 \ \ldots \ \boldsymbol{a}_{k-1} \ \boldsymbol{b} \ \boldsymbol{a}_{k+1} \ldots \boldsymbol{a}_n]$$

where $\boldsymbol{a}_i$ is the ith column of $\boldsymbol{A}$, i.e. it is the determinant of the matrix produced by replacing the kth column by the vector $\boldsymbol{b}$.

Proof: The result can be derived immediately by using the above form of the inverse of $\boldsymbol{A}$ to evaluate: $\boldsymbol{x} = \boldsymbol{A}^{-1}\boldsymbol{b}$.

Again this procedure is generally not an efficient one for solving simultaneous equation systems with more than three variables.

9. If $\boldsymbol{A}$ and $\boldsymbol{B}$ are two $n \times n$ matrices and $\boldsymbol{C} = \boldsymbol{AB}$, then $|\boldsymbol{C}| = |\boldsymbol{A}| . |\boldsymbol{B}|$.

Proof: There are two possible cases. First let us suppose that either $\boldsymbol{A}$ or $\boldsymbol{B}$ is singular. Without loss of generality let $r(\boldsymbol{A}) = m < n$. As a result we know that $r(\boldsymbol{C}) \leqslant m < n$. In other words $\boldsymbol{C}$ is singular and $|\boldsymbol{C}| = 0$, while $|\boldsymbol{A}| \,.\, |\boldsymbol{B}| = 0$ since $|\boldsymbol{A}| = 0$.

Now we assume that both $\boldsymbol{A}$ and $\boldsymbol{B}$ are non-singular. To begin with suppose that $\boldsymbol{B}$ is an elementary matrix representing some elementary column operation. Then:

(i) If $\boldsymbol{B}$ interchanges two columns we know that $|\boldsymbol{B}| = -1$ – since it is obtained by performing the appropriate operation on $\boldsymbol{I}_n$ – while $|\boldsymbol{C}| = -|\boldsymbol{A}|$.

(ii) If $\boldsymbol{B}$ multiplies a column by the scalar λ, then $|\boldsymbol{B}| = \lambda$ and $|\boldsymbol{C}| = \lambda \,.\, |\boldsymbol{A}|$.

(iii) If $\boldsymbol{B}$ adds λ times column j to column i, then $|\boldsymbol{B}| = 1$ and $|\boldsymbol{C}| = |\boldsymbol{A}|$. Thus for each type of elementary matrix we have $|\boldsymbol{C}| = |\boldsymbol{A}| \,.\, |\boldsymbol{B}|$. But we know that any non-singular matrix may be written as the product of elementary matrices. Thus if

$$\boldsymbol{B} = \boldsymbol{F}_1 \boldsymbol{F}_2 \ldots \boldsymbol{F}_k,$$

we have:

$$|\boldsymbol{B}| = |\boldsymbol{F}_1| \,.\, |\boldsymbol{F}_2| \ldots |\boldsymbol{F}_k|$$

and

$$\begin{aligned} |\boldsymbol{C}| &= |\boldsymbol{A}\boldsymbol{F}_1 \ldots \boldsymbol{F}_{k-1}| \,.\, |\boldsymbol{F}_k| \\ &= |\boldsymbol{A}| \,.\, |\boldsymbol{F}_1| \ldots |\boldsymbol{F}_k| \\ &= |\boldsymbol{A}| \,.\, |\boldsymbol{B}|. \end{aligned}$$

Q.E.D.

8.1 Problems

8.1. Prove that a sufficient condition for det $\boldsymbol{A} = 0$ is that $a_{ij} = 0$ for more than $n^2 - n$ elements, where $\boldsymbol{A}$ is an $(n \times n)$ matrix.

8.2. What is the determinant of each of the following matrices?

(i) a diagonal matrix $\boldsymbol{A} = \|a_i \delta_{ij}\|$;

(ii) a triangular matrix $\boldsymbol{A} = \|a_{ij}\|$ with $a_{ij} = 0 \qquad j < i$.

8.3. Prove that the determinants of a skew-symmetric matrix of order (2×2) and (4×4) are perfect squares. Can you show that the result is true for all skew-symmetric matrices of even order?

8.4. Suppose $\boldsymbol{A}$ and $\boldsymbol{B}$ are two matrices, neither of which have all elements equal to zero. Prove that, if $\boldsymbol{AB} = \boldsymbol{0}$, det $\boldsymbol{A}$ = det $\boldsymbol{B} = 0$.

8.5. Consider the matrix

$$\begin{bmatrix} 1 & 4 & 7 \\ 3 & 2 & 1 \\ 4 & -4 & 1 \end{bmatrix}$$

Construct the adjoint matrix and hence the inverse. Check your result by obtaining the inverse by a series of elementary operations.

8.6. Prove that the determinant of a skew-symmetric matrix of odd order is zero.

8.7. Prove that, if $\boldsymbol{A} = ||a_{ij}||$ and $\boldsymbol{B} = ||\alpha_i a_{ij}||$, $\det \boldsymbol{B} = \alpha_i \ldots \alpha_n \det \boldsymbol{A}$.

Is the result unaffected if $\boldsymbol{B} = \|\beta_j a_{ij}\|$?

8.8. Show that

$$\begin{vmatrix} 1 & 1 & 1 \\ a & b & c \\ a^2 & b^2 & c^2 \end{vmatrix} = (b - a)(c - b)(c - a).$$

8.9. Show that an expansion of a determinant by the ith row in terms of the cofactors for the kth row vanishes unless $i = k$.

8.10. Prove that two similar matrices have the same determinant.

8.11. Prove that the determinant of an orthogonal matrix must equal ± 1.

9 Eigenvalues and Eigenvectors

In this chapter we consider the existence and nature of solutions to a special system of linear equations. The results thus derived enable us to establish other useful properties of linear transformations and their matrices. The system of equations is:

$$\boldsymbol{A}\boldsymbol{x} = \lambda\boldsymbol{x} \tag{9.1}$$

where $\boldsymbol{A}$ is a square matrix and λ is a scalar. $\boldsymbol{A}$ must be square since both its range and its domain must both be subsets of the same space. Given this we are looking for a vector which the transformation represented by $\boldsymbol{A}$ 'stretches' or 'contracts' by the multiple λ. In other words $\boldsymbol{A}$ transforms $\boldsymbol{x}$ into a new vector colinear with $\boldsymbol{x}$.

D.82. *Let* $\mathbf{A}$ *be a square matrix,* $\mathbf{x}$ *a non-null vector, and* λ *a scalar. If* $\mathbf{Ax} = \lambda\mathbf{x}$, *then* $\mathbf{x}$ *is said to be an EIGENVECTOR of* $\mathbf{A}$, *and* λ *is its associated EIGENVALUE.*

Note: (i) Alternative terms for eigenvector are characteristic vector, invariant direction, or invariant subspace. Other terms for eigenvalues are characteristic value, proper value, or latent root. (ii) Any square matrix has the trivial eigenvector $\boldsymbol{x} = \mathbf{0}$, since $\boldsymbol{A}\mathbf{0} = \lambda\mathbf{0}$ for any λ. We are interested only in non-trivial eigenvectors.

The terms invariant direction or subspace are applied to eigenvectors because of the following result:

T.41. *If* $\mathbf{x}$ *is an eigenvector of a matrix* $\mathbf{A}$, *then so is* $\mu\mathbf{x}$ *for any scalar* μ. *Moreover the eigenvalue associated with* $\mu\mathbf{x}$ *is the same as that associated with* $\mathbf{x}$.

Proof: We know that for some λ, $\boldsymbol{A}\boldsymbol{x} = \lambda\boldsymbol{x}$. Hence:

$$\boldsymbol{A}(\mu\boldsymbol{x}) = \mu \,.\, \boldsymbol{A}\boldsymbol{x} = \mu \,.\, \lambda\boldsymbol{x} = \lambda(\mu\boldsymbol{x}).$$

Q.E.D.

Thus any scalar multiple of an eigenvector is an eigenvector, and so associated with any eigenvector is a one-dimensional subspace named as above.

It should be noted that there might be several distinct eigenvectors associated with a particular eigenvalue. Thus we may have: $\boldsymbol{Ax}_1 = \lambda \boldsymbol{x}_1$, $\boldsymbol{Ax}_2 = \lambda \boldsymbol{x}_2$ where $\boldsymbol{x}_1$, $\boldsymbol{x}_2$ are not scalar multiples of each other. In the light of this it may be shown that T.41 is a special case of a more general result.

T.42. *The set of all eigenvectors of the matrix* **A** *associated with a given eigenvalue* λ *is a vector space.*

Proof: Suppose that $\boldsymbol{x}_1$, $\boldsymbol{x}_2$ are eigenvectors associated with the scalar λ. We will prove that any L.C. of these – i.e. $\boldsymbol{y} = \mu_1 \boldsymbol{x}_1 + \mu_2 \boldsymbol{x}_2$ – is also an eigenvector associated with λ.

$$\begin{aligned} \boldsymbol{Ay} &= \boldsymbol{A}\mu_1 \boldsymbol{x}_1 + \boldsymbol{A}\mu_2 \boldsymbol{x}_2 \\ &= \mu_1 \lambda \boldsymbol{x}_1 + \mu_2 \lambda \boldsymbol{x}_2 \\ &= \lambda \boldsymbol{y} \end{aligned}$$

Q.E.D.

Later we will derive the dimension of this vector space.

Before examining the general problem of finding the eigenvalues and eigenvectors of a matrix, we will briefly consider as examples some special cases:

(i) All the eigenvalues of $\boldsymbol{I}_n$ are 1 and any vector $\boldsymbol{x} \in R^n$ is an eigenvector.

(ii) The L.T. in R^2 that rotates each vector through 90° may be represented by the matrix $\begin{bmatrix} 0 & -1 \\ 1 & 0 \end{bmatrix}$. It has complex eigenvalues – $\pm\sqrt{-1}$ – and complex eigenvectors.

(iii) The L.T. in R^2 that rotates each vector through 180° may be represented by the matrix $\begin{bmatrix} -1 & 0 \\ 0 & -1 \end{bmatrix}$. All of its eigenvalues are -1 with any $\boldsymbol{x} \in R^2$ as an eigenvector.

(iv) The transformation of R^n represented by the diagonal matrix $\boldsymbol{D} = \|\lambda_i \delta_{ij}\|$ has eigenvalues λ_i with the unit vectors as eigenvectors.

Now in the general case we need to find a scalar λ and a non-null $\boldsymbol{x}$ such that:

$$\boldsymbol{Ax} = \lambda \boldsymbol{x}$$

i.e.

$$\boldsymbol{Ax} = \lambda \boldsymbol{I} \,.\, \boldsymbol{x}$$

i.e.
$$[\boldsymbol{A} - \lambda \boldsymbol{I}] \cdot \boldsymbol{x} = \boldsymbol{0}. \tag{9.2}$$

Thus we have a homogeneous system of equations involving the nth order square matrix $[\boldsymbol{A} - \lambda\boldsymbol{I}]$. We know that if a non-trivial solution $\boldsymbol{x}$ is to exist the matrix $[\boldsymbol{A} - \lambda\boldsymbol{I}]$ must be singular. This implies the condition:

$$\det[\boldsymbol{A} - \lambda\boldsymbol{I}] = 0$$

or

$$\begin{bmatrix} a_{11} - \lambda & a_{12} & \dots & a_{1n} \\ a_{21} & a_{22} - \lambda & \dots & a_{2n} \\ \cdot & \cdot & & \\ \cdot & \cdot & & \\ \cdot & \cdot & & \\ a_{n1} & a_{n2} & \dots & a_{nn} - \lambda \end{bmatrix} = 0$$

Expanding this determinant will give an nth degree polynomial equation in λ – it must be nth degree because the highest order term in λ will be the product of the diagonal terms.

D.83. *The polynomial* f(λ) *given by:*

$$\mathrm{f}(\lambda) = (-\lambda)^n + b_{n-1}(-\lambda)^{n-1} + b_{n+2} + \dots + b_1(-\lambda) + b_0$$
$$= \det[\mathbf{A} - \lambda\mathbf{I}] \tag{9.3}$$

is called the CHARACTERISTIC POLYNOMIAL of the square n × n *matrix* **A**, *and the equation:*

$$\mathrm{f}(\lambda) = 0 \tag{9.4}$$

is the CHARACTERISTIC EQUATION of **A**.

Any value of λ which satisfies the characteristic equation will be an eigenvalue for $\boldsymbol{A}$. The associated eigenvector(s) may be found by solving the system of equations using this eigenvalue. From the basic theory of polynomials we know that this equation will have n roots $\lambda_1, \dots, \lambda_n$. Some of these λ_i may be equal, i.e. the roots are not distinct; others may be conjugate pairs of complex roots – i.e. $\alpha + \beta i$, $\alpha - \beta i$ where $i = \sqrt{-1}$.

In the remainder of this book we will concentrate on the real eigenvalues and their eigenvectors. In general the eigenvectors associated with complex eigenvalues will have complex components. It may be shown that the eigenvectors of a pair of conjugate complex eigenvalues will themselves be complex conjugates. Further the various properties of eigenvalues proved in subsequent theorems apply equally to complex eigenvalues. However, since complex numbers play no part in mathematical economics we will ignore them here.

Whether eigenvalues are distinct or not plays an important part in later analysis. The reason for this is made clear by the following theorem:

T.43. *If each eigenvector in a set of eigenvectors of* A *corresponds to a distinct eigenvalue, then the set will be L.I.*

Proof: The proof proceeds by induction on n, the number of eigenvectors. The theorem is true for $n = 1$; we will show that if it is true for $(n - 1)$ eigenvectors corresponding to distinct eigenvalues, then it is also true for n such eigenvectors.

Assume the contrary – i.e. that eigenvectors $\boldsymbol{x}_1, \ldots, \boldsymbol{x}_n$ corresponding to eigenvalues $\lambda_1, \ldots, \lambda_n$, all distinct, are L.D. Hence there exist μ_i, $i = 1, \ldots, n$, not all zero, such that:

$$\sum_{i=1}^{n} \mu_i \boldsymbol{x}_i = \boldsymbol{0}. \tag{9.5}$$

Suppose, without loss of generality, that $\mu_1 \neq 0$. Multiplying (9.5) by $\boldsymbol{A}$ we have:

$$\begin{aligned} &\mu_1 \boldsymbol{A}\boldsymbol{x}_1 + \mu_2 \boldsymbol{A}\boldsymbol{x}_2 \ldots + \mu_n \boldsymbol{A}\boldsymbol{x}_n \\ &= \mu_1 \lambda_1 \boldsymbol{x}_1 + \mu_2 \lambda_2 \boldsymbol{x}_2 \ldots + \mu_n \lambda_n \boldsymbol{x}_n \\ &= \boldsymbol{0}. \end{aligned}$$

In addition if we multiply (9.5) by λ_n, and subtract it from the above we obtain:

$$\mu_1(\lambda_1 - \lambda_n)\boldsymbol{x}_1 + \mu_2(\lambda_2 - \lambda_n)\boldsymbol{x}_2 \ldots + \mu_{n-1}(\lambda_{n-1} - \lambda_n)\boldsymbol{x}_{n-1} = \boldsymbol{0}.$$

But by the induction assumption $\boldsymbol{x}_1, \ldots, \boldsymbol{x}_{n-1}$ are L.I.; hence all the terms $\mu_i(\lambda_i - \lambda_n)$ must be zero. But $\mu_1 \neq 0$ by assumption, so $\lambda_1 = \lambda_n$. This violates the assumption of distinct eigenvalues.

Q.E.D.

9.1 The Diagonalization of Matrices

In Chapter 7 we saw how the matrix representation of a linear transformation was altered by changing the bases for the domain and range of the transformation. In this section we will be concerned to find the matrix representation of a linear transformation which is as close as possible to being a diagonal matrix. Since we are discussing square matrices, that is linear transformations of R^n into itself, we focus on matrices which are similar to the original matrix. Just as a similarity transformation of a matrix leaves the rank of the matrix unaffected the next theorem shows that it also leaves the eigenvalues unaffected.

T.44. *If* **A** *and* **B** *are similar matrices, then they have the same eigenvalues.*

Proof: Suppose $\boldsymbol{B} = \boldsymbol{S}^{-1}\boldsymbol{A}\boldsymbol{S}$, and $\boldsymbol{A}\boldsymbol{x} = \lambda\boldsymbol{x}$.

For any non-singular matrix $\boldsymbol{P}$,

$$\boldsymbol{P}\boldsymbol{A}\boldsymbol{x} = \lambda\boldsymbol{P}\boldsymbol{x}$$

and

$$\boldsymbol{x} = \boldsymbol{P}^{-1}\boldsymbol{P}\boldsymbol{x}.$$

Hence

$$\boldsymbol{P}\boldsymbol{A}\boldsymbol{P}^{-1}\boldsymbol{P}\boldsymbol{x} = \lambda\boldsymbol{P}\boldsymbol{x}.$$

Put $\boldsymbol{y} = \boldsymbol{P}\boldsymbol{x}$, and $\boldsymbol{S} = \boldsymbol{P}^{-1}$ to get:

$$\boldsymbol{S}^{-1}\boldsymbol{A}\boldsymbol{S}\boldsymbol{y} = \boldsymbol{B}\boldsymbol{y} = \lambda\boldsymbol{y}.$$

In other words if λ is an eigenvalue of $\boldsymbol{A}$, it must also be one of $\boldsymbol{B}$. The reverse can easily be proved. If $\boldsymbol{x}$ is the associated eigenvector for $\boldsymbol{A}$, then $\boldsymbol{y} = \boldsymbol{S}^{-1}\boldsymbol{x}$ is the associated one for $\boldsymbol{B}$. Of course, $\boldsymbol{y}$ is just the original eigenvector stated in terms of the new basis.

Q.E.D.

Note that the implication of this is that if $\boldsymbol{A}$ and $\boldsymbol{B}$ are similar, then so are the matrices $[\boldsymbol{A} - \lambda\boldsymbol{I}]$ and $[\boldsymbol{B} - \lambda\boldsymbol{I}]$. We can see this directly by:

$$\boldsymbol{B} - \lambda\boldsymbol{I} = \boldsymbol{S}^{-1}\boldsymbol{A}\boldsymbol{S} - \lambda\boldsymbol{I} = \boldsymbol{S}^{-1}(\boldsymbol{A} - \lambda\boldsymbol{I})\boldsymbol{S}.$$

The implication of this theorem is that, like the rank, the eigenvalues are fundamentally associated with the linear transformation represented by the similar matrices. In the same way we see that the eigenvectors are also fundamentally linked to the linear transformation. Their representation, of course, must depend upon the basis for R^n being used. In the theorem $\boldsymbol{P}$ represented the change of basis so that if $\boldsymbol{x}_i$ was an eigenvector of $\boldsymbol{A}$ associated with eigenvalue λ_i, then $\boldsymbol{y}_i = \boldsymbol{P}\boldsymbol{x}_i$ would be the eigenvector of $\boldsymbol{B}$ associated with λ_i. Both $\boldsymbol{y}_i$ and $\boldsymbol{x}_i$ represent the same fundamental vector in terms of the different bases or co-ordinate systems.

Now a necessary and sufficient condition for an $n \times n$ matrix $\boldsymbol{A}$ to be similar to a diagonal matrix may be proved.

T.45. *Let* **A** *be an* n × n *matrix, and let* T *be the linear transformation of* R^n *that has matrix* **A** *with respect to some basis for* R^n. *The matrix* **A** *is similar to a diagonal matrix* $\mathbf{D} = ||\lambda_i\delta_{ij}||$, *where* $\lambda_1, \lambda_2, \ldots, \lambda_n$ *are real numbers, if and only if there is a basis of* R^n *consisting of eigenvectors of* T.

Proof: $\boldsymbol{A}$ is similar to $\boldsymbol{D}$ iff there is a basis $\boldsymbol{f}_1, \ldots, \boldsymbol{f}_n$ of R^n such that T has the matrix $\boldsymbol{D}$ with respect to this basis. For any basis $\boldsymbol{f}_1, \ldots, \boldsymbol{f}_n$ the co-ordinates of $T(\boldsymbol{f}_i)$ are the elements in the ith column of the matrix with respect to this basis. Thus T has matrix $\boldsymbol{D}$ iff

$$T(\boldsymbol{f}_i) = \sum_{j=1}^{n} \lambda_i \delta_{ij} \boldsymbol{f}_j$$
$$= \lambda_i \boldsymbol{f}_i$$

for $i = 1, \ldots, n$. But $T(\boldsymbol{f}_i) = \lambda_i \boldsymbol{f}_i$ if and only if $\boldsymbol{f}_i$ is a eigenvector of T.

Q.E.D.

Thus the similarity transformation to diagonalise a matrix is the one which changes the basis to a set of eigenvectors for the linear transformation. The resulting diagonal matrix will have the eigenvalues of the linear transformation as its diagonal elements.

The theorem just proved established a necessary and sufficient condition for the matrix $\boldsymbol{A}$ to be similar to a diagonal matrix in terms of the eigenvectors. In order to diagonalize a matrix we must therefore discover whether this condition is satisfied. One result follows trivially from T.43.

T.46. *Let* T *be a linear transformation of* R^n *to* R^n, *and suppose that* T *has* n *distinct eigenvalues* λ_i(i = 1, . . . , n). *Then* T *can be represented by a diagonal matrix whose diagonal elements are the* λ_i. *Any other matrix* **A** *representing* T *may be diagonalized by an appropriate similarity transformation.*

We will also prove another result, which essentially restates T.45, because it indicates how we should set about diagonalizing a matrix in practice.

T.47. *Let* $\mathbf{A}$ *be an* n × n *matrix with* n *L.I. eigenvectors* $\mathbf{x}_1, \ldots, \mathbf{x}_n$ *and eigenvalues* $\lambda_i (i = 1, \ldots, n)$ *– not necessarily distinct. Then there exists a non-singular matrix* $\mathbf{X}$ *such that the similarity transformation gives:*

$$\mathbf{X}^{-1}\mathbf{A}\mathbf{X} = \|\lambda_i \delta_{ij}\|.$$

Proof: Let $\boldsymbol{X} = [\boldsymbol{x}_1, \ldots, \boldsymbol{x}_n]$. Clearly it is non-singular, since the columns $\boldsymbol{x}_i$ are L.I. by assumption. Now:

$$\begin{aligned} \boldsymbol{AX} &= [\boldsymbol{Ax}_1 \ \boldsymbol{Ax}_2 \ldots \boldsymbol{Ax}_n] \\ &= [\lambda_1 \boldsymbol{x}_1 \ \lambda_2 \boldsymbol{x}_2 \ldots \lambda_n \boldsymbol{x}_n]. \end{aligned}$$

Put

$$\boldsymbol{D} = \| \lambda_i \delta_{ij} \|$$

and let $\boldsymbol{e}_1, \ldots, \boldsymbol{e}_n$ be the unit vectors. Then:

$$\begin{aligned} \boldsymbol{XD} &= \boldsymbol{X}[\lambda_1 \boldsymbol{e}_1 \ldots \lambda_n \boldsymbol{e}_n] \\ &= [\lambda_1 \boldsymbol{Xe}_1 \ldots \lambda_n \boldsymbol{Xe}_n] \\ &= [\lambda_1 \boldsymbol{x}_1 \ldots \lambda_n \boldsymbol{x}_n]. \end{aligned}$$

Thus $$\boldsymbol{XD} = \boldsymbol{AX},$$

i.e. $$\boldsymbol{D} = \boldsymbol{X}^{-1}\boldsymbol{AX}$$

Q.E.D.

Implicitly this proof treats the basis for the transformation represented by $\boldsymbol{A}$ as the unit vectors. It then follows that the eigenvectors of $\boldsymbol{A}$ for this basis, if they are L.I., provide the matrix to perform the requisite change of basis directly, since it is the matrix whose columns are n L.I. eigenvectors of $\boldsymbol{A}$. Another way of viewing the same procedure is to note that ,v' ıı we have diagonalized the matrix the new eigenvectors will be the unit vectors. Thus we need to find the matrix performing this transformation. Suppose it is $\boldsymbol{P}$ so that

$$\begin{aligned} \boldsymbol{Px}_1 &= \boldsymbol{e}_1 \\ \boldsymbol{Px}_2 &= \boldsymbol{e}_2 \\ &\ldots \\ \boldsymbol{Px}_n &= \boldsymbol{e}_n \end{aligned}$$

i.e. $$\boldsymbol{PX} = \boldsymbol{I}$$

$$\boldsymbol{P} = \boldsymbol{X}^{-1}$$

Now: $$\boldsymbol{A}\boldsymbol{x}_i = \lambda_i \boldsymbol{x}_i \qquad (i = 1, \ldots, n)$$

and we wish to find $\boldsymbol{D}$ such that

$$\boldsymbol{D}\boldsymbol{e}_i = \lambda_i \boldsymbol{e}_i \qquad (i = 1, \ldots, n)$$

Substituting $\boldsymbol{x}_i = \boldsymbol{P}^{-1}\boldsymbol{e}_i$ we get:

$$\boldsymbol{P}\boldsymbol{A}\boldsymbol{P}^{-1}\boldsymbol{e}_i = \lambda_i \boldsymbol{e}_i \qquad (i = 1, \ldots, n)$$

and hence $\boldsymbol{D} = \boldsymbol{X}^{-1}\boldsymbol{A}\boldsymbol{X}$.

Example: We will find the eigenvalues, eigenvectors and then diagonalize the matrix $\boldsymbol{A}$ given by:

$$\boldsymbol{A} = \begin{bmatrix} 2 & 1 & -1 \\ 0 & 1 & 1 \\ 2 & 0 & -2 \end{bmatrix}.$$

The characteristic polynomial is:

$$\begin{aligned} f(\lambda) &= \det[\boldsymbol{A} - \lambda \boldsymbol{I}] \\ &= (2 - \lambda)[(1 - \lambda)(-2 - \lambda)] + 2[1 + (1 - \lambda)] \\ &= (2 - \lambda)[-2 + \lambda + \lambda^2 + 2] \\ &= \lambda(2 - \lambda)(1 + \lambda). \end{aligned}$$

Thus the eigenvalues are $\lambda_1 = 0$, $\lambda_2 = 2$, $\lambda_3 = -1$. Since they are distinct we know that the associated eigenvectors will be L.I. Note that one eigenvalue is equal to zero; this implies that $\det(\boldsymbol{A}) = 0$, in other words that $r(\boldsymbol{A}) < 3$. We will only derive an eigenvector for $\lambda_2 = 2$; the others may be found similarly.

$$[\boldsymbol{A} - 2\boldsymbol{I}]\boldsymbol{x}_2 = \boldsymbol{0}$$

i.e. $$\begin{bmatrix} 0 & 1 & -1 \\ 0 & -1 & 1 \\ 2 & 0 & -4 \end{bmatrix} \begin{bmatrix} x_{12} \\ x_{22} \\ x_{32} \end{bmatrix} = \boldsymbol{0}.$$

Thus $x_{12} = 2x_{22} = 2x_{32}$. We can choose one of these arbitrarily, so let us put $x_{32} = 1$ giving $\boldsymbol{x}_2 = (2, 1, 1)$. The other two eigenvectors are $\boldsymbol{x}_1 = (1, -1, 1)$ and $\boldsymbol{x}_3 = (1, -1, 2)$. The matrix of eigenvectors $\boldsymbol{X}$ is therefore:

$$\boldsymbol{X} = \begin{bmatrix} 1 & 2 & 1 \\ -1 & 1 & -1 \\ 1 & 1 & 2 \end{bmatrix}.$$

We can confirm that the vectors are L.I. by checking that $\boldsymbol{X}$ is non-singular. We obtain: $\det(\boldsymbol{X}) = 1(2+1) + 1(4-1) + 1(-2-1) = 3$. Thus $\boldsymbol{X}$ is indeed non-singular, and

$$\boldsymbol{X}^{-1} = \begin{bmatrix} 1 & -1 & -1 \\ \frac{1}{3} & \frac{1}{3} & 0 \\ -\frac{2}{3} & \frac{1}{3} & 1 \end{bmatrix}.$$

If we form the product $\boldsymbol{X}^{-1}\boldsymbol{AX}$, we obtain the diagonal matrix:

$$\boldsymbol{D} = \begin{bmatrix} 0 & 0 & 0 \\ 0 & 2 & 0 \\ 0 & 0 & -1 \end{bmatrix}.$$

It will not always be possible to find a similarity transformation to diagonalize a matrix. If an eigenvalue has a multiplicity of greater than one, i.e. for some $i, j, k, \ldots, \lambda_i = \lambda_j = \lambda_k = \ldots$, then only under special circumstances will it be possible to find linearly independent eigenvectors associated with the multiple eigenvalue. However, with some difficulty it can be shown that any square matrix may be transformed by a similarity transformation to *Jordan canonical form*. This has the following structure:

$$\begin{bmatrix} \lambda_1 & 0 & & & & & & & & \\ & \lambda_2 & 0 & & & & & & & \\ & & \cdot & & & & & & & \\ & & & \cdot & & & & & & \\ & & & & \lambda_h & \alpha_1 & 0 & & & \\ & & & & & \lambda_h & \alpha_2 & 0 & & \\ & & & & & & \lambda_h & 0 & & \\ & & & & & & & \lambda_i & & \\ & & & & & & & & \cdot & \\ & & & & & & & & & \lambda_m \end{bmatrix}$$

i.e. $\boldsymbol{C} = \|c_{ij}\|$ where $c_{i,i-j} = 0, j > 0$; $c_{ii} = \lambda_i$, some $j \in \{1, \ldots, m\}$; and, if $c_{ii} = c_{i+1,i+1}$, then $c_{i,i+1} = \alpha_g$; otherwise $c_{i,i+j} = 0, j > 0$. The elements α_g will take the values 0 or 1 depending on whether there are L.I. eigenvectors associated with the multiple eigenvalue or not. The possibility of achieving this transformation will not be proved here; a proof will be found in Gantmacher (1959).

The relationship between a linear transformation and its eigenvalues and eigenvectors may be further elucidated by considering an $n \times n$ matrix $\boldsymbol{A}$ with n L.I. eigenvectors. Now consider the product $\boldsymbol{Ay}$ where $\boldsymbol{y}$ is an arbitrary vector in R^n. The eigenvectors span R^n so we can write:

$$\boldsymbol{y} = \sum_{i=1}^{n} \mu_i \boldsymbol{x}_i.$$

So

$$\boldsymbol{Ay} = \sum_{i=1}^{n} \lambda_i \mu_i \boldsymbol{x}_i.$$

Thus $\boldsymbol{A}$ transforms $\sum_{i=1}^{n} \mu_i \boldsymbol{x}_i$ into $\sum_{i=1}^{n} \lambda_i \mu_i \boldsymbol{x}_i$; the action of $\boldsymbol{A}$ may therefore be resolved into action along each of the n L.I. directions defined by the n eigenvectors. In each such direction $\boldsymbol{A}$ has the effect of stretching or contracting a vector by a factor λ_i. To find the total effect of $\boldsymbol{A}$ on any vector we resolve it into components along each of the directions $(\mu_i \boldsymbol{x}_i)$, look at the effect of $\boldsymbol{A}$ on each component (transforming $\mu_i \boldsymbol{x}_i$ to $\lambda_i \mu_i \boldsymbol{x}_i$), and add up the results. Finally it is clear that if the directions $\boldsymbol{x}_i$ are taken as the axes of the co-ordinate system, then the effect of $\boldsymbol{A}$ is that of a diagonal matrix.

9.2 Symmetric Matrices

Symmetric matrices have a number of useful properties with respect to their eigenvalues and eigenvectors. These play an important role in the application of the theory of maximisation subject to constraints to economic problems.

T.48. *If* **A** *is a symmetric matrix, then all its eigenvalues are real.*

Proof: Suppose not, in other words, that $\lambda = a + bi$, $\lambda^* = a - bi$ are eigenvalues of $\boldsymbol{A}$. Thus:

$$\boldsymbol{Ax} = \lambda \boldsymbol{x}, \tag{9.6}$$

$$\boldsymbol{Ax}^* = \lambda^* \boldsymbol{x}^*. \tag{9.7}$$

Premultiply (9.6) by $(\boldsymbol{x}^*)'$ and (9.7) by $\boldsymbol{x}'$, and then subtract: $(\boldsymbol{x}^*)'\boldsymbol{Ax} - \boldsymbol{x}'\boldsymbol{Ax}^* = (\lambda - \lambda^*)\boldsymbol{x}'\boldsymbol{x}^*$, since $\boldsymbol{x}'\boldsymbol{x}^* = (\boldsymbol{x}^*)'\boldsymbol{x}$. Note that $\boldsymbol{x}'\boldsymbol{Ax}^*$ is a scalar whose transpose is equal to itself. Thus, using $\boldsymbol{A} = \boldsymbol{A}'$, $\boldsymbol{x}'\boldsymbol{Ax}^* = (\boldsymbol{x}'\boldsymbol{Ax}^*)' = (\boldsymbol{x}^*)'\boldsymbol{Ax}$.

Hence
$$(\lambda - \lambda^*)\boldsymbol{x}'\boldsymbol{x}^* = 0. \tag{9.8}$$

In addition
$$\boldsymbol{x}'\boldsymbol{x}^* = \sum_{i=1}^{n} \boldsymbol{x}_i\boldsymbol{x}_i^*.$$

It has already been noted that the eigenvectors associated with a pair of conjugate complex eigenvalues will themselves be complex conjugates. Thus if $\boldsymbol{x} = (x_1 + y_1 i,\ x_2 + y_2 i, \dots, x_n + y_n i)$, then $\boldsymbol{x}^* = (x_1 - y_1 i,\ x_2 - y_2 i, \dots, x_n - y_n i)$. Hence $\boldsymbol{x}'\boldsymbol{x}^*$ must be a real positive number. Therefore in (9.8) we must have $\lambda = \lambda^*$, which implies $b = 0$ in $\lambda = a + bi$. In other words the roots are all real.

Q.E.D.

T.49. *If* **A** *is symmetric the eigenvectors of* **A** *corresponding to distinct eigenvalues are orthogonal.*

Proof: Suppose $\boldsymbol{Ax}_i = \lambda_i\boldsymbol{x}_i$, $\boldsymbol{Ax}_j = \lambda_j\boldsymbol{x}_j$ and $\lambda_i \neq \lambda_j$. Then
$$\boldsymbol{x}_j'\boldsymbol{Ax}_i = \lambda_i\boldsymbol{x}_j'\boldsymbol{x}_i, \tag{9.9}$$
$$\boldsymbol{x}_i'\boldsymbol{Ax}_j = \lambda_j\boldsymbol{x}_i'\boldsymbol{x}_j. \tag{9.10}$$

we get:
$$(\lambda_i - \lambda_j)\boldsymbol{x}_j'\boldsymbol{x}_i = 0.$$

Thus
$$\boldsymbol{x}_j'\boldsymbol{x}_i = 0 \text{ since } \lambda_i \neq \lambda_j.$$

Q.E.D.

T.50. *If* **A** *is symmetric with all its eigenvalues distinct, then we can choose a set of eigenvectors such that the matrix* **X** *of eigenvectors is orthogonal.*

Proof: We have already proved that $\boldsymbol{x}_j'\boldsymbol{x}_i = 0$ for all $i \neq j$, provided that the eigenvalues are distinct. Further we know that if $\boldsymbol{x}$ is an eigenvector associated with the eigenvalue λ, so is $\mu\boldsymbol{x}$. Hence we can normalize each $\boldsymbol{x}_i$ by choosing its scale such that:
$$\boldsymbol{x}_i'\boldsymbol{x}_i = \sum_{k=1}^{n} x_{ik}^2 = 1, \text{ each } i.$$

Thus we can ensure that $\boldsymbol{x}_j'\boldsymbol{x}_i = \delta_{ij}$.

Q.E.D.

This result directly confirms that we can use the matrix $\boldsymbol{X}$ to diagonalise $\boldsymbol{A}$, since if $\boldsymbol{D} = \| \lambda_i\delta_{ij} \|$, we have:
$$\boldsymbol{AX} = \boldsymbol{XD}$$

i.e. $$X^{-1}AX = X^{-1}XD,$$

$\therefore$ $$X^{-1}AX = D.$$

That is the orthogonal similarity transformation X will diagonalise the matrix A. In geometric terms this means that by changing the basis for R^n from the unit vectors to the orthonormal set $x_1, \ldots, x_n$ we have diagonalised the transformation. In other words the diagonalisation was achieved by an appropriately chosen rotation of our co-ordinate system.

To extend the analysis we must now consider symmetric matrices with roots of multiplicity greater than one.

T.51. *The eigenvectors of a symmetric matrix* **A** *associated with an eigenvalue with multiplicity* k *span a subspace of* R^n *of dimension* k.

Proof: Suppose that λ_j is an eigenvalue with multiplicity k, and that u_j is a normalised eigenvector associated with λ_j. We know that we can choose $(n-1)$ vectors $v_1, \ldots, v_{n-1}$ such that the set u_j, $v_1, \ldots, v_{n-1}$ is an orthonormal basis for R^n. Let P be the matrix whose columns are these n orthonormal basis vectors, i.e.

$$P = [u_j \ v_1 \ v_2 \ \ldots \ v_{n-1}].$$

By construction P is orthogonal.

We consider:

$$P'AP = P'[\lambda_j u_j \ Av_1 \ldots Av_{n-1}]$$
$$= \begin{bmatrix} \lambda_j & \mathbf{0} \\ \mathbf{0} & B_1 \end{bmatrix} \tag{9.11}$$

where B_1 is an $(n-1)$th order square matrix whose (ih)th element is $v_i'Av_h$. This follows because $v_i'u_j = 0$ and $u_j'Av_i = (u_j'Av_i)' = v_i'Au_j = \lambda_j v_i'u_j = 0$. Note that B_1 is symmetric because with A symmetric $(v_i'Av_h)' = v_h'Av_i$. Since P is orthogonal, the matrix $A_1 = P'AP$ is similar to A and thus must have the same eigenvalues as A. From (9.11) we see that:

$$\det[A_1 - \lambda I_n] = (\lambda_j - \lambda)\det[B_1 - \lambda I_{n-1}].$$

Thus if λ_j has multiplicity $k \geqslant 2$, it follows that $\det[B_1 - \lambda_j I_{n-1}]$ must vanish. This is because if $f(\lambda)$ is the characteristic polynomial of A, then

$$f(\lambda) = (\lambda_j - \lambda)^k(\lambda_1 - \lambda)\ldots(\lambda_i - \lambda)$$

where $\lambda_1, \ldots, \lambda_i$ are the other eigenvalues of $\boldsymbol{A}$. Further the characteristic polynomial of $\boldsymbol{A}_1$ must be the same, since $\boldsymbol{A}_1$ has the same eigenvalues. Hence:

$$\det[\boldsymbol{A}_1 - \lambda \boldsymbol{I}_n] = (\lambda_j - \lambda)\det[\boldsymbol{B}_1 - \lambda \boldsymbol{I}_{n-1}]$$
$$= (\lambda_j - \lambda)^k(\lambda_1 - \lambda)\ldots(\lambda_i - \lambda).$$

i.e. $$\det[\boldsymbol{B}_1 - \lambda \boldsymbol{I}_{n-1}] = (\lambda_j - \lambda)^{k-1}(\lambda_1 - \lambda)\ldots(\lambda_i - \lambda).$$

With $\det[\boldsymbol{B}_1 - \lambda_j \boldsymbol{I}_{n-1}] = 0$ we see that all minors of order $(n-1)$ of the matrix

$$[\boldsymbol{A}_1 - \lambda_j \boldsymbol{I}_n] = \begin{bmatrix} 0 & \mathbf{0} \\ \mathbf{0} & \boldsymbol{B}_1 - \lambda_j \boldsymbol{I}_{n-1} \end{bmatrix}$$

vanish. In other words $r(\boldsymbol{A}_1 - \lambda_i \boldsymbol{I}_n) \leqslant n - 2$, which implies that $r(\boldsymbol{A} - \lambda_j \boldsymbol{I}_n) \leqslant 2$ since similar matrices have identical ranks. Thus the nullity of $[\boldsymbol{A} - \lambda_j \boldsymbol{I}_n]$ is greater than or equal to 2, and we can find another vector $\hat{\boldsymbol{u}}_j$ orthogonal to $\boldsymbol{u}_j$ in the null space of $[\boldsymbol{A} - \lambda_j \boldsymbol{I}_n]$. That is, we can find another eigenvector of $\boldsymbol{A}$ associated with the eigenvalue λ_j which is orthogonal to the first one $\boldsymbol{u}_j$.

If $k = 2$ we can stop, while if $k \geqslant 3$ we can choose a new orthogonal basis for R^n $\boldsymbol{u}_j, \hat{\boldsymbol{u}}_j, \hat{\boldsymbol{v}}_1, \ldots, \hat{\boldsymbol{v}}_{n-2}$. We put:

$$\boldsymbol{Q} = [\boldsymbol{u}_j \ \hat{\boldsymbol{u}}_j \ \hat{\boldsymbol{v}}_1 \ \ldots \ \hat{\boldsymbol{v}}_{n-2}],$$

where $\boldsymbol{Q}$ is orthogonal, and

$$\boldsymbol{A}_2 = \boldsymbol{Q}'\boldsymbol{A}\boldsymbol{Q} = \begin{bmatrix} \lambda_j & 0 & \mathbf{0} \\ 0 & \lambda_j & \mathbf{0} \\ \mathbf{0} & \mathbf{0} & \boldsymbol{B}_2 \end{bmatrix}$$

with $\boldsymbol{B}_2 = \| \hat{\boldsymbol{v}}_i'\boldsymbol{A}\hat{\boldsymbol{v}}_h \|$, a square matrix of order $(n-2)$. Proceeding as above we see that $n(\boldsymbol{A} - \lambda_j \boldsymbol{I}_n] \geqslant 3$, and so we continue until we have $n(\boldsymbol{A} - \lambda_j \boldsymbol{I}_n) \geqslant k$.

Finally, since any two eigenvectors associated with distinct eigenvalues are orthogonal, there cannot be more than k L.I. or orthogonal eigenvectors associated with an eigenvalue of multiplicity k as that would require a set of more than k L.I. vectors in R^n.

Q.E.D.

Comments: (i) The proof that $n(\boldsymbol{A} - \lambda_j \boldsymbol{I}_n) \leqslant k$ applies to all matrices. Thus, in general the subspace spanned by the eigenvectors associated with an eigenvalue of multiplicity k is of dimension less than or equal to k.

(ii) If we use the approach in the proof above we can easily construct an orthonormal set of eigenvectors for a symmetric matrix $\boldsymbol{A}$. Thus, every symmetric matrix has at least one set of orthonormal eigenvectors $\boldsymbol{u}_1, \ldots, \boldsymbol{u}_n$. Put:

$$\boldsymbol{P} = [\boldsymbol{u}_1 \ \boldsymbol{u}_2 \ \ldots \ \boldsymbol{u}_n]$$

so that $\boldsymbol{P}$ is orthogonal and

$$\begin{aligned} \boldsymbol{P}'\boldsymbol{A}\boldsymbol{P} &= \| \boldsymbol{u}_i'\boldsymbol{A}\boldsymbol{u}_j \| \\ &= \| \lambda_j \boldsymbol{u}_i'\boldsymbol{u}_j \| \\ &= \| \lambda_j \delta_{ij} \|. \end{aligned}$$

In other words $\boldsymbol{P}$ gives an orthogonal similarity transformation which diagonalizes $\boldsymbol{A}$. Formally we may state:

T.52. *Any symmetric matrix* **A** *can be diagonalized by an orthogonal similarity transformation using a matrix whose columns are an orthogonal set of eigenvectors for* **A**. *The resulting matrix has as its diagonal elements the eigenvalues of* **A**.

9.3 Quadratic Forms

D.84. *Given a vector* $\mathbf{x} \in \mathrm{R}^{\mathrm{n}}$ *and an* $\mathrm{n} \times \mathrm{n}$ *matrix* **A**, *the function*

$$\mathrm{Q}(\mathbf{x}, \mathbf{x}) = \mathbf{x}'\mathbf{A}\mathbf{x}$$

is called a QUADRATIC FORM.

If we expand the equation for $Q(\boldsymbol{x}, \boldsymbol{x})$ we get:

$$\begin{aligned} Q(\boldsymbol{x}, \boldsymbol{x}) &= \boldsymbol{x}'\boldsymbol{A}\boldsymbol{x} \\ &= \boldsymbol{x}' . \begin{bmatrix} \sum_j a_{1j}x_j \\ \vdots \\ \sum_j a_{nj}x_j \end{bmatrix} \end{aligned}$$

$$= \sum_i x_i (\sum_j a_{ij}x_j)$$

$$= a_{11}x_1^2 + a_{12}x_1x_2 + a_{13}x_1x_3 + \ldots + a_{1n}x_1x_n$$

$$+ a_{21}x_2x_1 + a_{22}x_2^2 + a_{23}x_2x_3 + \ldots + a_{2n}x_2x_n$$

$$+ a_{31}x_3x_1 + a_{32}x_3x_2 + a_{33}x_3^2 + \ldots$$
$$+ a_{n1}x_nx_1 + a_{n2}x_nx_2 + \ldots + a_{nn}x_n^2. \tag{9.12}$$

Quadratic forms are a particular example of a more general type of mapping.

D. 85. *A mapping* B *from ordered pairs of vectors in* R^n *to the real numbers* (R^1) *is called a BILINEAR MAPPING if* B *satisfies:*

$$\begin{aligned}&\mathrm{B}(\alpha_1\mathbf{u}_1 + \alpha_2\mathbf{u}_2, \beta_1\mathbf{v}_1 + \beta_2\mathbf{v}_2)\\ &= \alpha_1\beta_1\mathrm{B}(\mathbf{u}_1, \mathbf{v}_1) + \alpha_1\beta_2\mathrm{B}(\mathbf{u}_1, \mathbf{v}_2)\\ &+ \alpha_2\beta_1\mathrm{B}(\mathbf{u}_2, \mathbf{v}_1) + \alpha_2\beta_2\mathrm{B}(\mathbf{u}_2, \mathbf{v}_2),\end{aligned}$$

for any $\mathbf{u}_1, \mathbf{u}_2, \mathbf{v}_1, \mathbf{v}_2 \in \mathrm{R}^n$ *and scalars* $\alpha_1, \alpha_2, \beta_1, \beta_2$.

In a similar manner to the proof of T.29 it can be shown that any bilinear mapping $B(\;)$ may be represented with respect to a given basis for R^n by some matrix $\boldsymbol{A}$, such that:

$$B(\boldsymbol{u}, \boldsymbol{v}) = \boldsymbol{u}'\boldsymbol{A}\boldsymbol{v},$$

where $\boldsymbol{u}$, $\boldsymbol{v}$ are the representations of the vectors in the domain in terms of the basis. Beside quadratic forms defined above another type of bilinear mapping is the scalar product of two vectors, since

$$\begin{aligned}&(\alpha_1\boldsymbol{u}_1 + \alpha_2\boldsymbol{u}_2)'(\beta_1\boldsymbol{v}_1 + \beta_2\boldsymbol{v}_2)\\ &\qquad = \alpha_1\beta_1\boldsymbol{u}_1'\boldsymbol{v}_1 + \alpha_1\beta_2\boldsymbol{u}_1'\boldsymbol{v}_2 + \alpha_2\beta_1\boldsymbol{u}_2'\boldsymbol{v}_1 + \alpha_2\beta_2\boldsymbol{u}_2'\boldsymbol{v}_2.\end{aligned}$$

The matrix representation of this bilinear mapping is $\boldsymbol{I}_n$ since:

$$\boldsymbol{u}'\boldsymbol{v} = \boldsymbol{u}'\boldsymbol{I}_n\boldsymbol{v}.$$

Returning to quadratic forms we note that the coefficient of each term x_ix_j $(i \neq j)$ in (9.12) is $a_{ij} + a_{ji}$. Thus without loss of generality we can alter the representation of the form by defining new coefficients:

$$b_{ij} = b_{ji} = \tfrac{1}{2}(a_{ij} + a_{ji}), \qquad (i \neq j) \tag{9.13a}$$

$$b_{ii} = a_{ii}. \tag{9.13b}$$

Then $Q(\boldsymbol{x}, \boldsymbol{x}) = \boldsymbol{x}'\boldsymbol{A}\boldsymbol{x} = \boldsymbol{x}'\boldsymbol{B}\boldsymbol{x}$, where $\boldsymbol{B} = \|b_{ij}\|$ is a symmetric matrix. Thus we can always assume that the matrix in a quadratic form is symmetric. If in an actual problem it is not symmetric, then by using (9.13*a*) and (9.13*b*) the conversion to symmetry is easily performed.

The fundamental property of quadratic forms which we need to establish is the sign they take for different vectors $\boldsymbol{x}$.

D.86. (*a*) $Q(\mathbf{x}, \mathbf{x})$ *is said to be POSITIVE DEFINITE (NEGATIVE DEFINITE) if* $Q(\mathbf{x}, \mathbf{x}) > 0$ ($Q(\mathbf{x}, \mathbf{x}) < 0$) *for all* $\mathbf{x} \neq \mathbf{0}$.

(*b*) $Q(\mathbf{x}, \mathbf{x})$ *is POSITIVE SEMI-DEFINITE (NEGATIVE SEMI-DEFINITE) if* $Q(\mathbf{x}, \mathbf{x}) \geqslant 0$ ($Q(\mathbf{x}, \mathbf{x}) \leqslant 0$) *for all* $\mathbf{x}$.

In discussing quadratic forms it is frequently useful to transform the matrix of the form by transforming the vectors in the domain. Suppose $\boldsymbol{x} = \boldsymbol{S}\boldsymbol{y}$, then we have:

$$\begin{aligned} Q(\boldsymbol{x}, \boldsymbol{x}) &= \boldsymbol{x}'\boldsymbol{A}\boldsymbol{x} \\ &= \boldsymbol{y}'\boldsymbol{S}'\boldsymbol{A}\boldsymbol{S}\boldsymbol{y} = Q(\boldsymbol{y}, \boldsymbol{y}). \end{aligned}$$

Note that if $\boldsymbol{A}$ is symmetric, then so is $\boldsymbol{S}'\boldsymbol{A}\boldsymbol{S}$. Provided that $\boldsymbol{S}$ is one-to-one and onto, the range of values taken by $Q(\boldsymbol{x}, \boldsymbol{x})$ and $Q(\boldsymbol{y}, \boldsymbol{y})$ must be identical. In other words, if we apply a congruence transformation on $\boldsymbol{A}$ using the non-singular matrix $\boldsymbol{S}$ we can simplify the task of discovering the properties of the quadratic form.

T.53. *Every quadratic form can be transformed into canonical form*:

$$Q(\mathbf{y}, \mathbf{y}) = \sum_{i=1}^{n} \lambda_i y_i^2$$

by an appropriate similarity transformation. The λ_i *are the eigenvalues of the matrix of the quadratic form.*

Proof: Put $Q(\boldsymbol{x}, \boldsymbol{x}) = \boldsymbol{x}'\boldsymbol{A}\boldsymbol{x}$, and let $\boldsymbol{X}$ be the matrix whose columns are an orthonormal set of eigenvectors for $\boldsymbol{A}$. We know that $\boldsymbol{X}$ exists, and that $\boldsymbol{X}' = \boldsymbol{X}^{-1}$. Now put:

$$\boldsymbol{y} = \boldsymbol{X}^{-1}\boldsymbol{x}, \text{ where } \boldsymbol{y} \in R^n,$$

i.e.

$$\boldsymbol{x} = \boldsymbol{X}\boldsymbol{y}.$$

Then

$$\begin{aligned} Q(\boldsymbol{x}, \boldsymbol{x}) &= \boldsymbol{y}'\boldsymbol{X}'\boldsymbol{A}\boldsymbol{X}\boldsymbol{y} \\ &= \boldsymbol{y}' . \boldsymbol{D}\boldsymbol{y} \end{aligned}$$

where $\boldsymbol{D} = \| \lambda_i \delta_{ij} \|$ and the λ_i are the eigenvalues of $\boldsymbol{A}$ as in T.47. Hence we may write:

$$Q(\boldsymbol{x}, \boldsymbol{x}) = \sum_{i=1}^{n} \lambda_i y_i^2.$$

Q.E.D.

Directly from this we have the result:

T.54. *The quadratic form associated with the matrix* **A** *is positive definite iff all the eigenvalues of* **A** *are strictly positive, and it is negative definite iff all the eigenvalues are strictly negative.*

Generally we say that the matrix A is positive or negative definite if either of these conditions is satisfied. The matrix will be positive (negative) semi-definite if all $\lambda_i \geqslant 0$ ($\lambda_i \leqslant 0$) and some $\lambda_i = 0$.

It is often not convenient to discover the sign of a quadratic form by examining the eigenvalues of the matrix. There is an alternative approach which involves calculating the minors of the matrix A. In order to demonstrate this we need a simple lemma.

Lemma: If $D = X'AX$, where X is an orthogonal matrix, then $\det(D) = \det(A)$.

Proof: $\det(D) = \det(X'AX)$

$$= \det(X)^2 \,.\, \det(A)$$

as $\det(X') = \det(X)$. But $X' = X^{-1}$, so $\det(X') = \det(X^{-1}) = 1/\det(X)$. Hence $\det(X) = \pm 1$, and the result follows. Note that we have shown that an orthogonal matrix must have a determinant equal to either 1 or -1.

T.55. (*a*) *A necessary and sufficient condition for the quadratic form* $\mathbf{x}'\mathbf{A}\mathbf{x}$ *to be positive definite is that the principal minors of* **A** *are all positive; i.e.*

$$a_{11} > 0, \qquad \begin{vmatrix} a_{11} & a_{12} \\ a_{21} & a_{22} \end{vmatrix} > 0, \qquad \begin{vmatrix} a_{11} & a_{12} & a_{13} \\ a_{21} & a_{22} & a_{23} \\ a_{31} & a_{32} & a_{33} \end{vmatrix} > 0,$$

$$\ldots, \det(\mathbf{A}) > 0.$$

(*b*) *The quadratic form* $\mathbf{x}'\mathbf{A}\mathbf{x}$ *is negative definite iff for every* $i = 1, \ldots, n$ *the principal minor of order* i *has sign* $(-1)^i$; *i.e.*

$$a_{11} < 0, \qquad \begin{vmatrix} a_{11} & a_{12} \\ a_{21} & a_{22} \end{vmatrix} > 0, \qquad \begin{vmatrix} a_{11} & a_{12} & a_{13} \\ a_{21} & a_{22} & a_{23} \\ a_{31} & a_{32} & a_{33} \end{vmatrix} < 0,$$

$$\ldots, [\det(\mathbf{A})](-1)^n > 0$$

Proof: We will prove (*a*) only since (*b*) follows from an identical argument.

Let $x'Ax = y'Dy$ after the appropriate orthogonal similarity transformation with D being the diagonal matrix of eigenvalues of A. By the lemma we know det (A) = det (D); in other words:

$$\det(A) = \lambda_1\lambda_2 \ldots \lambda_n.$$

Now suppose we put $x = (x_1, \ldots, x_{n-1}, 0)$, then $y = Xx$ will be of the form $(y_1, \ldots, y_{n-1}, 0)$ and:

$$x'Ax = (x^*)'A^*x^* = (y^*)'D^*y^* = y'Dy$$

where A^*, D^* are $(n - 1)$th order square matrices formed by omitting the nth row and column of A and D, and x^*, y^* are $(n - 1)$-vectors formed by omitting the zero element in x, y. But D^* may be obtained from A^* by the orthogonal similarity transformation represented by the matrix X^* – i.e. X with the nth row and column omitted. Hence:

$$\det(A^*) = \det(D^*) = \lambda_1\lambda_2 \ldots \lambda_{n-1}$$

where det (A^*) is the $(n - 1)$th order principal minor of A. Generalising this we see that the ith order principal minor of A must equal the product of the first i eigenvalues of A.

Now if A is positive definite, then for all i, $\lambda_i > 0$, and so every principal minor of A must be strictly positive. Obversely, if any principal minor of A is negative, then at least one eigenvalue must be negative and so the matrix cannot be positive definite.

Q.E.D.

Corollary: The quadratic form $x'Ax$ is positive (negative) semidefinite if det (A) = 0 and all other principal minors of A are either positive (of sign $(-1)^i$) or zero.

We have, so far, considered quadratic forms for which x could be arbitrarily chosen from R^n. In many applications of quadratic forms we may only be interested in the value of the quadratic form taken for $x \in V$ where V is some defined subset of R^n. A particular case of this is when V is the set of all solutions to the equation system $Bx = c$, where B is an $m \times n$ matrix. We will only state sufficient conditions for the quadratic form $x'Ax$ to be positive or negative definite subject to the specified constraint. These conditions are derived in Bellman (1960), or Samuelson (1947) (Appendix A).

T.56. *A sufficient condition that the quadratic form* $\mathbf{x}'\mathbf{A}\mathbf{x}$ *be positive definite for all* $\mathbf{x}$ *satisfying the constraints* $\mathbf{B}\mathbf{x} = \mathbf{c}$ *is that det* $(\mathbf{A})$ *and the determinants given by:*

$$\begin{vmatrix} a_{11} & a_{12} \ldots & a_{1k} & b_{11} \ldots & b_{m1} \\ & & & & \\ a_{k1} & \ldots & a_{kk} & b_{1k} \ldots & b_{mk} \\ b_{11} & \ldots & b_{1k} & 0 \ldots & 0 \\ & & & & \\ b_{m1} & \ldots & b_{mk} & 0 \ldots & 0 \end{vmatrix} = |\mathbf{A}_k|$$

are such that $(-1)^m$ *det* $(\mathbf{A}) > 0$ *and* $(-1)^m . |\mathbf{A}_k| > 0$ *for* $k = m + 1, \ldots, n$*; in this,* m *is the number of constraints and* n *the number of elements in* $\mathbf{x}$.

A sufficient condition for the constrained quadratic form to be negative definite is that $(-1)^n$ *det* $(\mathbf{A}) > 0$ *and* $(-1)^k . |\mathbf{A}_k| > 0$ *for* $k = m + 1, \ldots, n$.

9.4 Problems

9.1. Find the eigenvalues and hence the eigenvectors of the matrix

$$\boldsymbol{A} = \begin{vmatrix} 1 & 0 & 2 \\ 6 & -1 & 3 \\ 0 & 0 & 2 \end{vmatrix}.$$

How would your answer differ if $a_{21} = a_{23} = 0$? How do you explain this different result?

9.2. Prove by induction that if $\boldsymbol{x}$ is an eigenvector of matrix $\boldsymbol{A}$ associated with eigenvalue λ,

$$\boldsymbol{A}^k \boldsymbol{x} = \lambda^k \boldsymbol{x}.$$

Furthermore, show that for any polynomial $f(\alpha)$,

$$f(\boldsymbol{A})\boldsymbol{x} = f(\lambda)\boldsymbol{x}.$$

9.3. A matrix $\boldsymbol{A}$ is said to be idempotent if $\boldsymbol{A}^n = \boldsymbol{A}$ for all $n > 0$. What values can the eigenvalues of an idempotent matrix take?

9.4. Prove that, if λ is an eigenvalue of an orthogonal matrix $\boldsymbol{A}$, then so is $1/\lambda$.

9.5. Prove that, for any two square matrices, $\boldsymbol{AB}$ and $\boldsymbol{BA}$ have the same eigenvalues.

9.6. Prove that the rank of a symmetric matrix is $n - k$ where k is the multiplicity of the eigenvalue equal to zero. Show that this result holds for the following matrices:

(i) $\begin{bmatrix} 1 & 1 & 1 \\ 1 & 1 & 1 \\ 1 & 1 & 1 \end{bmatrix}$ (ii) $\begin{bmatrix} 2 & 1 & 1 \\ 1 & 3 & -2 \\ 1 & -2 & 3 \end{bmatrix}$ (iii) $\begin{bmatrix} 0 & 1 & 1 \\ 1 & 0 & 1 \\ 1 & 1 & 0 \end{bmatrix}$.

9.7. Show that if $\boldsymbol{x}$ is an eigenvector of $\boldsymbol{A}$ with eigenvalue α and $\boldsymbol{y}$ is an eigenvector of $\boldsymbol{A}'$ with eigenvalue β ($\beta \neq \alpha$), then $\boldsymbol{y}'\boldsymbol{x} = 0$. Show that eigenvalues of $\boldsymbol{A}'$ are the same as those of $\boldsymbol{A}$. Are the eigenvectors also the same?

9.8. Show that, if the symmetric matrix $\boldsymbol{A}$ is either positive or negative semi-definite, then $\det(\boldsymbol{A}) = 0$.

9.9. Prove that, if $\boldsymbol{x}'\boldsymbol{A}\boldsymbol{x}$ is positive definite and $\boldsymbol{A}$ is non-singular, then $\boldsymbol{x}'\boldsymbol{A}^{-1}\boldsymbol{x}$ is also positive definite.

9.10. Show that the symmetric matrix $\boldsymbol{A}$ is positive definite if and only if there exists a non-singular matrix $\boldsymbol{X}$ such that $\boldsymbol{X}'\boldsymbol{X} = \boldsymbol{A}$. What is $\boldsymbol{X}$?

9.11. If λ is the largest eigenvalue of the symmetric matrix $\boldsymbol{A}$, prove that

$$\lambda_1 = \max_{\boldsymbol{x}} \frac{\boldsymbol{x}' . \boldsymbol{A}\boldsymbol{x}}{\boldsymbol{x}'\boldsymbol{x}}$$

when $\boldsymbol{x}$ is allowed to range over all R^n.

9.12. Let $\boldsymbol{A}$ be the matrix representation of a linear transformation on a finite-dimensional vector space. Prove that the product of the eigenvalues of $\boldsymbol{A}$ is equal to the determinant of $\boldsymbol{A}$.

9.13. Prove that

$$\boldsymbol{A} = \begin{bmatrix} \cos\theta & \sin\theta \\ -\sin\theta & \cos\theta \end{bmatrix}$$

is an orthogonal matrix. Find the eigenvalues and eigenvectors of $\boldsymbol{A}$. What effect does $\boldsymbol{A}$ have on (i) the length of any vector, and (ii) the axes which are rotated by $\boldsymbol{A}$?

10 Non-negative Square Matrices

In many economic problems we will be concerned with matrices distinguished by the characteristic that all of the elements of the matrix are greater than or equal to zero. For instance, in the Leontief system introduced in Chapter 5, if each industry produces one good only the input matrix A – i.e. the matrix of coefficients a_{ij} giving the (constant) amount of good i required to produce one unit of good j – has all its elements greater than or equal to zero, since every a_{ij} must be either zero or positive.

D.87. *A matrix* $\mathbf{A}$ *is said to be:*
(*a*) *NON-NEGATIVE iff every element* $a_{ij} \geqslant 0$;
(*b*) *SEMI-POSITIVE iff every row and every column of* $\mathbf{A}$ *is a semi-positive vector, i.e.* $\mathbf{a}_i \geqslant \mathbf{0}, \mathbf{a}^i \geqslant \mathbf{0}$ *for all* i – *that is every* $a_{ij} \geqslant 0$ *and at least one element of each row and each column is strictly positive;*
(*c*) *POSITIVE iff every element* $a_{ij} > 0$.

Returning to the Leontief system we showed that, given A and the final demand vector f, we wish to find a solution vector x to the equation system:

$$(I - A)x = f.$$

Clearly if the inverse $(I - A)^{-1}$ exists we can find the solution from:

$$x = (I - A)^{-1}f.$$

Now if we expand the inverse using the expansion of $(I - A)^{-1}$ as a power series we get:

$$x = (I + A + A^2 + \dots)f$$

i.e.

$$x = (\sum_{t=0}^{\infty} A^t)f. \quad (10.1)$$

Thus the nature of the solution will depend upon the powers of A and on the asymptotic behaviour of A^t.

Before we focus specifically on non-negative matrices we will examine the general question of power series and the asymptotic behaviour of A^t for any matrix A.

10.1 Matrix Power Series

We can easily extend the idea of a polynomial function of some scalar λ defined by:

$$f(\lambda) = b_n\lambda^n + b_{n-1}\lambda^{n-1} + \ldots + b_1\lambda + b_0$$

to polynomial functions of an $n \times n$ square matrix A by defining:

$$f(A) = b_nA^n + b_{n-1}A^{n-1} + \ldots + b_1A + b_0I$$

where $f(A)$ is another $n \times n$ square matrix. Mathematicians have developed a substantial body of analysis relating to polynomial and other functions of matrices. The best known theorem is the Cayley–Hamilton theorem which is stated below; a full discussion of the field may be found in Gantmacher (1959).

T.57. *(Cayley–Hamilton) Every square matrix* $\mathbf{A}$ *satisfies its own characteristic equation. In other words if det* $(\mathbf{A} - \lambda\mathbf{I}) = \mathrm{f}(\lambda)$, *then* $\mathrm{f}(\mathbf{A}) = \mathbf{0}$.

A useful result which follows from this theorem is:

T.58. *Let* λ_i $(i = 1, \ldots, n)$ *be the eigenvalues of an* $n \times n$ *matrix* $\mathbf{A}$ *and let* $\mathbf{B}$ *be given by some polynomial function of* $\mathbf{A}$, *i.e.* $\mathbf{B} = \mathrm{f}(\mathbf{A})$. *Then* $\mathrm{f}(\lambda_i)$ $(i = 1, \ldots, n)$ *will be the eigenvalues of* $\mathbf{B}$.

In some economic models we will be interested in polynomial functions which are infinite power series, as for example in (10.1). Then the results above require convergence of the series, and this focuses our attention on the asymptotic behaviour of A^t. First we will examine:

$$\lim_{t\to\infty} A^t z$$

where z is an arbitrary n-vector. Suppose that the eigenvectors and eigenvalues of A are $x_1, \ldots, x_n, \lambda_1, \ldots, \lambda_n$ respectively and that we can write:

$$z = \sum_{i=1}^{n} \alpha_i x_i. \tag{10.2}$$

Then

$$A^t z = \sum_{i=1}^{n} \alpha_i \lambda_i^t x_i.$$

Clearly as t gets large this sum will be dominated by the term involving the eigenvalue with the highest absolute value, provided that the associated coefficient α_i is not zero. Let us assume that this eigenvalue has the index $i = 1$, so that we can write:

$$\lim_{t\to\infty} A^t z = \alpha_1 x_1 \cdot (\lim_{t\to\infty} \lambda_1^t)$$

i.e.

$$A^t z \approx \alpha_1 \lambda_1^t x_1. \tag{10.3}$$

This will only converge to a vector with finite components if the absolute value of λ_1 is less than or equal to 1. Formally:

T.59. *Let* $\mathbf{A}$ *be an* $n \times n$ *matrix with eigenvalues* $\lambda_1, \ldots, \lambda_n$, *where* $|\lambda_1| \geq |\lambda_j|$ *all* $j = 2, \ldots, n$, *and eigenvectors* $\mathbf{x}_1, \ldots, \mathbf{x}_n$ *which form a basis for* R^n. *Then given any* $\mathbf{z} \in R^n$ *with* $\mathbf{z} = \sum \alpha_i \mathbf{x}_i$,

$$\mathbf{A}^t\mathbf{z} \approx \alpha_1 \lambda_1^t \mathbf{x}_1$$

(*or* $\mathbf{A}^t\mathbf{z} \approx \alpha_1\lambda_1^t\mathbf{x}_1 + \alpha_k\lambda_k^t\mathbf{x}_k$ *for* $k \neq 1$ *if* $|\lambda_1| = |\lambda_k|$). $\mathbf{A}^t\mathbf{z}$ *will converge asymptotically iff* $|\lambda_1| \leq 1$.

We will now examine the asymptotic behaviour of A^t itself. To extend the discussion leading to T.59 we will prove a lemma.

Lemma: Let A be an $n \times n$ matrix, x an n-vector, and α, λ real numbers. Then

$$\lim_{t\to\infty} A^t z = \alpha\lambda^t x$$

for all $z \in R^n$ iff

$$\lim_{t\to\infty} A^t = \lambda^t x y'$$

where $\alpha = y'z$.

Proof: As z is independent of t, $\lim A^t z = (\lim A^t)z$. Thus, if

$$\lim_{t\to\infty} A^t = \lambda^t x y', \quad \lim_{t\to\infty} A^t z = (\lambda^t x y')z = \lambda^t x \,.\, y'z = \alpha\lambda^t x,$$

which proves sufficiency.

Now suppose that $\lim_{t\to\infty} A^t = \lambda^t x y' + E$ where $E \neq \mathbf{0}$ is an $n \times n$

matrix. Then $\lim_{t \to \infty} A^t z = (\lambda^t x y' + E)z = \alpha \lambda^t x + Ez$. For arbitary z we must therefore have $E = 0$.

Q.E.D.

T.60. *Let* **A** *be an* n × n *matrix with* n *L.I. eigenvectors. If* **A** *has a unique eigenvalue of largest absolute value, say* λ_1, *with corresponding eigenvector* $\mathbf{x}_1$, *then*

$$\lim_{t \to \infty} \mathbf{A}^t = \lambda_1^t \mathbf{x}_1 \mathbf{y}_1'$$

where $\mathbf{y}_1$ *is the eigenvector of* $\mathbf{A}'$ *corresponding to the eigenvalue* λ_1.

Proof: We know that A and A' must have the same eigenvalues, and thus λ_1 is the eigenvalue of largest absolute value for A' as well as A. Hence by T.59

$$\lim_{t \leftarrow \infty} (A')^t z = \beta_1 \lambda_1^t y_1$$

for any $z = \Sigma \beta_i y_i$. From the lemma

$$\lim_{t \to \infty} {}'(A')^t = \lambda_1^t y_1 w'. \tag{10.4}$$

Now $(A')^t = (A^t)'$, and from T.59 and the lemma $(\lim A^t)' = \lambda_1^t (x_1 u')'$

i.e.

$$\lim_{t \to \infty} (A')^t = \lambda_1^t \, u \mathbf{u}'. \tag{10.5}$$

From (10.2) and (10.3) we can put $w = x_1$, $u = y_1$. Q.E.D.

This theorem can be generalised to cover matrices whose eigenvectors do not form a basis for R^n. One immediate corollary of this result which also holds for the general case is as follows:

T.61. *Lim* $\mathbf{A}^t = 0$ *iff all the eigenvalues of* **A** *are less than unity in absolute value.*

To obtain the solution to the Leontief system expressed as a power series in (10.1) it was assumed that the power series converged. For the scalar case of $(1 - \alpha)^{-1}$ we know that a necessary and sufficient condition for convergence is $|\alpha| < 1$. The next theorem states the equivalent condition for a matrix series.

T.62. $(\mathbf{I} - \mathbf{A})^{-1} = \sum_{t=0}^{\infty} \mathbf{A}^t$ *iff* $\lim_{t \to \infty} \mathbf{A}^t = 0$.

Proof: We examine the effect of pre- or post-multiplying $(I - A)$ by the first t terms of the series and show that these products tend to the identity matrix if A satisfies the condition specified.

$$(I - A)(I + A + A^2 + \ldots + A^{t-1}) = I - A^t,$$

so that

$$\lim_{t \to \infty} \{(I - A)(I + A + A^2 + \ldots + A^{t-1})\} = \lim_{t \to \infty} (I - A^t),$$

and thus

$$(I - A)(\sum_{t=0}^{\infty} A^t) = I \text{ iff } \lim A^t = 0.$$

A similar argument applies if the order of multiplication is reversed.

Q.E.D.

10.2 Indecomposable Matrices

In order to discuss the properties of non-negative matrices we need to introduce a fundamental concept relating to the structure of a matrix. In other words we must examine the pattern of the coefficients which make up the matrix, in particular to discover whether the system generating the matrix can be reorganised so that the zero elements in the matrix form a special block. If we consider the system of equations:

$$Ax = \lambda x$$

we can reorder the variables – for instance interchanging x_i with x_j – by reordering both the columns of the matrix A and the order of the equations (i.e. the rows of A) in the same manner. Thus to interchange x_i with x_j we would interchange the ith and jth rows and the same columns in the matrix. In general, any reordering of variables may be achieved by appropriately permuting the rows and columns of the matrix together.

D.88. *The square matrix* **A** *is said to be DECOMPOSABLE if we can permute its rows and columns together in such a way to give a matrix of the form:*

$$\begin{bmatrix} \mathbf{A}_{11} & \mathbf{A}_{12} \\ \mathbf{0} & \mathbf{A}_{22} \end{bmatrix}$$

where $\mathbf{A}_{11}$, $\mathbf{A}_{22}$ *are square submatrices,* $\mathbf{0}$ *is a rectangular null submatrix, and* $\mathbf{A}_{12}$ *a rectangular submatrix. If the matrix cannot be reordered in this form, then it is INDECOMPOSABLE.*

Note: (*a*) The terms *reducible, irreducible* are sometimes used instead of decomposable, indecomposable.

(*b*) If by continued permutation of rows and columns the matrix can be reordered to give a matrix of the form:

$$\begin{bmatrix} \boldsymbol{A}_{11} & \mathbf{0} & \mathbf{0} \\ \mathbf{0} & \boldsymbol{A}_{22} & \mathbf{0} \\ \mathbf{0} & \mathbf{0} & \boldsymbol{A}_{33} \end{bmatrix}$$

where the submatrices $\boldsymbol{A}_{11}, \boldsymbol{A}_{22}, \boldsymbol{A}_{33}, \ldots,$ are square and indecomposable, then we say that the matrix is *completely decomposable.*

We will show later that indecomposable matrices have a number of properties which do not apply to decomposable matrices. Thus it will be useful to establish the implications of these different matrix structures. Consider a Leontief model in which final demand is given as a proportion α of gross output ($\alpha < 1$), so that we have:

$$[\boldsymbol{I} - \boldsymbol{A}]\boldsymbol{x} = \alpha\boldsymbol{x}$$

or

$$\boldsymbol{A}\boldsymbol{x} = (1 - \alpha)\boldsymbol{x}.$$

Further suppose $\boldsymbol{A}$ is decomposable so that we have:

$$\boldsymbol{A} = \begin{bmatrix} \boldsymbol{A}_{11} & \boldsymbol{A}_{12} \\ \mathbf{0} & \boldsymbol{A}_{22} \end{bmatrix}$$

and let us partition $\boldsymbol{x}$ into $(\boldsymbol{x}_1, \boldsymbol{x}_2)$ where if $\boldsymbol{A}_{11}$ is $k \times k$, $\boldsymbol{A}_{22}$ is $(n - k) \times (n - k)$, then $\boldsymbol{x}_1$ is a k-vector, $\boldsymbol{x}_2$ an $(n - k)$-vector. In equation form we can now write the system as:

$$\boldsymbol{A}_{11}\boldsymbol{x}_1 + \boldsymbol{A}_{12}\boldsymbol{x}_2 = (1 - \alpha)\boldsymbol{x}_1$$

$$\boldsymbol{A}_{22}\boldsymbol{x}_2 = (1 - \alpha)\boldsymbol{x}_2.$$

In other words the industries indexed by $k + 1, \ldots, n$ can be separated out and their gross output levels determined without reference to the behaviour of the other industries. This is only possible if none of the goods produced by this second set of industries is purchased by any industry in the first set for use as an input, though if $\boldsymbol{A}_{12} \neq \mathbf{0}$ the goods produced by the first set of industries are purchased by those in the second set. Clearly if $\boldsymbol{A}$ were completely decomposable, i.e. if $\boldsymbol{A}_{12} = \mathbf{0}$, then we can separate the industries into two groups which do not trade and can be treated as if they were totally independent economies.

This idea of interdependence may be formalized by considering three possibilities.

(i) If we can partition our variables so that each variable depends only on the value taken by other members of the set and not at all on any other variables, then the system is really a set of autonomous or independent subsystems. The matrix of the system will be completely decomposable.

(ii) Suppose a partition of variables can be made such that x_i depends upon x_j for any $j > i$, but x_j does not depend on x_i. Then we have one-way dependence – i.e. $x_j \rightarrow x_i$ – and a decomposable matrix.

(iii) Finally there is two-way dependence in which every x_i depends on every other x_j – i.e. $x_i \rightleftarrows x_j$ – for which the matrix is indecomposable. It should be noted that the idea of dependence does not refer to direct interrelationships alone. Thus industry i may not directly sell to industry j, but if it does sell to industry k which in turn sells to industry j then the gross output of i must depend on that of j.

10.3 The Frobenius–Perron Theorem

This section is devoted to the exposition and proof of a series of results concerning the eigenvalues and eigenvectors of non-negative matrices. We will, in particular, be interested in the existence of a semi-positive or strictly positive eigenvector and of a positive largest eigenvalue. Since there are a number of interrelated results formal proofs for each one will not be given, but instead the main results will be derived and then all of them will be stated as one theorem. The discussion will be algebraic—largely following that in Lancaster (1968); alternative proofs relying on topological concepts (i.e. fixed points of point-set mappings) may be found in Debreu and Herstein (1953), Nikaido (1970), and Schwartz (1961).

The discussion is based upon a fundamental lemma:

Lemma. Let $Z(\boldsymbol{x})$ denote the number of zero components of the vector $\boldsymbol{x}$. Then, if $\boldsymbol{A}$ is semi-positive and indecomposable, and $\boldsymbol{x}$ is semi-positive, $Z[(\boldsymbol{I} + \boldsymbol{A})\boldsymbol{x}] < Z(\boldsymbol{x})$.

Proof: Put $\boldsymbol{y} = (\boldsymbol{I} + \boldsymbol{A})\boldsymbol{x}$. Since $\boldsymbol{I} + \boldsymbol{A} > \boldsymbol{0}$, it is clear that $Z(\boldsymbol{y}) \leqslant Z(\boldsymbol{x})$. Suppose that $Z(\boldsymbol{y}) = Z(\boldsymbol{x})$. Then as $\boldsymbol{y} \geqslant \boldsymbol{x}$ (from $\boldsymbol{I} + \boldsymbol{A} \geqslant \boldsymbol{I}$), the zero components of $\boldsymbol{y}$ must be the same as those of $\boldsymbol{x}$. Without loss of generality let these occupy the last r elements, so that we can write $\boldsymbol{y} = (\hat{\boldsymbol{y}}, \boldsymbol{0})$, $\boldsymbol{x} = (\hat{\boldsymbol{x}}, \boldsymbol{0})$ where $\hat{\boldsymbol{x}}$, $\hat{\boldsymbol{y}}$ each have $(n - r)$ elements and are strictly positive. Then:

$$\begin{bmatrix} \hat{\boldsymbol{y}} \\ \boldsymbol{0} \end{bmatrix} = \begin{bmatrix} \boldsymbol{I} + \boldsymbol{A}_{11} & \boldsymbol{A}_{12} \\ \boldsymbol{A}_{21} & \boldsymbol{I} + \boldsymbol{A}_{22} \end{bmatrix} \begin{bmatrix} \hat{\boldsymbol{x}} \\ \boldsymbol{0} \end{bmatrix}$$

i.e.

$$\hat{\boldsymbol{y}} = (\boldsymbol{I} + \boldsymbol{A}_{11})\hat{\boldsymbol{x}}$$

$$\boldsymbol{0} = \boldsymbol{A}_{21}\hat{\boldsymbol{x}}.$$

This requires $\boldsymbol{A}_{21} = \boldsymbol{0}$, since $\hat{\boldsymbol{x}} > \boldsymbol{0}$, which contradicts the assumption of indecomposability.

Q.E.D.

Corollary: If $\boldsymbol{A}$ is semi-positive and indecomposable of order n, then $(\boldsymbol{I} + \boldsymbol{A})^{n-1} > \boldsymbol{0}$.

Proof: If we take any semi-positive vector $\boldsymbol{x}$ and apply the lemma above repeatedly, then $(\boldsymbol{I} + \boldsymbol{A})^{n-1}\boldsymbol{x}$ can have no zero components. As $\boldsymbol{x}$ is arbitrary we must have $(\boldsymbol{I} + \boldsymbol{A})^{n-1} > \boldsymbol{0}$.

Q.E.D.

The discussion now proceeds by defining a number $r(\boldsymbol{v}^*)$ associated with the matrix $\boldsymbol{A}$ and demonstrating its properties. The number is defined by:

$$r(\boldsymbol{v}^*) = \max_{\boldsymbol{v} \in V} \left\{ \min_i \frac{(\boldsymbol{A}\boldsymbol{v})_i}{v_i} \right\} \tag{10.6}$$

where $V = \{\boldsymbol{v} | \boldsymbol{v} \geqslant \boldsymbol{0}, \sum_{i=1}^{n} v_i = 1\}$ and $(\boldsymbol{A}\boldsymbol{v})_i$ is the ith component of the vector $\boldsymbol{A}\boldsymbol{v}$; $\boldsymbol{v}^*$ is the vector for which the maximum occurs. In words $r(\boldsymbol{v}^*)$ is found by taking weighted sums of the rows of $\boldsymbol{A}$ and choosing the row i with the lowest ratio of this weight to the weight for the ith element of each row (i.e. the ith column); then we maximise this value over all possible weightings. Now since $\boldsymbol{A}, \boldsymbol{v} \geqslant \boldsymbol{0}$, we can easily show that $r(\boldsymbol{v}^*) > 0$. Let $\boldsymbol{v} = \boldsymbol{u} = (1/n, \ldots, 1/n) \in V$. Then:

$$\begin{aligned} r(\boldsymbol{u}) &= \min_i \frac{(\boldsymbol{A}\boldsymbol{u})_i}{\boldsymbol{u}_i} \\ &= \min_i \sum_j a_{ij} \\ &> 0 \quad \text{since } \boldsymbol{A} \text{ is semi-positive.} \end{aligned}$$

By definition

$$r(\boldsymbol{v}^*) \geqslant r(\boldsymbol{u}) > 0.$$

Thus as well as showing that $r(\boldsymbol{v}^*) > 0$ we see that it must be greater than or equal to the minimum row sum of the matrix.

We now show that $r(\boldsymbol{v}^*)$ gives us the maximum value which might be taken by an eigenvalue of $\boldsymbol{A}$; in other words $r(\boldsymbol{v}^*)$ is the largest number satisfying the inequality:

$$\boldsymbol{A}\boldsymbol{v} \geqq r\boldsymbol{v}.$$

The kth component of the inequality gives:

$$\frac{(\boldsymbol{A}\boldsymbol{v})_k}{v_k} \geqslant r$$

i.e.

$$r \leqslant \min_k \frac{(\boldsymbol{A}\boldsymbol{v})_k}{v_k}.$$

Clearly for a maximum of r we will have equality with $r = r(\boldsymbol{v}^*)$. It follows that

$$[\boldsymbol{A}\boldsymbol{v}^* - r(\boldsymbol{v}^*)\boldsymbol{v}^*] \geqq \mathbf{0}.$$

If this is not an equality, then $[\boldsymbol{A}\boldsymbol{v}^* - r(\boldsymbol{v}^*)\boldsymbol{v}^*]$ is a semi-positive vector. We multiply it by the strictly positive matrix $(\boldsymbol{I} + \boldsymbol{A})^{n-1}$ to obtain

$$(\boldsymbol{I} + \boldsymbol{A})^{n-1}[\boldsymbol{A}\boldsymbol{v}^* - r(\boldsymbol{v}^*)\boldsymbol{v}^*] > \mathbf{0}.$$

Noting that $(\boldsymbol{I} + \boldsymbol{A})^{n-1}\boldsymbol{A} = \boldsymbol{A}(\boldsymbol{I} + \boldsymbol{A})^{n-1}$ and putting $\boldsymbol{y} = (\boldsymbol{I} + \boldsymbol{A})^{n-1}\ \boldsymbol{v}^*$ we get:

$$\boldsymbol{A}\boldsymbol{y} - r(\boldsymbol{v}^*)\boldsymbol{y} > \mathbf{0}.$$

However, this contradicts the fact that $r(\boldsymbol{v}^*)$ is the maximum over all r, so that we must have equality in $\boldsymbol{A}\boldsymbol{v}^* \geqq r(\boldsymbol{v}^*)\boldsymbol{v}^*$ – in other words $r(\boldsymbol{v}^*)$ is an eigenvalue of $\boldsymbol{A}$ and $\boldsymbol{v}^*$ the associated eigenvector.

If $r(\boldsymbol{v}^*)$ is an eigenvalue of $\boldsymbol{A}$, $1 + r(\boldsymbol{v}^*)$ must be an eigenvalue of $(\boldsymbol{I} + \boldsymbol{A})$, and thus $[1 + r(\boldsymbol{v}^*)]^{n-1}$ will be an eigenvalue of $[\boldsymbol{I} + \boldsymbol{A}]^{n-1}$ with $\boldsymbol{v}^*$ as the eigenvector in each case. Since $[\boldsymbol{I} + \boldsymbol{A}]^{n-1}$ is strictly positive we have:

$$[1 + r(\boldsymbol{v}^*)]^{n-1}\boldsymbol{v}^* = [\boldsymbol{I} + \boldsymbol{A}]^{n-1}\boldsymbol{v}^* > \mathbf{0}$$

which implies that $\boldsymbol{v}^* > 0$, as $r(\boldsymbol{v}^*) > 0$.

Now consider any other eigenvalue λ with eigenvector $\boldsymbol{x}$ so that $\boldsymbol{Ax} = \lambda\boldsymbol{x}$. Take the absolute values and put $\boldsymbol{x}^+ = (|x_1|, |x_2|, \ldots, |x_n|)$ so that we get:

$$|\lambda| \,.\, \boldsymbol{x}^+ \leqq \boldsymbol{Ax}^+$$

since $|a| \,.\, |b| \leqslant |ab|$† and $|\boldsymbol{Ax}| = \boldsymbol{Ax}^+$ by the non-negativity of $\boldsymbol{A}$. But $r(\boldsymbol{v}^*)$ is the largest number satisfying this inequality. Hence

$$r(\boldsymbol{v}^*) \geqslant |\lambda|$$

for every eigenvalue of $\boldsymbol{A}$; we will call $r(\boldsymbol{v}^*)$ the dominant root of $\boldsymbol{A}$ and denote it by λ^* from now on. Further it is clear that λ^* cannot be a repeated eigenvalue. Suppose not, so that there was another vector $\boldsymbol{x}^*$ – which would have to be strictly positive by the above argument – not equal to $\boldsymbol{v}^*$ such that $\boldsymbol{Ax}^* = \lambda^*\boldsymbol{x}^*$. Now we can choose $\boldsymbol{x}^*$ such that $\sum_i \boldsymbol{x}_i^* = 1$, so that since $\boldsymbol{x}^* \neq \boldsymbol{v}^*$ for some i, $x_i^* > v_i^*$. Subtracting the two eigenvector equations we get:

$$\boldsymbol{A}(\boldsymbol{v}^* - \boldsymbol{x}^*) = \lambda^*(\boldsymbol{v}^* - \boldsymbol{x}^*).$$

In other words the vector $(\boldsymbol{v}^* - \boldsymbol{x}^*)$, which must have a negative element, is another eigenvector associated with λ^*. This contradicts the demonstration that the eigenvector associated with λ^* must be strictly positive. Hence λ^* cannot be a repeated eigenvalue.

If $\boldsymbol{A}$ is a strictly positive matrix we can also show that $\lambda^* > |\lambda|$ for all $\lambda \neq \lambda^*$. Suppose not, so that $\lambda^* = -\lambda_i$. Consider $\boldsymbol{B} = \boldsymbol{A} - \delta\boldsymbol{I}$ with two of its eigenvalues $\lambda^* - \delta$, $\lambda_i - \delta$. Since $\boldsymbol{A} > \boldsymbol{0}$, for small enough δ, $\boldsymbol{B} > \boldsymbol{0}$ so that its largest eigenvalue is $\lambda^* - \delta$. But $|\lambda_i - \delta| > |\lambda^* - \delta|$, which contradicts the fact that $\lambda^* - \delta$ is the dominant root. This shows that, if α is the smallest element in $\boldsymbol{A}$, then $\lambda^* - \alpha \geqslant |\lambda|$ for any $\lambda \neq \lambda^*$.

We will now prove that no other eigenvalue has an associated non-negative eigenvector. Suppose that the eigenvalue λ did have an eigenvector $\boldsymbol{v}$ which was non-negative. Now since $\boldsymbol{A}$ is semi-positive and indecomposable so is $\boldsymbol{A}'$, and, as a matrix and its transpose must have the same eigenvalues, λ^* is the dominant eigenvalue of $\boldsymbol{A}'$ associated with some strictly positive eigenvector $\boldsymbol{u}^*$. Thus:

$$\boldsymbol{Av} = \lambda\boldsymbol{v}, \qquad \boldsymbol{A}'\boldsymbol{u}^* = \lambda^*\boldsymbol{u}^*.$$

† This will be an equality if a, b are real and could be an inequality if both are complex.

Pre-multiply the first by $(\boldsymbol{u}^*)'$ and the second by $\boldsymbol{v}'$, so that we get:

$$(\boldsymbol{u}^*)'\boldsymbol{A}\boldsymbol{v} = \lambda(\boldsymbol{u}^*)'\boldsymbol{v}; \quad \boldsymbol{v}'\boldsymbol{A}'\boldsymbol{u}^* = \lambda^*\boldsymbol{v}'\boldsymbol{u}^*.$$

The two quadratic forms are equal so that subtraction gives:

$$(\lambda^* - \lambda) \,.\, \boldsymbol{v}'\boldsymbol{u}^* = 0,$$

i.e.

$$\boldsymbol{v}'\boldsymbol{u}^* = 0 \text{ as } \lambda \neq \lambda^*.$$

But this is not possible with $\boldsymbol{v} \geqslant \boldsymbol{0}$, $\boldsymbol{u}^* > \boldsymbol{0}$; hence $\boldsymbol{v}$ cannot be non-negative.

Now we consider the matrix $(\mu\boldsymbol{I} - \boldsymbol{A})^{-1} = \mu^{-1}(\boldsymbol{I} - \mu^{-1}\boldsymbol{A})^{-1}$, for $\mu > \lambda^*$. The dominant eigenvalue of $\mu^{-1}\boldsymbol{A}$ is $\lambda^*/\mu < 1$, so by T.61 and T.62 we can expand the matrix to give the convergent infinite series:

$$(I - \mu^{-1}\boldsymbol{A})^{-1} = \boldsymbol{I} + \mu^{-1}\boldsymbol{A} + \mu^{-2}\boldsymbol{A}^2 + \ldots$$

We have already shown that for any i, j the (i, j)th element of $\boldsymbol{A}^r$ is positive for some $r < n$. As $\mu > 0$ this implies that every element of $(\boldsymbol{I} - \mu^{-1}\boldsymbol{A})^{-1}$ is strictly positive, so that $(\mu\boldsymbol{I} - \boldsymbol{A})^{-1}$ is a positive matrix for all $\mu > \lambda^*$.

This completes the derivation of the principal results. This was framed in terms of the properties of indecomposable semi-positive matrices. Usually the Frobenius – Perron theorem which embodies the result is stated in terms of indecomposable non-negative matrices. This is merely a terminological difference, since a non-negative matrix must be semi-positive at least if it is indecomposable. Before stating this theorem weaker results for the more general case of any non-negative matrix are given.

T.63. *Let* $\mathbf{A}$ *be a non-negative square matrix. Then:*

(i) $\mathbf{A}$ *has a real eigenvalue* $\lambda^* \geqslant 0$.

(ii) *If* $\mathbf{x}^*$ *is an eigenvector corresponding to* λ^*, *then* $\mathbf{x}^* > \mathbf{0}$.

(iii) *For any other eigenvalue* λ *of* $\mathbf{A}$, $\lambda^* \geqslant |\lambda|$.

(iv) *The value of* λ^* *does not decrease with the increase of any element* a_{ij} *of* $\mathbf{A}$.

(v) *The matrix* $(\mu\mathbf{I} - \mathbf{A})^{-1}$ *is non-negative iff* $\mu > \lambda^*$.

T.64. *(Frobenius–Perron). Let* $\mathbf{A}$ *be a non-negative square indecomposable matrix. Then:*

(i) $\mathbf{A}$ *has a real eigenvalue* $\lambda^* > 0$ *which is not a repeated eigenvalue; this is called the dominant eigenvalue.*

(ii) *For any other eigenvalue* λ *of* $\mathbf{A}$, $\lambda^* \geqslant |\lambda|$; *if* $\mathbf{A}$ *is a strictly positive matrix, then* $\lambda^* > |\lambda|$.

(iii) *If* $\mathbf{x}^*$ *is the eigenvector corresponding to* λ^*, *then* $\mathbf{x}^* > \mathbf{0}$.

(iv) *There is no non-negative eigenvector other than* $\mathbf{x}^*$.

(v) *The value of* λ^* *increases with the increase of any element* a_{ij} *of* $\mathbf{A}$.

(vi) *If* s *is the smallest, and* S *the largest, of the row sums of* $\mathbf{A}$ (*i.e.* $s = \min_i \sum_j a_{ij}$, $S = \max_i \sum_j a_{ij}$), *then* $s < \lambda^* < S$, *unless* $a = S$ *in which case* $s = \lambda^* = S$. *The same relationship holds for column sums.*

(vii) *The only non-negative solution of either of the inequality systems* $\mathbf{Ax} \leqq \lambda^*\mathbf{x}$, $\mathbf{Ax} \geqq \lambda^*\mathbf{x}$ *is* $\mathbf{x}^*$. *The only non-negative solution of either of the inequality systems* $\mathbf{Ax} \leqq k\mathbf{x}$, $\mathbf{Ax} \geqq k\mathbf{x}$ *where at least one equation holds with equality is* $k = \lambda^*$, $\mathbf{x} = \mathbf{x}^*$.

(viii) *The matrix* $(\mu\mathbf{I} - \mathbf{A})^{-1}$ *is positive iff* $\mu > \lambda^\cdot$.

10.4 Stochastic Matrices

We will conclude this chapter by outlining the properties and uses of two special types of matrices which arise in different economic models. In particular the focus is on the nature of their eigenvalues. First we consider stochastic matrices which are special non-negative matrices defined as follows·

D.89. *A STOCHASTIC MATRIX is a non-negative matrix in which the sum of the elements in each column is equal to unity.*

The definition might equally have been phrased so that a stochastic matrix has row sums which are unity, but the column form is more usual. The name is derived from the fact that stochastic matrices are usually encountered in the study of stochastic processes. To illustrate this in an economic context consider the following model.

At any time t the distribution of wealth in a community is described by a vector $\boldsymbol{z}_t$, where each element $z_j(t)$ gives the proportion of the population whose wealth falls into the predefined wealth class j. Further we suppose that changes in the ownership of wealth may be described by a known and unchanging stochastic process. Let p_{ij} be the probability that an individual with wealth in class j at time t has wealth in class i at time $(t + 1)$. For a large community this may be regarded as describing the relative frequency of transition from class j to class i. Thus we do not know what will happen to any particular individual, but of the original proportion $z_j(t)$ in class j at t, $p_{ij}z_j(t)$ will be in class i at $(t + 1)$. In other words by writing $\boldsymbol{P}$ as the matrix of all the p_{ij} we can derive the wealth distribution at $(t + 1)$ from that at t by:

$$z_{t+1} = \boldsymbol{P}z_t. \qquad (10.7)$$

Further the matrix $\boldsymbol{P}$ must be a stochastic matrix provided that the stochastic process has been so defined that every individual in class j at t must move to some class i for $i = 1, \ldots, n$ at $t + 1$. This ensures that $\sum_i p_{ij} = 1$. By repeated application of the transition given by (10.7) we can trace the evolution of the wealth distribution through time. If we suppose that the initial distribution was $\boldsymbol{z}_0$, then:

$$\boldsymbol{z}_t = \boldsymbol{P}^t \boldsymbol{z}_0.$$

Using (10.3) on the assumption that $\boldsymbol{x}_1, \ldots, \boldsymbol{x}_n$ are the eigenvectors of $\boldsymbol{P}$, $\lambda_1, \ldots, \lambda_n$ are the eigenvalues with λ_1 being the dominant one, we get:

$$\boldsymbol{z}_t \approx \mu_1 \lambda_1^t \boldsymbol{x}_1 \tag{10.8}$$

where $\boldsymbol{z}_0 = \sum_i \mu_i \boldsymbol{x}_i$. In other words the distribution of wealth converges to a given pattern independent of the initial distribution and determined completely by the eigenvector associated with the dominant eigenvalue. The time path of convergence depends on the term $\mu_1 \lambda_1^t$ and on the other eigenvalues of the matrix.

As the above discussion shows, the magnitude of the dominant eigenvalue of a stochastic matrix is of critical importance.

T.65. *A stochastic matrix* **P** *has at least one eigenvalue equal to unity.*

Proof: Consider the transpose of $\boldsymbol{P}$. If we post-multiply it by a vector $\boldsymbol{w}$ each of whose elements is 1, the result must be the vector $\boldsymbol{w}$ since all the row sums of $\boldsymbol{P}'$ are equal to 1. Thus $\boldsymbol{w}$ is an eigenvector of $\boldsymbol{P}'$ with 1 as the eigenvalue. But the eigenvalues of a matrix and its transpose are the same.

Q.E.D.

Corollaries: (*a*) The eigenvalue of a stochastic matrix $\boldsymbol{P}$ equal to 1 is the dominant eigenvalue, and the associated eigenvector is non-negative.

Proof: Suppose there is another eigenvalue $\mu > 1$, and let $\boldsymbol{P}\boldsymbol{v} = \mu \boldsymbol{v}$. Further we have $\boldsymbol{w}'\boldsymbol{P} = \boldsymbol{w}' \neq \boldsymbol{0}$. Multiplying the first by $\boldsymbol{w}'$, the second by $\boldsymbol{v}$ and subtracting gives:

$$(\mu - 1)\boldsymbol{w}'\boldsymbol{v} = 0.$$

If μ is the dominant eigenvalue, $\boldsymbol{v} \geqslant \boldsymbol{0}$ which is not compatible with the requirement that $\boldsymbol{w}'\boldsymbol{v} = 0$. Hence 1 must be the dominant eigenvalue, and the rest follows. Note that there may be eigenvalues equal to -1, or 1 may be a repeated eigenvalue since in general we know only that $\lambda^* \geqslant |\lambda|$.

(*b*) If $\boldsymbol{P}$ is a stochastic indecomposable matrix, then 1 is the unique dominant eigenvalue.

The example of the behaviour of the wealth distribution over time is a specific type of stochastic process known as an *homogeneous Markov Chain.* The results just proved show that if the transition matrix $\boldsymbol{P}$ is indecomposable, then we would have in (10.8):

$$z_t \approx \mu_1 \boldsymbol{x}_1$$

where $\boldsymbol{x}_1$ is the eigenvector associated with the eigenvalue 1. Since μ_1 appears simply as a constant of proportionality we can choose the scale of $\boldsymbol{x}_1$ such that $\sum_i x_{i1} = 1/\mu_1$. Thus we can write:

$$z_t \approx z, \text{ where } \sum_j z_j = 1$$

for all initial distributions of wealth, and we see that the asymptotic distribution of wealth in the community is entirely determined by the transition matrix describing the Markov chain. It is possible to introduce complications into the framework of this model of the evolution of a distribution in order to allow for births and deaths, upper or lower barriers, and other features. Such models have been used to discuss the distributions of income and of wealth, the size distribution of firms, and in the analysis of unemployment. However, it should be noted that if the chain does not converge quickly the assumption that the transition probabilities are the same for every step is a very strong and rather implausible one from an economist's point of view.

10.5 Dominant Diagonal Matrices

The type of matrix to be considered in this section is usually encountered in studies of the stability of systems of equations – for example the stability of the adjustment process for markets which are out of equilibrium.

D.90. *A square matrix* A *of order* $\mathrm{n} \times \mathrm{n}$ *is called a DOMINANT DIAGONAL MATRIX if there exist numbers* $\mathrm{d_j} > 0$ *such that:* $\mathrm{d_j}|\mathrm{a_{jj}}| > \sum_{\mathrm{i} \neq \mathrm{j}} \mathrm{d_i}|\mathrm{a_{ij}}|$ *for* $\mathrm{j} = 1, \ldots, \mathrm{n}$.

This definition specifies a matrix with column dominance, i.e. the weighted absolute value of the diagonal element exceeds the weighted sum of the absolute values of all other elements in the column. We could alternatively have used a definition in terms of row dominance – the two are equivalent for the purpose of the results stated below.

The properties of dominant diagonal matrices will be stated without proof; full details of the proofs may be found in McKenzie (1960).

T.66. *Suppose* **A** *is a dominant diagonal matrix. Then:*

(*a*) **A** *is non-singular.*

(*b*) *If* **A** *has a dominant negative diagonal, all its eigenvalues have negative real parts.*

(*c*) *If* **A** *has column dominance, no eigenvalue has an absolute value exceeding the largest column sum of absolute values* ($\max_i \sum_j |a_{ij}|$), *and if it has row dominance no eigenvalue has an absolute value greater than the largest row sum of absolute values.*

Part (*c*) of this theorem provides a link with the Frobenius–Perron theorem since (vi) of that in part relies on this result. In fact, as will be seen, many of the results concerning the Leontief model or other models which rely on magnitude and sign of the dominant eigenvalue may alternatively be proved by the use of the theory of dominant diagonal matrices.

We will first return again to the Leontief model. However, in addition to the material inputs required in production given by the matrix $\boldsymbol{A}$, we will assume that per unit output of the ith industry an amount m_i of labour is required, so that the vector $\boldsymbol{m}$ describes unit labour inputs. Now let us suppose that we observe a competitive equilibrium in the economy with all industries operating with price $p_i > 0$ $(i = 1, \ldots, n)$. If workers are paid a wage of w, for each industry j the competitive assumption implies:

$$p_j = \sum_i p_i a_{ij} + w m_j. \tag{10.9}$$

We will replace the matrix $[\boldsymbol{I} - \boldsymbol{A}]$ by $\boldsymbol{B} = \| b_{ij} \|$; so long as the wage rate is positive and $\boldsymbol{m} \geqq \boldsymbol{0}$ (10.9) implies:

$$\sum_i p_i b_{ij} > 0$$

or

$$p_j b_{jj} > \sum_j p_i |b_{ij}|$$

since $\quad b_{jj} = 1 - a_{jj} > 0, \quad b_{ij} = -a_{ij} < 0 \quad \text{for } i \neq j.$

In other words $\boldsymbol{B} = [\boldsymbol{I} - \boldsymbol{A}]$ is a dominant diagonal matrix.

T.67. *Let* **B** *be a square matrix with* $b_{ii} > 0$ *all* i *and* $b_{ij} < 0$ *for* $i \neq j$. *A necessary and sufficient condition for* $\mathbf{Bx} = \mathbf{y}$ *to have a unique solution* $\mathbf{x} \geqslant$ *for every* $\mathbf{y} \geqslant \mathbf{0}$ *is that* **B** *is a dominant diagonal matrix.*

Corollary: If all industries appear in a competitive equilibrium with positive output levels and there is a positive wage in a Leontief model, then any non-negative bill of goods can be achieved in the system.

This provides yet another condition guaranteeing the existence of a non-negative solution for the general Leontief system.

The second use of matrices with dominant diagonals which we will consider is in the analysis of a multi-sector or multi-country multiplier model. Suppose that there are n countries trading with each other and that the spending in period t may be related to income in the previous period $t - 1$. Then we can describe the incremental flow of spending by:

$$y_i(t) = \sum_{j=1}^{n} d_{ij} y_j(t-1) \qquad (i = 1, \ldots, n)$$

where $y_i(t)$ is the difference between income in period t and the equilibrium income for country i. The coefficients d_{ij} give the marginal propensity of country j to spend on country i's goods. Clearly we analyse the evolution of this system in the same way as that of the distribution of wealth, so that writing the difference equation system as:

$$\boldsymbol{y}_t = \boldsymbol{D} \boldsymbol{y}_{t-1} \tag{10.10}$$

we get:

$$\boldsymbol{y}_t = \boldsymbol{D}^t \boldsymbol{y}_0.$$

In other words it will converge to equilibrium – that is, $\lim_{t \to \infty} \boldsymbol{y}_t = \mathbf{0}$ – if and only if all the eigenvalues of $\boldsymbol{D}$ are less than 1 in absolute value. Using (vi) of the Frobenius–Perron theorem this will be the case if $\boldsymbol{D} \geqq \mathbf{0}$ and all the column sums of $\boldsymbol{D}$ are less than 1. But note that the column sum d_j is given by $d_j = \sum_{i=1}^{n} d_{ij}$, so that it gives the total marginal propensity to spend of country j. Thus the difference equation system is stable if the total marginal propensity to spend of each country is less than 1.

T.68. *The many country multiplier model (10.10) is stable if all the marginal propensities are non-negative and the total marginal propensity of each country is less than 1.*

Finally we will examine the stability of a price adjustment mechanism in a multi-market system. The model is taken from Arrow (1960), who discusses a number of more complex models related to the one presented here. We suppose that there are n markets for each of n commodities with p_i the price in the ith market. Supply and demand functions for each good depend on all prices and may be written as:

$$\text{Supply: } S_i = S_i(p_1, \ldots, p_n) \text{ with } \frac{\partial S_i}{\partial p_i} > 0, \frac{\partial S_i}{\partial p_j} \leqslant 0 \text{ for all } i \neq j.$$

$$\text{Demand: } D_i = D_i(p_1, \ldots, p_n) \text{ with } \frac{\partial D_i}{\partial p_i} < 0, \frac{\partial D_i}{\partial p_j} \geqslant 0 \text{ for } i \neq j.$$

We assume that these functions may be represented by linear approximations, so that:

$$S_i = \sum_{j=1}^{n} a_{ij}p_j + c_i. \qquad a_{ii} > 0, a_{ij} \leqslant 0 \text{ for } i \neq j.$$

$$D_i = \sum_j b_{ij}p_j + d_i. \qquad b_{ii} < 0, b_{ij} \geqslant 0 \text{ for } i \neq j.$$

For each market we can define the excess demand as the difference between supply and demand, i.e.

$$X_i = D_i - S_i.$$

Now we assume that the price in market i responds to the excess demand (excess supply if $X_i < 0$) by increasing if X_i is positive, falling if X_i is negative, and not changing if $X_i = 0$. To a linear approximation:

$$\dot{p}_i = k_i X_i \qquad (k_i > 0)$$

where the dot denotes differentiation with respect to time. Substituting for X_i we get:

$$\dot{p}_i = k_i \sum_j m_{ij}p_j + k_i n_i$$

where $m_{ij} = b_{ij} - a_{ij}$, $n_i = d_i - c_i$ and $m_{ii} < 0$, $m_{ij} \geqslant 0$ for $i \neq j$. In matrix notation:

$$\dot{\boldsymbol{p}} = \boldsymbol{KMp} + \boldsymbol{Kn} \tag{10.11}$$

where $\boldsymbol{K}$ is a diagonal matrix with the k_i as diagonal elements. Here we have a system of first order differential equations rather than the first order difference equation systems such as (10.7) and (10.10).

Before we can establish conditions for stability of this multi-market system we can simplify (10.11) by introducing the equilibrium vector of prices $\boldsymbol{p}^*$, assumed to be non-negative. This is found when the prices are such that none is changing; i.e.

$$\dot{\boldsymbol{p}} = \boldsymbol{0} = \boldsymbol{KMp}^* + \boldsymbol{Kn}$$

so that if $\boldsymbol{M}$ is non-singular

$$\boldsymbol{p}^* = -\boldsymbol{M}^{-1}\boldsymbol{n}.$$

Thus we can write (10.11) in terms of deviations from equilibrium:

$$\dot{\boldsymbol{p}} = \boldsymbol{KM}(\boldsymbol{p} - \boldsymbol{p}^*)$$

or writing $\boldsymbol{x} = \boldsymbol{p} - \boldsymbol{p}^*$

$$\dot{\boldsymbol{x}} = \boldsymbol{KMx}. \tag{10.12}$$

Now it is a standard result that a system such as (10.12) is stable – i.e. $\lim_{t\to\infty} \boldsymbol{x} = \boldsymbol{0}$ – if and only if all the eigenvalues of the matrix $\boldsymbol{KM}$ have negative real parts. Such a matrix is often called a *stable matrix*. But from (*b*) of T.66 this is ensured if $\boldsymbol{KM}$ has a dominant negative diagonal; clearly this requires that $\boldsymbol{M}$ be a dominant diagonal matrix since it has all its diagonal elements negative and, as $\boldsymbol{K}$ is a non-negative diagonal matrix, $\boldsymbol{KM}$ must have a dominant diagonal if $\boldsymbol{M}$ has one. We will now show that $n_i > 0$ all i is a sufficient condition for the system to be stable with a strictly positive equilibrium price vector $\boldsymbol{p}^*$. Note that at equilibrium:

$$X_i = \sum_j p_j^* m_{ij} + n_i = 0 \qquad (i = 1, \ldots, n)$$

so that for $n_i > 0$,

$$\sum_j p_j^* m_{ij} < 0 \qquad (i = 1, \ldots, n)$$

or

$$-p_i^* m_{ii} > \sum_{i \neq j} p_j^* m_{ij}.$$

But $m_{ii} < 0$, $m_{ij} \geqslant 0$ for $i \neq j$ so that this implies:

$$p_i^* |m_{ii}| > \sum_{i \neq j} p_j^* |m_{ij}|$$

i.e. that $\boldsymbol{M}$ has a dominant diagonal provided that $\boldsymbol{p}^* > \boldsymbol{0}$. But $-\boldsymbol{Mp}^* = \boldsymbol{n}$ and $-\boldsymbol{M}$ fulfils the conditions on $\boldsymbol{B}$ in T.67, so that $\boldsymbol{p}^*$ must be strictly positive so long as $\boldsymbol{n}$ is also strictly positive. Hence the sufficiency of the condition $\boldsymbol{n} > \boldsymbol{0}$ follows. The economic implication of $\boldsymbol{n} > 0$ is that if all goods were free there would be positive excess demand for every good. This would seem a reasonable assumption to make.

Before concluding this section on dominant diagonal matrices it is worth noting that many of the results involving dominant diagonals are simply ways of formulating theorems which we have already encountered. For instance:

(*a*) We have noted that stability requires a matrix whose eigenvalues all have negative real parts. This is ensured by the matrix having a dominant negative diagonal. Equivalently it follows iff the matrix is negative definite. Thus a matrix with a dominant negative diagonal must be negative definite.

(*b*) It has been shown that a set of conditions guaranteeing the existence of a solution to the Leontief system can be formulated using these matrices. From T.67 it follows that a non-negative square matrix $\boldsymbol{A}$ has all its eigenvalues less than 1 in absolute value iff $[\boldsymbol{I} - \boldsymbol{A}]$ has a dominant positive diagonal. But another set of necessary and sufficient conditions is the famous Hawkins–Simon requirement that all the principal minors of $[\boldsymbol{I} - \boldsymbol{A}]$ be positive. Thus any dominant diagonal matrix with positive diagonal elements and negative off-diagonal elements must be positive definite. Further, not only are all its eigenvalues less than 1 in absolute value, but they also all have positive real parts.

11 Linear Economic Models

11.1 The Static Leontief Model

The static Leontief model has already been discussed in various contexts in Chapters 5 and 10. To recap, the model is described by the set of equations:

$$[\boldsymbol{I} - \boldsymbol{A}]\boldsymbol{x} = \boldsymbol{f}$$

in which $\boldsymbol{A}$ is the non-negative matrix of input coefficients, $\boldsymbol{f}$ is a non-negative vector of final demands, and we wish to find a non-negative gross output vector $\boldsymbol{x}$ which will fulfil the final demands. A number of alternative necessary and sufficient conditions for the existence of a non-negative solution $\boldsymbol{x}$ have been proved. Clearly they are all equivalent, and to bring them together they are listed here:

(i) $\boldsymbol{x} = [\sum_{t=0}^{\infty} \boldsymbol{A}^t]\boldsymbol{f}$ iff $\lim_{t\to\infty} \boldsymbol{A}^t = \boldsymbol{0}$.

(ii) $\boldsymbol{x} = [\boldsymbol{I} - \boldsymbol{A}]^{-1}\boldsymbol{f} \geqslant \boldsymbol{0}$ iff the dominant eigenvalue of $\boldsymbol{A}$ is less than 1 in absolute value.

(iii) A non-negative solution for any $\boldsymbol{f} > \boldsymbol{0}$ exists iff $[\boldsymbol{I} - \boldsymbol{A}]$ has a positive dominant diagonal.

(iv) A non-negative solution exists iff all the principal minors of $[\boldsymbol{I} - \boldsymbol{A}]$ are positive.

That $\boldsymbol{x}$ is non-negative for conditions (i) and (ii) was not proved, but it follows immediately from the observation that if $\boldsymbol{A}$ is non-negative then any power of $\boldsymbol{A}$ must also be non-negative. Hence the sum of the power series in $\boldsymbol{A}$ must be non-negative, and multiplication of a non-negative matrix by a non-negative vector gives another non-negative vector. Note further that if $\boldsymbol{A}$ is indecomposable, then the gross output vector will be strictly positive for $\boldsymbol{f} \geqslant \boldsymbol{0}$, since we know that at least $\boldsymbol{A}^{n-1} > \boldsymbol{0}$ if $\boldsymbol{A}$ is $n \times n$.

We saw in Chapter 10 that a non-negative square matrix has at least one positive eigenvalue with an associated positive eigenvector.

Let $\boldsymbol{y}$ be such an eigenvector for a matrix $\boldsymbol{A}$ which satisfies condition (ii); then as the eigenvalues are less than 1:

$$\boldsymbol{A}\boldsymbol{y} = \lambda\boldsymbol{y} \text{ implies } \boldsymbol{A}\boldsymbol{y} < \boldsymbol{y} \text{ or } \boldsymbol{y} - \boldsymbol{A}\boldsymbol{y} > \boldsymbol{0}.$$

If $\boldsymbol{y}$ represents a vector of outputs, then the L.H.S. of the inequality here gives the difference between the gross outputs produced and the inputs of produced goods needed by the various industries to sustain these gross outputs. The inequality therefore assures us that there is some gross output vector associated with a positive net output of each good. Given this, it follows that by scaling up the activities of the economy it will be possible to produce any desired quantity of a good. The property that there exists some non-negative $\boldsymbol{y}$ such that $\boldsymbol{y} > \boldsymbol{A}\boldsymbol{y}$ provides a formal definition of the term *productive* used for matrices which satisfy the conditions on $\boldsymbol{A}$ for a non-negative solution of the Leontief system.

The equation

$$\boldsymbol{x} = \left(\sum_{t=0}^{\infty} \boldsymbol{A}^t\right)\boldsymbol{f}$$

can be given an interesting interpretation. It may be written

$$\boldsymbol{x} = \boldsymbol{I}\boldsymbol{f} + \boldsymbol{A}\boldsymbol{f} + \boldsymbol{A}^2\boldsymbol{f} + \boldsymbol{A}^3\boldsymbol{f} + \dots \tag{11.1}$$

This says that the vector of gross outputs $\boldsymbol{x}$ needed to produce the final outputs $\boldsymbol{f}$ is the sum of a number of terms:

(i) $\boldsymbol{I}\boldsymbol{f}$, or $\boldsymbol{f}$ itself.
(ii) $\boldsymbol{A}\boldsymbol{f}$, the intermediate goods needed to produce $\boldsymbol{f}$.
(iii) $\boldsymbol{A}^2\boldsymbol{f}$, the intermediate goods needed to produce $\boldsymbol{A}\boldsymbol{f}$, etc.

We can easily see in intuitive terms why there is an infinite series here. To produce a net output of n trucks we obviously need to produce the n trucks themselves. But in doing this we have to produce the iron and steel that go into them, and this will in its turn use trucks – say $m \,.\, n$ – for transportation, giving a total of $n + m \,.\, n$ trucks. Of course the extra $m \,.\, n$ trucks need more iron and steel and so more trucks, $m^2 \,.\, n$ of them. The extra $m^2 \,.\, n$ trucks need more metal, more trucks, and so on. Inverting the matrix $(\boldsymbol{I} - \boldsymbol{A})$ in effect involves summing a series of this type for each input to each produced good.

Let us now augment the fundamental Leontief system by the addition of the extra input labour. The non-negative row n-vector $\boldsymbol{m}$ represents the labour requirements per unit output in each industry. In competitive equilibrium market prices – given by the row vector $\boldsymbol{p}$ – must be such that the cost of production just equals the price of the output. We will assume that all prices are measured in terms of labour as the numeraire. In other words the wage is 1 and each p_j represents the price of good j as a multiple of the wage. By the competitive assumption:

$$\boldsymbol{p} = \boldsymbol{m} + \boldsymbol{pA}$$

as unit materials input costs for good j are $\sum_i p_i a_{ij}$. Thus $\boldsymbol{p}[\boldsymbol{I}-\boldsymbol{A}]=\boldsymbol{m}$. It follows that, if and only if the eigenvalues of $\boldsymbol{A}$ are less than unity in absolute value, we can write

$$\begin{aligned}\boldsymbol{p} &= \boldsymbol{m} \sum_{t=0}^{\infty} \boldsymbol{A}^t \\ &= \boldsymbol{m} + \boldsymbol{mA} + \boldsymbol{mA}^2 + \boldsymbol{mA}^3 + \ \dots \end{aligned} \tag{11.2}$$

To understand this in economic terms, recall (11.1) and its interpretation. By analogy, we can see that $\boldsymbol{m}$ represents the labour costs of producing one unit of each good; $\boldsymbol{mA}$ represents the labour costs of producing the materials used as inputs to the production of one unit of each good; $\boldsymbol{mA}^2$ gives the labour costs of producing these, etc. (11.2) can thus be interpreted as a statement that the market price of a good will equal the total direct and indirect labour costs of producing that good – in effect a labour theory of value.

Another way of reaching the same conclusion is to consider $\boldsymbol{pf}$, the value of final demand at market prices.

Since $\boldsymbol{f} = [\boldsymbol{I} - \boldsymbol{A}]\boldsymbol{x}$, we get:

$$\boldsymbol{pf} = \boldsymbol{p}[\boldsymbol{I} - \boldsymbol{A}]\boldsymbol{x} = \boldsymbol{mx} \text{ as } \boldsymbol{p}[\boldsymbol{I} - \boldsymbol{A}] = \boldsymbol{m}.$$

Hence $\boldsymbol{pf} = \boldsymbol{mx}$ – the market value of final demand equals the total labour cost of gross output needed to produce it. From (11.2):

$$\boldsymbol{pf} = \boldsymbol{mx} = \boldsymbol{mf} + \boldsymbol{mAf} + \boldsymbol{mA}^2\boldsymbol{f} + \dots.$$

Clearly the verification of a labour theory of value does depend crucially on the special features of the model we are dealing with – in particular, on the assumption that there is only one scarce factor, labour. It is, perhaps, not surprising that when there is only one scarce factor the prices of goods reflect the amounts of that factor used in producing them. The introduction of a second factor alters matters considerably, as will be shown in the next section.

Before moving to a two-factor model, it is worth noting that the vector of relative prices $\boldsymbol{p}$ defined by equation (11.2) is completely independent of demand conditions and depends only on technology as represented by the coefficients of the matrix $\boldsymbol{A}$. This observation provides the basis for various *non-substitution theorems*, and is no longer valid in the two-factor case considered below.

11.2 Two Factors in a Static Linear Model

Consider the introduction into the economy of a second scarce factor – land – with $\boldsymbol{h}$ as the row vector of unit land requirements and the rest of the technology as before. We will now let p_{n+1} be the price of land, p_{n+2} that of labour, and $\boldsymbol{p} = (p_1, p_2, \ldots, p_n)$ the row vector of produced goods prices. Note that because we have introduced the price of labour explicitly, rather than using it as the numeraire, the vector $\boldsymbol{p}$ has a slightly different interpretation. Under perfect competition with market prices equal to production costs it would be the case that:

$$\boldsymbol{p} = p_{n+1}\boldsymbol{h} + p_{n+2}\boldsymbol{m} + \boldsymbol{pA}$$

which, under the appropriate conditions on the eigenvalues of $\boldsymbol{A}$, can be solved to yield:

$$\boldsymbol{p} = p_{n+1}\boldsymbol{h} + p_{n+2}\boldsymbol{m} + (p_{n+1}\boldsymbol{h} + p_{n+2}\boldsymbol{m})\boldsymbol{A} + (p_{n+1}\boldsymbol{h} + p_{n+2}\boldsymbol{m})\boldsymbol{A}^2 + \ldots \tag{11.3}$$

which implies that market prices are now determined by the total direct and indirect land and labour costs involved in producing a unit of a good. The system of equations (11.3) can be used to calculate the vector $\boldsymbol{p}$ of goods prices once the two factor prices p_{n+1} and p_{n+2} are known, but of course it cannot also be used to find these factor prices. The model as it stands is incomplete: to complete it, and determine factor prices and thus the distribution of income, it is necessary to take account of the facts that final demand depends on the prices of both factors and goods, that the supply of and demand for factors depend on all prices, and that the demand for each factor should not exceed its supply. For illustrative purposes we shall complete the model in the simplest possible way, assuming that all the remaining dependencies are linear. Thus f_i, the final demand for good i, is given by

$$f_i = f_{i1}p_1 + f_{i2}p_2 + \ldots + f_{i,n+1}p_{n+1} + f_{i,n+2}p_{n+2}$$

and in general

$$f = F\hat{p}'$$

where F is the $n \times n + 2$ matrix of f_{ij} and $\hat{p} = (p, p_{n+1}, p_{n+2})$. Similarly the supply of labour will be assumed given by:

$$\text{Labour supply} = \sum_{i=1}^{n} s_i p_i + s_{n+1} p_{n+1} + s_{n+2} p_{n+2} = s\hat{p}'$$

where s is a row vector describing the dependence of total labour supply on goods prices and the prices of land and labour. The supply of land is taken as a constant $\bar{h}$. The complete model can now be set out as:

$$x = (I - A)^{-1} F\hat{p}' \tag{11.4}$$

$$mx = s\hat{p}' \tag{11.5}$$

$$hx = \bar{h} \tag{11.6}$$

$$p = (p_{n+1}h + p_{n+2}m)[I - A]^{-1}. \tag{11.7}$$

(11.4) simply states the usual relationship between gross outputs and net output or final demand, which is now a function of the price vector p. (11.5) and (11.6) ensure that the factor markets clear, and (11.7) gives the relationship that must exist between goods prices p and factor prices p_{n+1} and p_{n+2} in a competitive market. Using (11.4) in (11.5) and (11.6) gives

$$m[I - A]^{-1} F\hat{p}' = s\hat{p}' \tag{11.8}$$

$$h[I - A]^{-1} F\hat{p}' = h \tag{11.9}$$

and (11.7) can be used to remove $\hat{p}$ from these by substituting:

$$\hat{p} = \{(p_{n+1}h + p_{n+2}m)[I - A]^{-1}, p_{n+1}, p_{n+2}\}.$$

Thus we have two equations in only two unknowns, p_{n+1} and p_{n+2}, the two factor prices. If they have a solution, then it can be substituted into (11.7) to find the remaining prices. It is worth noting that in this model it is no longer true that relative prices are independent of demand conditions, as goods prices depend on factor prices via (11.7) and factor prices depend on demand conditions via the matrix F which appears in equations (11.8) and (11.9).

11.3 Dynamic Linear Models: Balanced Growth

We now proceed to consider a dynamic model, or growth model, very similar in spirit to the static Leontief model of the previous sections. There will, however, be one substantial difference in the specification: we shall consider a *closed* model, that is to say, a model in which there is no use of goods and services for personal consumption or export. Outputs may be used only as inputs to production, or to augment capital stocks. In such a framework, if we want to consider consumption at all, we have to consider it as an input to production, the corresponding output being labour. Such a treatment of labour is very much in the spirit of Marx and Malthus. Likewise, exports could be considered as an input to the production of commodities such as foreign exchange or goods available only by importation.

It is assumed that there are n different types of goods, and two broad categories of inputs to production, capital goods, which are not used up in production, and current inputs, which are, of course, used up. Let $\boldsymbol{y}(t)$ be the vector of total outputs in period t, and $\boldsymbol{D}$ an $n \times n$ matrix of capital input requirements. $\boldsymbol{d}_{ij}$ is the stock of the ith good needed in the form of capital equipment to produce one unit of the jth output, and $\boldsymbol{k}(t) \in R^n$ will be the vector of quantities of the n goods available as capital equipment in period t. On a growth path where all capital stocks are fully employed, the following equation must hold:

$$\boldsymbol{D}\boldsymbol{y}(t) = \boldsymbol{k}(t).$$

If $\boldsymbol{y}(t + 1)$ is the output vector in period $t + 1$, capital input requirements then are $\boldsymbol{D}\boldsymbol{y}(t + 1)$, so that if $\boldsymbol{y}(t + 1)$ is feasible in period $t + 1$ and capital stocks are fully employed, investment in period t must satisfy

$$\boldsymbol{k}(t + 1) - \boldsymbol{k}(t) = \boldsymbol{D}[\boldsymbol{y}(t + 1) - \boldsymbol{y}(t)].$$

As before the $n \times n$ matrix $\boldsymbol{A}$ will be the matrix of current input requirements. As neither consumption nor exports feature explicitly in the model, the equality of supply and demand for each good requires that its total output should equal intermediate demand plus investment demand, i.e.

$$\boldsymbol{y}(t) = \boldsymbol{A}\boldsymbol{y}(t) + \boldsymbol{D}[\boldsymbol{y}(t + 1) - \boldsymbol{y}(t)]$$

which can be solved for $\boldsymbol{y}(t+1)$ to give

$$\boldsymbol{y}(t+1) = [\boldsymbol{I} + \boldsymbol{D}^{-1}(\boldsymbol{I} - \boldsymbol{A})]\boldsymbol{y}(t) \qquad (11.10)$$

assuming that $\boldsymbol{D}$ has an inverse. This is a difference equation describing the evolution of the output vectors over time, and yields

$$\boldsymbol{y}(t+1) = [\boldsymbol{I} + \boldsymbol{D}^{-1}(\boldsymbol{I} - \boldsymbol{A})]^2\boldsymbol{y}(t-1)$$

or

$$\boldsymbol{y}(t+1) = [\boldsymbol{I} + \boldsymbol{D}^{-1}(\boldsymbol{I} - \boldsymbol{A})]^{t+1}\boldsymbol{y}(0). \qquad (11.11)$$

In the context of such models, it is interesting to ask the following question: is the model capable of *balanced growth* – i.e. of growth along a path on which all outputs grow at the same proportional rate so that the composition of final output is constant? Formally, this involves asking whether there exists some solution path such that for some $\lambda > 1$,

$$\boldsymbol{y}(t+1) = \lambda\boldsymbol{y}(t),\ \boldsymbol{y}(t+1) = \lambda^2\boldsymbol{y}(t-1)$$

and

$$\boldsymbol{y}(t+1) = \lambda^{t+1}\boldsymbol{y}(0).$$

For simplicity let $\boldsymbol{E} = \boldsymbol{I} + \boldsymbol{D}^{-1}(\boldsymbol{I} - \boldsymbol{A})$. In this case (11.10) becomes:

$$\boldsymbol{y}(t+1) = \boldsymbol{E}\boldsymbol{y}(t).$$

This describes a growth path for $\boldsymbol{y}(t)$. If it is balanced we have $\boldsymbol{y}(t+1) = \lambda\boldsymbol{y}(t)$, so that:

$$\boldsymbol{E}\boldsymbol{y}(t) = \lambda\boldsymbol{y}(t).$$

Suppose that the matrix $\boldsymbol{E}$ has a positive eigenvector $\boldsymbol{y}^*$ with an associated eigenvalue λ^* greater than 1, then:

$$\boldsymbol{E}\boldsymbol{y}^* = \lambda^*\boldsymbol{y}^*.$$

If $\boldsymbol{y}(0) = \boldsymbol{y}^*$:

$$\boldsymbol{y}(1) = \boldsymbol{E}\boldsymbol{y}^* = \lambda^*\boldsymbol{y}^*, \text{ etc.}$$

Hence: $\boldsymbol{y}(t+1) = \boldsymbol{E}\boldsymbol{y}(t) = (\lambda^*)^{t+1}\boldsymbol{y}^*$, and we have indeed found a balanced growth path. Thus the growth of a dynamic linear model of the type considered here – known as the *dynamic Leontief* model – depends on the eigenvalues and eigenvectors of the matrix $\boldsymbol{E}$.

A sufficient condition to guarantee the existence of a balanced growth path for this model is provided in the following theorem:

T.69. *The dynamic Leontief system of (11.10) is capable of balanced growth if the input matrix* **A** *is indecomposable and has its dominant eigenvalue less than 1 in absolute value.*

Proof: If the conditions are satisfied we know from the Frobenius–Perron theorem that $(\boldsymbol{I} - \boldsymbol{A})^{-1}$ is strictly positive. $\boldsymbol{D}$ is semi-positive by the assumption that its inverse exists, since this requires that every row and column of $\boldsymbol{D}$ contains at least one non-zero element and we assume that it is non-negative. Hence $(\boldsymbol{I} - \boldsymbol{A})^{-1}\boldsymbol{D}$ must be positive – and thus also indecomposable – which means that it will have positive dominant eigenvalue ρ and a positive associated eigenvector $\boldsymbol{y}^*$. But note that if $(\boldsymbol{I} - \boldsymbol{A})^{-1}\boldsymbol{D}\boldsymbol{y}^* = \rho\boldsymbol{y}^*$, then:

$$\boldsymbol{D}^{-1}(\boldsymbol{I} - \boldsymbol{A})\boldsymbol{y}^* = \frac{1}{\rho}\boldsymbol{y}^* \text{ and } [\boldsymbol{I} + \boldsymbol{D}^{-1}(\boldsymbol{I} - \boldsymbol{A})]\boldsymbol{y}^* = \left(1 + \frac{1}{\rho}\right)\boldsymbol{y}^*.$$

In other words $\boldsymbol{E}$ has an eigenvalue greater than 1 associated with a positive eigenvector. Further, the Frobenius–Perron theorem tells us that $\boldsymbol{y}^*$ is the only positive eigenvector of $(\boldsymbol{I} - \boldsymbol{A})^{-1}\boldsymbol{D}$ and thus of $\boldsymbol{E}$ as well. So under the specified conditions the dynamic Leontief model has a unique balanced growth path with positive outputs given by $\boldsymbol{y}^*$ and a rate of expansion $\lambda^* = 1 + \dfrac{1}{\rho}$.

Q.E.D.

11.4 Prices in Dynamic Linear Models

We can use techniques similar to those of the previous section to analyse the behaviour of prices in a dynamic Leontief model. The costs of production are now of two types – costs of capital inputs, and those of current inputs. We shall suppose that the production of an output in period $(t + 1)$ requires capital goods to be held for this purpose during period t, and requires current inputs to be supplied in period $t + 1$. Then the cost of producing one unit of good j in period $t + 1$ is:

$$\sum_{i=1}^{n} a_{ij}p_i(t + 1) + (1 + r(t)) \sum_{i=1}^{n} d_{ij}p_i(t)$$

where $r(t)$ is the interest rate ruling in period t, and $p_i(t)$ is the cost of good i in period t, etc. The first term here represents the cost of current inputs in period $t + 1$, and the second represents the total cost of providing the required capital inputs during period t. This total is made up of the cost of buying the goods, plus the opportunity cost of interest foregone on money invested in these goods. In a competitive economy this cost will equal the value of one unit of good j in $t + 1$, $p_j(t + 1)$, plus the resale value of the capital goods acquired in period t, which is $\sum_{i=1}^{n} d_{ij}p_i(t + 1)$. Equating these gives

$$p_j(t + 1) + \sum_{i=1}^{n} d_{ij}p_i(t + 1) = \sum_{i=1}^{n} a_{ij}p_i(t + 1) + (1 + r(t)) \sum_{i=1}^{n} d_{ij}p_i(t). \tag{11.12}$$

The interpretation of (11.12) might be clearer if it is written as

$$\{p_j(t + 1) - \sum_{i=1}^{n} a_{ij}p_i(t + 1)\} + \sum_{i=1}^{n} d_{ij}\{p_i(t + 1) - p_i(t)\} = r(t) \sum_{i=1}^{n} d_{ij}p_i(t).$$

This requires that the surplus of the price of good j over its variable cost, plus the capital gains on its capital inputs, should equal the interest foregone in investing in the production of j. There will be n equations such as (11.12), and in matrix form they can be written

$$\boldsymbol{p}(t + 1)(\boldsymbol{I} + \boldsymbol{D}) = \boldsymbol{p}(t + 1)\boldsymbol{A} + (1 + r(t))\boldsymbol{p}(t)\boldsymbol{D}$$

where the $\boldsymbol{p}(\ )$'s are row vectors of prices. Simple rearrangement gives:

$$\boldsymbol{p}(t + 1)[\boldsymbol{I} - \boldsymbol{A} + \boldsymbol{D}] = (1 + r(t))\boldsymbol{p}(t)\boldsymbol{D}.$$

Post-multiplying both sides by $\boldsymbol{D}^{-1}$, and then by $[\boldsymbol{I} + (\boldsymbol{I} - \boldsymbol{A})\boldsymbol{D}^{-1}]^{-1}$,

$$\boldsymbol{p}(t + 1) = (1 + r(t))\boldsymbol{p}(t)[\boldsymbol{I} + (\boldsymbol{I} - \boldsymbol{A})\boldsymbol{D}^{-1}]^{-1}$$

or

$$\boldsymbol{p}'(t + 1) = (1 + r(t))\{[\boldsymbol{I} + (\boldsymbol{I} - \boldsymbol{A})\boldsymbol{D}^{-1}]^{-1}\}'\boldsymbol{p}'(t) \tag{11.13}$$

as the transpose of the product of two matrices equals the product of their transposes in reverse order. Note that:

$$\{[\boldsymbol{I} + (\boldsymbol{I} - \boldsymbol{A})\boldsymbol{D}^{-1}]^{-1}\}' = [\boldsymbol{I} + (\boldsymbol{D}^{-1})'(\boldsymbol{I} - \boldsymbol{A})']^{-1}$$

because $\boldsymbol{I}$ is diagonal and $\{(\boldsymbol{I} - \boldsymbol{A})\boldsymbol{D}^{-1}\}' = (\boldsymbol{D}^{-1})'(\boldsymbol{I} - \boldsymbol{A})'$. Therefore (11.13) may be written as:

$$\boldsymbol{p}'(t + 1) = (1 + r(t))[\boldsymbol{I} + (\boldsymbol{D}^{-1})'(\boldsymbol{I} - \boldsymbol{A})']^{-1}\boldsymbol{p}'(t). \quad (11.14)$$

This difference equation describes the evolution of competitive prices over time and its properties are closely related to those of (11.10) describing the evolution of outputs.

The relationship between the price and quantity systems for dynamic Leontief models are analysed in *Dual Stability Theorems.* These go beyond the scope of this chapter. Here we will examine the dual problem to the existence of a balanced growth path, that is whether there is some equilibrium price vector $\boldsymbol{p}^* > \boldsymbol{0}$ and interest rate $r^* > 0$ which are compatible with the unchanging pattern of a balanced growth path. Thus we wish to find $\boldsymbol{p}^*$ and r^* such that if for all $t, r(t) = r^*$, then $\boldsymbol{p}(t) = \boldsymbol{p}^*$ for all t. Rearranging (11.14), this implies:

$$[\boldsymbol{I} + (\boldsymbol{D}^{-1})'(\boldsymbol{I} - \boldsymbol{A})'](\boldsymbol{p}^*)' = (1 + r^*)(\boldsymbol{p}^*)'$$

or

$$\boldsymbol{E}'(\boldsymbol{p}^*)' = (1 + r^*)(\boldsymbol{p}^*)'.$$

But we know that, if the conditions in T.69 are satisfied, $\boldsymbol{E}$ is a positive matrix with a dominant eigenvalue $\left(1 + \frac{1}{\rho}\right)$. Therefore, $\boldsymbol{E}'$ also has a dominant eigenvalue $\left(1 + \frac{1}{\rho}\right)$ – greater than 1 – and associated with it a single positive eigenvector. Thus if the model is capable of balanced growth, then there must also exist an equilibrium price vector $\boldsymbol{p}^* > \boldsymbol{0}$ and interest rate $r^* > 0$. Note further that the interest rate and the growth rate $\left(\frac{1}{\rho}\right)$ are identical, so that the balanced growth path satisfies the so-called *Golden Rule.*

Before moving on to other dynamic linear models it should be noted that the results proved above for the closed dynamic Leontief system also hold for balanced growth paths in the open Leontief system. In other words we can introduce final demand for consumption or export into the system and still find a balanced growth path. However, one restriction on it is that the final demand vector must grow at the same rate at the gross output vector as a whole. Thus we could assume that a constant fraction of gross output goes to final demand in each period. If we suppose that this fraction is f_i for the ith industry and $\boldsymbol{F} = \| f_i \delta_{ij} \|$, we have:

$$\boldsymbol{y}(t) = \boldsymbol{A}\boldsymbol{y}(t) + \boldsymbol{D}[\boldsymbol{y}(t+1) - \boldsymbol{y}(t)] + \boldsymbol{F}\boldsymbol{y}(t)$$

i.e.

$$\boldsymbol{y}(t+1) = [\boldsymbol{I} + \boldsymbol{D}^{-1}(\boldsymbol{I} - \boldsymbol{A} - \boldsymbol{F})]\boldsymbol{y}(t). \tag{11.15}$$

Equation (11.15) is the same as (11.10) with the replacement of $\boldsymbol{A}$ by $\boldsymbol{A} + \boldsymbol{F}$ and so long as $\boldsymbol{A} + \boldsymbol{F}$ satisfies the condition in T.69 identical results can be demonstrated. An alternative assumption is that the coefficients f_i are the constant proportions of net output which go to final consumption or export demand. Then in place of (11.15) we would obtain:

$$\boldsymbol{y}(t+1) = [\boldsymbol{I} + \boldsymbol{D}^{-1}(\boldsymbol{I} - \boldsymbol{F})(\boldsymbol{I} - \boldsymbol{A})]\boldsymbol{y}(t). \tag{11.16}$$

A number of such models can be formulated by incorporating different assumptions, and under the appropriate conditions each will be capable of balanced growth.

11.5 The Von Neumann Model

In this section we examine a rather different and more general linear model than those based on the Leontief framework. As for the Leontief model, the discussion will focus on the existence and characteristics of a balanced growth path. This model – known as the Von Neumann model after the author who first formulated it – is a closed model in the same way as the model in section 11.3 was closed. We suppose that there are a finite number of production activities indexed by $j = 1, \ldots, m$. The jth activity when operated at unit level requires inputs $(a_{1j}, \ldots, a_{nj})$ of the n commodities and produces outputs $(b_{1j}, \ldots, b_{nj})$. This formulation allows joint production since several of the b_{ij} may be positive. It is well suited to the discussion of a true capital model with depreciation since activities and commodities can be specified so that activity j has among its inputs some capital good of age s – commodity s – and produces among its outputs the same capital good of age $s + 1$. Thus by distinguishing capital goods by age as well as type the full effects of capital depreciation can be incorporated. If labour is to be included in the model we assume that one activity takes inputs of various consumption goods and produces as its output a unit of labour of a given quality. In this way we can distinguish many different types of labour. Notice, however, that labour is a produced good in this framework; there are no scarce factors, such as land, which are used in production but whose supply is exogeneously determined. None the less the model is significantly more general than the previous ones.

The production possibilities may be described by two $n \times m$ matrices $\boldsymbol{A} = \|a_{ij}\|$, $\boldsymbol{B} = \|b_{ij}\|$. We will assume that every activity requires at least one good as an input and produces at least one good as an output – i.e. $\boldsymbol{a}_{j}, \boldsymbol{b}_{j} \geqslant \boldsymbol{0}$, since we also assume that both matrices are non-negative. Further, we assume that for any good i there is at least one activity j for which $b_{ij} > 0$; that is, every commodity can be produced by some activity. We can now define the transformation set for the economy in terms of two vectors $\boldsymbol{x}, \boldsymbol{y}$ which represent total inputs available at the beginning of the production period and total outputs available at the end. This gives:

$$T = \{(\boldsymbol{x}, \boldsymbol{y}) \mid \boldsymbol{x} \geqq \boldsymbol{A}\boldsymbol{z}, \boldsymbol{y} \leqq \boldsymbol{B}\boldsymbol{z} \text{ for some } \boldsymbol{z} \geqq \boldsymbol{0}, \boldsymbol{z} = (z_1, \ldots, z_m)\}.$$

In this $\boldsymbol{z}$ is the vector of levels at which each of the activities is operated. Indexing this by t to indicate the production period we have:

$$\boldsymbol{A}\boldsymbol{z}(t+1) \leqq \boldsymbol{B}\boldsymbol{z}(t)$$

since the output from period t forms the inputs available in $(t + 1)$.

Now if we focus on balanced growth our problem is one of finding a path such that $\alpha \boldsymbol{z}(t) = \boldsymbol{z}(t+1)$. If we drop the period indices and look for the fastest possible rate of balanced growth, this gives the problem of finding a maximum α for which there exists a $\boldsymbol{z} \geqslant \boldsymbol{0}$ such that:

$$\alpha \boldsymbol{A}\boldsymbol{z} \leqq \boldsymbol{B}\boldsymbol{z}$$

i.e. $$(\boldsymbol{B} - \alpha \boldsymbol{A})\boldsymbol{z} \geqq \boldsymbol{0}, \qquad \boldsymbol{z} \geqslant \boldsymbol{0}. \tag{11.17}$$

The dual problem to this is to find the minimum profit rate for which there exists a price vector such that no activity makes positive profits. Let $\boldsymbol{p}$ be a row vector of prices and $\beta = 1 + r$ be a profit factor. Then we wish to find the minimum β such that:

$$\beta \boldsymbol{p}\boldsymbol{A} \geqq \boldsymbol{p}\boldsymbol{B}, \qquad \boldsymbol{p} \geqslant \boldsymbol{0} \tag{11.18}$$

since all input costs ($\sum_i p_i a_{ij}$ for activity j) are incurred at the beginning of the period so that the profit rate must be applied to their total.

If we examine (11.17) it is clear that we can find some positive α

to satisfy the constraints given some $z \geqslant 0$. This is because $Bz > 0$ since every good is the output of some activity. On the other hand there is an upper bound on α since by making it large enough we can ensure that $(B - \alpha A)z$ contains at least one negative element for every $z \geqslant 0$. Thus a maximum for α exists; we will denote it by α^* and the associated activity vector by z^*. By the same argument a minimum for β exists which we denote by β^* and the associated price vector by p^*. We can now show that $\beta^* \leqslant \alpha^*$. Consider the inequality $(B - \alpha^* A)z > 0$; it cannot have a non-negative solution for z since this would have allowed us to increase α^*, contradicting our assumption that it is a maximum. Using a property of linear inequalities – Farkas lemma – we can therefore say that $p(B - \alpha^* A) \leqq 0$ has a semi-positive solution. But, since β^* is the minimum of all β's satisfying $p(B - \beta A) \leqq 0$ for $p \geqslant 0$, we have $\beta^* \leqslant \alpha^*$.

This completes our review of the fundamental features of the model and the basic theorem can be stated:

T.70. *Von Neumann Theorem. For the model defined by (11.17) and (11.18) there exists a positive number* γ *and semi-positive vectors* $\mathbf{z}$, $\mathbf{p}$ *such that:*

$$\text{(i) } (\mathbf{B} - \gamma\mathbf{A})\mathbf{z} \geqslant 0; \text{ (ii) } \mathbf{p}(\mathbf{B} - \gamma\mathbf{A}) \leqslant 0; \text{ (iii) } \mathbf{p}(\mathbf{B} - \gamma\mathbf{A})\mathbf{z} = 0.$$

Proof: The results (i) and (ii) follow directly from our proof that $\beta^* \leqslant \alpha^*$ since we can choose $\beta^* \leqslant \gamma \leqslant \alpha^*$. Then γ with the vectors z^*, p^* will satisfy (i) and (ii). Consider $pB \leqslant \gamma pA$; if $z \geqslant 0$ it follows that $pBz \leqslant \gamma pAz$. But $Bz \geqslant \gamma Az$ so that, for $p \geqslant 0$, $pBz \geqslant \gamma pAz$. Hence we must have: $pBz = \gamma pAz$.

Q.E.D.

This proof implies that if $\beta^* \leqslant \alpha^*$ there are many values of γ which are solutions; thus there will be many of pairs of activity and price vectors other than the optimal pair z^*, p^*. In other words the solution to the model is not unique. If we consider the third part of the theorem two points emerge:

(*a*) Suppose that for some i we have $b^i z - \gamma a^i z > 0$ (where b^i, a^i are the ith rows of B, A respectively). Then $p(B - \gamma A)z = 0$ implies that for this i we must have $p_i = 0$. In other words any commodities which can be produced in excess of the standard growth factor must have zero prices, while those not being produced in excess may have a positive price.

(*b*) Suppose, now, that for some j we have $pb_j - \gamma pa_j < 0$ (where b_j, a_j are the jth columns of B and A respectively). Then we must have $z_j = 0$, which may be interpreted as saying that all those activities which make less than the required profit rate γ will not be used.

The Von Neumann theorem can be strengthened if we introduce a definition of indecomposability applicable to the present model.

D.91. *The Von Neumann system with input matrix* **A** *and output matrix* **B** *is said to be indecomposable if there is no subset of goods which can be produced without using at least one input not in the subset. If the matrix* **C** *is given by* $\mathbf{C} = \mathbf{A} + \mathbf{B}$, *then the system is indecomposable if there are no partitions* $\{I_1, I_2\}$ *of* $I = \{i | i = 1, \ldots, n\}$ *and* $\{J_1, J_2\}$ *of* $J = \{j | j = 1, \ldots, m\}$ *such that* $c_{ij} = 0$ *for* $i \in I_2$ *and* $j \in J_1$.

If the system is decomposable we can rearrange the columns and rows of $\boldsymbol{A}$ and $\boldsymbol{B}$ by renumbering goods and activities so that:

$$\boldsymbol{A} = \begin{bmatrix} \boldsymbol{A}_{11} & \boldsymbol{A}_{12} \\ \mathbf{0} & \boldsymbol{A}_{22} \end{bmatrix}, \quad \boldsymbol{B} = \begin{bmatrix} \boldsymbol{B}_{11} & \boldsymbol{B}_{12} \\ \mathbf{0} & \boldsymbol{B}_{22} \end{bmatrix},$$

and thus

$$\boldsymbol{C} = \begin{bmatrix} \boldsymbol{C}_{11} & \boldsymbol{C}_{12} \\ \mathbf{0} & \boldsymbol{C}_{22} \end{bmatrix}.$$

The value of this definition is shown in the next theorem:

T.71. *For the Von Neumann system with an indecomposable technology,* $\alpha^* = \gamma^* = \beta^*$.

Proof: We know that $\beta^* \leqslant \alpha^*$; thus we need to show that in this case $\beta^* \geqslant \alpha^*$. Now $\boldsymbol{z}^*, \boldsymbol{p}^* \geqslant \mathbf{0}$, so $\alpha^* \boldsymbol{p}^* \boldsymbol{A} \boldsymbol{z}^* \leqslant \boldsymbol{p}^* \boldsymbol{B} \boldsymbol{z}^* \leqslant \beta^* \boldsymbol{p}^* \boldsymbol{A} \boldsymbol{z}^*$, i.e. $(\beta^* - \alpha^*) \boldsymbol{p}^* \boldsymbol{A} \boldsymbol{z}^* \geqslant \mathbf{0}$. But we can show that $\boldsymbol{B} \boldsymbol{z}^* > \mathbf{0}$. Suppose not, that is, let $\boldsymbol{B} \boldsymbol{z}^* \geqslant \mathbf{0}$ with, for some i, $\boldsymbol{b}^i \boldsymbol{z}^* = 0$. Then from the inequality $\boldsymbol{B} \boldsymbol{z}^* \geqslant \alpha^* \boldsymbol{A} \boldsymbol{z}^*$ with $\alpha^* > 0$ it follows that $\boldsymbol{a}^i \boldsymbol{z}^* = 0$. This implies that the ith commodity is neither produced nor used by the activity vector $\boldsymbol{z}^*$, which would only be possible if the system were decomposable. Hence for the indecomposable system $\boldsymbol{B} \boldsymbol{z}^* > \mathbf{0}$, and, since $\boldsymbol{p}^* \geqslant \mathbf{0}$, $\boldsymbol{p}^* \boldsymbol{B} \boldsymbol{z}^* \geqslant 0$. But $\alpha^* \geqslant 0$ and $\alpha^* \boldsymbol{p}^* \boldsymbol{A} \boldsymbol{z}^* \geqslant \boldsymbol{p}^* \boldsymbol{B} \boldsymbol{z}^*$, so that $\boldsymbol{p}^* \boldsymbol{A} \boldsymbol{z}^* \geqslant 0$. Therefore $\beta^* \geqslant \alpha^*$.

Q.E.D.

For the indecomposable case we may strengthen our earlier interpretation:

(*a*) The output of each good is at least equal to γ^* times the input of the good, so that the availability of each good is increasing at least at the rate $\gamma^* - 1$. Any good whose output is growing faster than this will have a zero price, while all goods with positive prices will have the standard growth rate.

(*b*) The revenue from operating any activity is no more than γ^* times the cost of the inputs at the equilibrium prices $\boldsymbol{p}^*$. The amount $\gamma^* - 1$ is the shadow profit rate, as no activity which makes less than this profit rate will be used, while all activities which are used will have the same profit rate $\gamma^* - 1$.

(*c*) Finally it should be noted that γ^* is the maximum of α and the minimum of β satisfying the appropriate constraints. This maximin or saddle point property of variables such as γ is important in the theory of optimisation and other branches of economic theory.

Even with the assumption that the technology is indecomposable we have only proved the uniqueness of γ^*; it is still possible that there may be several pairs of compatible price and activity vectors. One way in which uniqueness can be ensured is by abandoning the possibility of joint production. Suppose that each activity produces one output only and that we order activities so that the first group includes all those having good 1 as output, the next group those with output of good 2, and so on. Then the matrix $\boldsymbol{B}$ will consist of sets of columns with 1 in the first row, then the second row, etc. Essentially this framework is a generalised Leontief model with several techniques available for producing each good, and may thus be called a *Von Neumann–Leontief* model.

From the matrix $\boldsymbol{A}$ we can form $n \times n$ square submatrices by taking one activity for producing each good – i.e. by forming a subtechnology. The submatrices will be assumed to be indecomposable so that we can find a positive dominant eigenvalue and associated positive row and column eigenvectors. After doing this for all possible subtechnologies we call the submatrix with the smallest dominant eigenvalue $\boldsymbol{A}^*$, its dominant eigenvalue λ^*, and the row and column eigenvectors $\boldsymbol{p}^*$, $\boldsymbol{x}^*$ respectively – remembering that $\boldsymbol{x}^*$ is an n-vector. Now define an activity vector for the whole model as follows: if the jth activity is not in $\boldsymbol{A}^*$, $z_j^* = 0$; if activity j does appear in $\boldsymbol{A}^*$, then put z_j^* equal to the appropriate element in $\boldsymbol{x}^*$. In other words all activities not in $\boldsymbol{A}^*$ are operated at zero level by $\boldsymbol{z}^*$ and those in $\boldsymbol{A}^*$ are operated at the levels indicated by $\boldsymbol{x}^*$. Thus we have;

$$\boldsymbol{B}\boldsymbol{z}^* = \boldsymbol{x}^*,$$

$$\boldsymbol{A}^*\boldsymbol{x}^* = \lambda^*\boldsymbol{x}^*.$$

From this, it is possible to derive the following theorem. It will not be proved here; a full proof may be found in either Lancaster (1968) or Morishima (1964).

T.72. *The Von Neumann–Leontief model has a unique growth factor* $\gamma^* = 1/\lambda^*$ *and unique price and activity vectors* $\mathbf{p}^*, \mathbf{z}^*$, *where* $\lambda^*, \mathbf{p}^*, \mathbf{z}^*$ *are as defined above. The output of each good grows at the rate* $\gamma^* - 1$ *so that* $\gamma^*\mathbf{A}^*\mathbf{x}^* = \mathbf{x}^*$ *and there are no surpluses – i.e. all prices are strictly positive. All activities in* $\mathbf{A}^*$ *break even at the profit rate* $\gamma^* - 1$ *and all other activities are unprofitable.*

From our knowledge of the Leontief system we know that $\lambda^* < 1$ if the input matrix $\boldsymbol{A}^*$ is productive, so that this confirms that a productive static model will be capable of a positive balanced rate of growth. Further, this result provides an analogue of the non-substitution theorem for balanced growth in that if the model follows the unique path $\boldsymbol{x}^*$, all activities not in $\boldsymbol{A}^*$ may be treated as if they did not exist.

This completes our brief survey of the most important linear economic models and their properties. The Von Neumann model in particular has been used in the discussion of optimal growth paths in models with many sectors, and thus the literature concerning it is substantial. A good and very important exposition may be found in Dorfman, Samuelson and Solow (1958); a more recent survey is given in Burmeister and Dobell (1970). The uses of the Leontief model, particularly for empirical work and in economic planning, have been manifold. A brief but thorough survey of the field is given in Yan (1969).

12 Linear Programming

12.1 An Example: Production with Fixed Resources

To introduce linear programming we will consider the following problem in which we investigate the optimal allocation of fixed resources for a firm engaged in production and trade. It can produce two goods X, Y, each of which requires inputs of capital (K), labour (L), and land (R) in production. The input requirements per unit of output of each good are given in the table below:

Per unit of output of	Input of	K	L	R
X		3	5	1
Y		4	2	3

The firm has endowments of these fixed resources of: 24 units of K, 30 units of L, and 15 units of R. It wishes to maximise the value of its output given that the competitive prices of X and Y are respectively £1 and £1.5.

This problem is very simple to solve graphically. Suppose that the output of X is x and of Y is y. Then the given endowments of the three imply that the following inequalities must be satisfied:

$$\begin{aligned} &\text{Capital:} \quad & 3x + 4y &\leqslant 24 \\ &\text{Labour:} \quad & 5x + 2y &\leqslant 30 \\ &\text{Land:} \quad & x + 3y &\leqslant 15 \end{aligned}$$

Given these the firm wishes to maximise

$$V = x + 1.5y.$$

Graphically the constraints restrict the production possibility set as shown in Figure 8. In addition to these three constraints we will assume that x, y must be non-negative, i.e. $x, y \geqslant 0$.

The lines K, L, R represent the constraints on each of the resources. Each constraint divides the $x - y$ space into a feasible closed half-space of all points on or beneath the line and an infeasible open half-space of all points above the line. The intersection of the closed half-spaces defined by the three constraints and the two axes for the non-negativity constraints gives the closed convex set $0ABCD$ which includes all feasible output combinations for the firm. We thus wish to maximise V over this set, i.e. subject to choosing an output combination within this set.

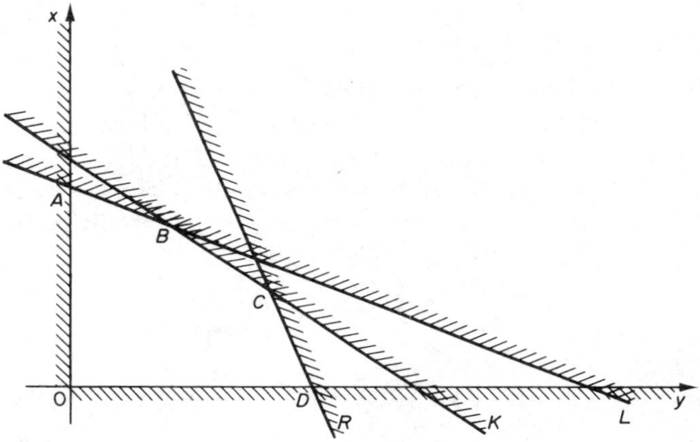

Figure 8

The dotted lines in Figure 9 are iso-revenue lines, each corresponding to some given value of V. To maximise V we must therefore choose the output combination in the set which is on the highest iso-revenue line. This is clearly the output mix given by C, which will thus be the optimal production plan for the firm. It will be observed that at C both the constraints on capital and land are binding, but that on labour is not. To find the exact outputs we can solve the simultaneous equations defined by the binding constraints, i.e.

$$3x + 4y = 24$$

$$x + 3y = 15$$

which gives as the optimal production:

$$x = 2{\cdot}4,\ y = 4{\cdot}2.$$

The optimal point C is an extreme point of the set. In general, it is clear that the solution to the problem must contain at least one extreme point. Suppose that the prices had been $p_x = 1$, $p_y = 1\frac{1}{3}$.

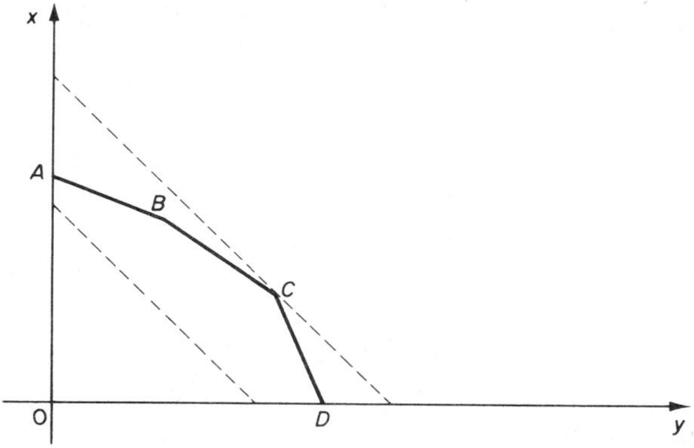

Figure 9

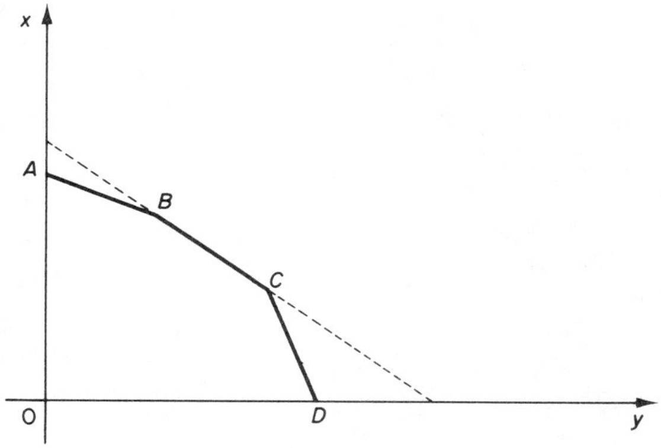

Figure 10

Then the problem would have been that in Figure 10. The iso-revenue lines are parallel to *BC*, so that any point on *BC* would be optimal. This must include both *B* and *C*, which are extreme points. In practice we will only be interested in these extreme points, since all the points between can be expressed as linear convex combinations of them.

12.2 The General Linear Programming Problem

Having introduced linear programming with the example above we now turn to a general discussion of it. The general L.P. problem may be formulated as follows:

$$\max V = \sum_{j=1}^{p} c_j x_j \tag{12.1}$$

subject to:

$$\sum_{j=1}^{p} a_{ij} x_j \leqslant b_i \qquad (i = 1, \ldots, m) \tag{12.2}$$

$$x_j \geqslant 0. \qquad (j = 1, \ldots, p) \tag{12.3}$$

The non-negativity constraints on the x_j are appropriate for many economic problems, but changing them to some other form would make no fundamental difference. Firstly, we note that the constraints in (12.2) may be rewritten by introducing *slack variables*. Let us define these as:

$$s_i = b_i - \sum a_{ij} x_j, \qquad (i = 1, \ldots, m) \tag{12.4}$$

so that the general L.P. problem becomes:

$$\max V = \Sigma\, c_j x_j$$

subject to

$$\Sigma\, a_{ij} x_j + s_i = b_i \qquad (i = 1, \ldots, m) \tag{12.2A}$$

$$x_j, s_i \geqslant 0. \qquad \text{all } i, j \tag{12.3A}$$

To express this in vector form we will use the conventions:

$$\begin{aligned} x_{p+i} &= s_i \\ a_{ij} &= 1 \qquad (j = p + i) \\ &= 0 \qquad (j \geqslant p + 1, j \neq p + i) \\ \boldsymbol{c} &= (c_1, c_2, \ldots, c_p, 0, \ldots, 0) \end{aligned}$$

so that we have:

$$\max V = \boldsymbol{cx} \tag{12.5}$$

S.T.

$$\boldsymbol{Ax} = \boldsymbol{b} \tag{12.6}$$

$$\boldsymbol{x} \geqq \boldsymbol{0}. \tag{12.7}$$

Note that $\boldsymbol{A}$ is $m \times n$, $\boldsymbol{x}$ is an n-vector where n is the sum of p and the number of inequality constraints, and $\boldsymbol{c}$ is a row n-vector whose last

$(n - p)$ components are all zero. We call (12.5) the valuation function for the linear programme as it defines the value of any solution vector $\boldsymbol{x}$. As expressed in (12.5)–(12.7) the L.P. problem is said to be in *canonical form.*

The next task is to establish some results about the nature of the feasible set – i.e. about the set of $\boldsymbol{x}$ which satisfy the constraints in (12.6) and (12.7).

T.73. *The feasible set of the L.P. problem formulated above is closed and convex.*

Proof: An exercise. [Hint – see T.1.]

For subsequent results we must make some assumptions about the equation system $\boldsymbol{Ax} = \boldsymbol{b}$. We will assume that:

(*a*) $$r(\boldsymbol{A}) = r(\boldsymbol{A}_b).$$

If this were not the case then there would be no solutions to this system, and hence none to the L.P. problem.

(*b*) $$r(\boldsymbol{A}) = m.$$

This implies that none of the equations are redundant in the sense that it is not possible to express any one of the equations as a linear combination of some of the others. Since for the general problem we have introduced one slack variable per constraint, this must be satisfied unless some of the constraints are equalities rather than inequalities. In that case some of the equalities could be L.D.; we assume that these have been eliminated to form a L.I. set. Further, if there are many equality constraints it is possible that we might have fewer variables than constraints, i.e. $n < m$. Then, if assumption (*a*) above is satisfied, some of the constraints must be L.D. and can be dropped to give us a system of n equations in the n variables. In both cases by dropping redundant equations we are left with a matrix $\boldsymbol{A}$ of full row rank, and an $m \times n$ equation system with $m \leqslant n$.

T.74. *Given a set of* m *simultaneous equations in* n *unknowns* (n $\geqslant$ *m*) $\mathbf{Ax} = \mathbf{b}$ *with* $r(\mathbf{A}) = $ m. *Then if there is a feasible solution* $\mathbf{x} \geqslant \mathbf{0}$, *there is a basic feasible solution.*

Proof: Assume that there exists a feasible solution with $p < n$ variables having positive values; number the variables so that these are the first p. Then:

$$\sum_{j=1}^{p} x_j \boldsymbol{a}_j = \boldsymbol{b}. \tag{12.8}$$

Now remember that a basic solution is one obtained by choosing m L.I. columns from $\boldsymbol{A}$, setting the variables ($n - m$ of them) not associated with these columns equal to zero, and then solving for the m variables. Such a basic solution will be degenerate if any of the m basic variables is equal to zero in this solution. Suppose that the $\boldsymbol{a}_j$ $(j = 1, \ldots, p)$ in (12.8) are L.I., so that $p \leqslant m$. If $p = m$ the solution is automatically a non-degenerate basic solution. Further, since $r(A) = m$ we know that if $p < m$, then there are $m - p$ columns of A which together with the p columns yield a non-singular matrix. Thus we can form a degenerate basic solution with $m - p$ of the basic variables equal to zero. In both cases these solutions must be feasible by our initial assumption.

Suppose that the $\boldsymbol{a}_j$ $(j = 1, \ldots, p)$ are L.D. Thus there exist α_j not all zero such that

$$\Sigma \alpha_j \boldsymbol{a}_j = \mathbf{0}. \tag{12.9}$$

$$\sum_{j=1}^{p} x_j \boldsymbol{a}_j = \boldsymbol{b}; \; x_j > 0 \qquad (j = 1, \ldots, p). \tag{12.10}$$

In a manner familiar from previous proofs we can use the L.D. condition (12.9) to reduce equation (12.10). Suppose $\alpha_r \neq 0$, then

$$\boldsymbol{a}_r = - \sum_{j \neq r} \frac{\alpha_j}{\alpha_r} \boldsymbol{a}_j,$$

i.e.

$$\sum_{j \neq r} \left(x_j - x_r \frac{\alpha_j}{\alpha_r} \right) \boldsymbol{a}_j = \boldsymbol{b}.$$

We have thus reduced the number of variables to $(p - 1)$, but it remains to check that they are all non-negative (i.e. that the solution is feasible). To ensure this α_r must be chosen appropriately. We need:

$$x_j - x_r \frac{\alpha_j}{\alpha_r} \geqslant 0 \qquad (j = 1, \ldots, p, j \neq r)$$

If $\alpha_j = 0$ this must hold. For non-zero α_j:

$$\frac{x_j}{\alpha_j} - \frac{x_r}{\alpha_r} \geqslant 0 \quad \text{if} \quad \alpha_j > 0$$

$$\frac{x_j}{\alpha_j} - \frac{x_r}{\alpha_r} \leqslant 0 \quad \text{if} \quad \alpha_j < 0$$

are the requirements. If we select the vector $\boldsymbol{a}_r$ using: $x_r/\alpha_r = \min_j \{x_j/\alpha_j, \alpha_j > 0\}$ these conditions will be met. In this way we can construct a solution with not more than $p - 1$ positive variables – all of the others being equal to zero. If the $(p - 1)$ columns $\boldsymbol{a}_j$ associated with this solution are L.I. then we can apply the previous analysis; if not then we reduce the variables to $p - 2$ positive ones and so on. Thus a basic feasible solution must exist.

Q.E.D.

T.75. *Every basic feasible solution is an extreme point of the set of feasible solutions. Further, every extreme point is a basic feasible solution to the set of constraints.*

Proof: Consider a basic feasible solution $\boldsymbol{x}$ to the set of constraints $\boldsymbol{Ax} = \boldsymbol{b}$. Let us assume that the variables have been numbered so that $\boldsymbol{x} = [\boldsymbol{x}_B, \boldsymbol{0}]$ where $\boldsymbol{x}_B = \boldsymbol{B}^{-1}\boldsymbol{b}$ with $\boldsymbol{B}$ as the non-singular matrix of m columns from $\boldsymbol{A}$ associated with the basic solution $\boldsymbol{x}$. We must show that there exist no feasible solutions $\boldsymbol{x}_1, \boldsymbol{x}_2$ different from $\boldsymbol{x}$ such that $\boldsymbol{x} = \lambda\boldsymbol{x}_1 + (1 - \lambda)\boldsymbol{x}_2$ $(0 < \lambda < 1)$. Suppose the contrary, and write $\boldsymbol{x}_1, \boldsymbol{x}_2$ as:

$$\boldsymbol{x}_1 = [\boldsymbol{u}_1, \boldsymbol{v}_1], \quad \boldsymbol{x}_2 = [\boldsymbol{u}_2, \boldsymbol{v}_2]$$

where $\boldsymbol{u}_1, \boldsymbol{u}_2$ are m-vectors, $\boldsymbol{v}_1, \boldsymbol{v}_2$ are $(n - m)$ vectors. For the last $(n - m)$ components of $\boldsymbol{x}$ we must have:

$$\boldsymbol{0} = \lambda\boldsymbol{v}_1 + (1 - \lambda)\boldsymbol{v}_2$$

which implies $\boldsymbol{v}_1 = \boldsymbol{v}_2 = \boldsymbol{0}$, since $\boldsymbol{v}_1, \boldsymbol{v}_2 \geqq \boldsymbol{0}$. Therefore we must have:

$$\boldsymbol{Ax}_1 = \boldsymbol{Bu}_1 = \boldsymbol{b}, \quad \boldsymbol{Ax}_2 = \boldsymbol{Bu}_2 = \boldsymbol{b},$$

since both $\boldsymbol{x}_1$ and $\boldsymbol{x}_2$ are feasible solutions. $\boldsymbol{B}$ is non-singular so that this implies

$$\boldsymbol{u}_1 = \boldsymbol{u}_2 = \boldsymbol{x}_B,$$

and

$$\boldsymbol{x}_1 = \boldsymbol{x}_2 = \boldsymbol{x}.$$

Hence there do not exist feasible solutions different from $\boldsymbol{x}$ such that $\boldsymbol{x}$ may be expressed as a convex combination of them. The first part of the theorem is thus proved.

For the second part we shall prove that the columns associated with the positive components of an extreme point $\boldsymbol{x}^*$ of the solution set are L.I. Assume that k components of $\boldsymbol{x}^*$ are non-zero – let these be the first k. Then:

$$\sum_{j=1}^{k} x_j^* \boldsymbol{a}_j = \boldsymbol{b}, \quad x_j^* > 0 \qquad (j = 1, \ldots, k).$$

If these columns $\boldsymbol{a}_j$ are L.D. there exist λ_j not all zero such that:

$$\sum_{j=1}^{k} \lambda_j \boldsymbol{a}_j = \boldsymbol{0}.$$

Now consider:

$$\eta = \min_i \frac{x_i^*}{|\lambda_i|}, \quad \lambda_i \neq 0 \qquad (i = 1, \ldots, k)$$

Note that η is a positive number. We select an ε, $0 < \varepsilon < \eta$, then

$$x_i^* + \varepsilon\lambda_i > 0 \text{ and } x_i^* - \varepsilon\lambda_i > 0 \qquad (i = 1, \ldots, k)$$

Define an n-component column vector $\boldsymbol{\lambda} \neq \boldsymbol{0}$ which has the λ_i in the first k positions and zero for the last $n - k$ components. Write

$$\boldsymbol{x}_1 = \boldsymbol{x}^* + \varepsilon\boldsymbol{\lambda}; \quad \boldsymbol{x}_2 = \boldsymbol{x}^* - \varepsilon\boldsymbol{\lambda}.$$

By definition $\boldsymbol{x}_1 \geqslant \boldsymbol{0}, \boldsymbol{x}_2 \geqslant \boldsymbol{0}$ and $A\boldsymbol{\lambda} = \boldsymbol{0}$. These imply that:

$$A\boldsymbol{x}_1 = \boldsymbol{b}; \quad A\boldsymbol{x}_2 = \boldsymbol{b}$$

It follows that $\boldsymbol{x}_1, \boldsymbol{x}_2$ are feasible solutions different from $\boldsymbol{x}^*$, and $\boldsymbol{x}^* = \frac{1}{2}\boldsymbol{x}_1 + \frac{1}{2}\boldsymbol{x}_2$; this contradicts the assumption that $\boldsymbol{x}^*$ is an extreme point. Hence the columns of $\boldsymbol{A}$ associated with the non-zero components of any extreme point of the convex set of feasible solutions must be L.I. There cannot be more than m L.I. columns of $\boldsymbol{A}$, and an extreme point cannot have more than m positive components. If an extreme point has less than m positive components, it can be interpreted as a degenerate basic solution.

Q.E.D.

T.76. *The optimum of a linear programming problem is reached either at an extreme point or a set of extreme points. In the latter case all convex combinations of the extreme points are also optimal.*

Proof: Every non-extreme point in the feasible set may be expressed as a convex combination of a number of extreme points $\boldsymbol{x}^k$. We choose the minimum number of extreme points necessary to define the point $\boldsymbol{x}$, so that none have zero weight; there must be at least two. Then

$$\boldsymbol{x} = \sum_k \alpha_k \boldsymbol{x}^k \qquad (\alpha_k > 0, \sum_k \alpha_k = 1)$$

Now consider $V = \boldsymbol{cx}$,

$$V = \boldsymbol{c}(\sum_k \alpha_k \boldsymbol{x}^k) = \sum_k \alpha_k(\boldsymbol{cx}^k). \tag{12.11}$$

Choose that $\boldsymbol{x}^k$ for which $\boldsymbol{cx}^k$ is the maximum – choosing one if several give the same maximum value. Denote this maximum value by V^*. It is clear that the R.H.S. of (12.11) cannot be reduced and may be increased if we substitute V^* for each $(\boldsymbol{cx}^k)$ – i.e. $\boldsymbol{cx} \leqslant V^*$. We have two possibilities:

(*a*) The maximum V^* is not reached at *all* the extreme points used to define $\boldsymbol{x}$, so that $\boldsymbol{cx} < V^*$, and $\boldsymbol{x}$ is not a maximum.

(*b*) The maximum V^* is equal to the value of V at all the extreme points so that $\boldsymbol{cx} = V^*$. If $\boldsymbol{x}$ is optimal, so are all the extreme points and also all other convex combinations of these extreme points.

Q.E.D.

Hence we have shown that we can always find an extreme point or several extreme points the value of which – that is $V^k = \boldsymbol{cx}^k$ – is at least as great as the value of any non-extreme point in the feasible set. Thus to find the overall or global optimum for the linear programme we need only investigate the extreme points of the feasible set. In other words we have only to explore the basic solutions of the constraint equations for the programme in canonical form – i.e. the basic solutions of $\boldsymbol{Ax} = \boldsymbol{b}$ for which $\boldsymbol{x} \geqslant \boldsymbol{0}$. From this an extremely useful and important result immediately follows:

T.77. *An optimal solution to an L.P. problem never needs to have more than* m *variables different from zero, where* m *is, of course, the number of constraint equations. If the optimal extreme point corresponds to a degenerate basic feasible solution, there will be less than* m *variables different from zero.*

The extreme points of the feasible set are generated by the conjunction of independent but consistent constraints. Thus suppose that the optimal solution is at an extreme point defined by $r(\leqslant m$ and $\leqslant p)$ independent and consistent binding constraints. The r slack variables associated with these will all be equal to zero, while the other $m - r$ slack variables will be positive. Since at most m variables can be non-zero, this means that at most $m - (m - r)$ – i.e. at most r – of the $x_j(j = 1, \ldots, p)$ can be non-zero. In the original problem in section 12.1 the optimal point C is defined by the intersection of the land and capital constraints. The slack variable associated with the labour constraint is positive as are the two variables x, y. Had the optimal point been either A or D defined respectively by labour or land constraints combined with the non-negativity requirements, then we have a basic solution with two of the slack variables positive – as may be seen in Figure 9.

The results outlined above provide the foundation for the usual method of solving linear programmes – the SIMPLEX METHOD. This starts from some basic feasible solution to the equation system and by using a directed and consistent pattern of search looks for other extreme points which have a higher value than the starting point. This procedure is repeated until the extreme point with maximum valuation is obtained. For full details of the simplex method and other computational aspects of linear programming readers should refer to one of: Dorfman, Samuelson and Solow (1958); Hadley (1962); Van de Panne (1971).

12.3 Duality

Associated with any linear programming problem 'max $\boldsymbol{cx}$ subject to $\boldsymbol{Ax} \leqq \boldsymbol{b}, \boldsymbol{x} \geqq \boldsymbol{0}$' is another L.P. problem known as the DUAL PROBLEM of the form:

$$\text{Minimise } \boldsymbol{yb} \text{ subject to } \boldsymbol{yA} \geqq \boldsymbol{c}, \boldsymbol{y} \geqq \boldsymbol{0}.$$

The original problem in its relationship to the second problem is known as the PRIMAL PROBLEM. The dual is formed from the primal by:

(i) replacing $\boldsymbol{x}$ by a new set of variables $y_i (i = 1, \ldots, m)$ as a row m-vector $\boldsymbol{y}$;

(ii) interchanging the constraint vector ($\boldsymbol{b}$) and the coefficients of the valuation function ($\boldsymbol{c}$);

(iii) minimising rather than maximising;

(iv) pre-multiplying $\boldsymbol{A}$ by $\boldsymbol{y}$;

(v) reversing the sense of the inequality in the constraints.

Thus we have:

Primal:	max $\boldsymbol{cx}$	S.T.	$\boldsymbol{Ax} \leqq \boldsymbol{b}, \boldsymbol{x} \geqq \boldsymbol{0}$.
Dual:	min $\boldsymbol{yb}$	S.T.	$\boldsymbol{yA} \geqq \boldsymbol{c}, \boldsymbol{y} \geqq \boldsymbol{0}$.

Clearly we can solve the dual like any other L.P. problem thus discovering the optimal values of the $y_i (i = 1, \ldots, m)$. However, there are a number of very important relationships between the primal and the dual which we will summarise in the next few theorems.

T.78. *The primal is the dual of the dual.*

Proof: Trivial.

T.79. *If* $\hat{\mathbf{x}}$ *is any feasible solution to the primal and* $\hat{\mathbf{y}}$ *any feasible solution to the dual, then:*

$$\hat{\mathbf{y}}\mathbf{b} \geqq \mathbf{c}\hat{\mathbf{x}}.$$

Proof: That $\hat{x}$, $\hat{y}$ are feasible implies:

$$A\hat{x} \leqq b; \quad \hat{y}A \geqq c.$$

Hence

$$\hat{y}A\hat{x} \leqslant \hat{y}b; \quad \hat{y}A\hat{x} \geqslant c\hat{x}.$$

Q.E.D.

T.80. *If the primal and dual problems both have feasible solutions, each has an optimal solution.*

Proof: If the primal problem has a feasible solution, its feasible set F is non-empty. By the previous theorem if the dual has a feasible solution, then the value of the dual valuation function at this solution provides an upper bound to values of the primal valuation function. Since F is closed and the valuation function cx is continuous over this set and bounded above, it follows that it must attain a maximum.

A similar argument establishes that the dual also has an optimal solution.

Q.E.D.

This theorem clarifies a difficulty relating to previous results – namely, under what circumstances do we know that a solution to a L.P. problem exists? Some problems may have an unbounded feasible set F. Thus in 'Max $[x_1 + x_2]$ subject to $x \geqq 0, a_{11}x_1 \leqslant b_1$' the maximand may be made indefinitely large. For such a problem there can be no feasible solution for the dual. If, on the other hand, we can find feasible solutions for the primal and dual problems, then we can be sure that optimal solutions to both exist.

T.81. *Duality Theorem. A feasible vector* $\mathbf{x}^*$ *of the primal problem is optimal if and only if the dual has a feasible vector* $\mathbf{y}^*$ *such that* $\mathbf{cx}^* = \mathbf{y}^*\mathbf{b}$. *The vector* $\mathbf{y}^*$ *is then optimal for the dual.*

Proof: (i) Sufficiency. Let x^*, y^* be feasible solutions such that $cx^* = y^*b$, and let x be any other vector which is feasible for the primal. Then by T. 79,

$$\begin{aligned} cx &\leqslant y^*b \\ &\leqslant cx^* \end{aligned}$$

so that x^* is optimal for the primal. The optimality of y^* in the dual follows from similar reasoning.

(ii) Necessity. To prove this requires the introduction of results going beyond the scope of this book. There are, in fact, two possible methods of proof. One, which uses the theory of linear inequalities, may be found in Gale (1960) or Nikaido (1970). The alternative, which follows from the Kuhn–Tucker theorem of non-linear programming and thus the theory of separating hyperplanes, may be found in Intriligator (1971).

Q.E.D.

An immediate corollary of this theorem is the necessity part of a stronger version of T.80 as follows:

T.80A. *Existence Theorem. The primal and dual problems have optimal solutions if and only if both have feasible solutions.*

T.82. *Complementary Slackness Conditions. Suppose* $\mathbf{x}^*$, $\mathbf{y}^*$ *are feasible for the primal and dual; then they are optimal iff:*

$$\text{(i)}\quad \mathbf{y}^*[\mathbf{A}\mathbf{x}^* - \mathbf{b}] = 0$$
$$\text{(ii)}\quad [\mathbf{y}^*\mathbf{A} - \mathbf{c}]\mathbf{x}^* = 0.$$

Together with the basic constraints in the L.P. problems these are known as Complementary Slackness conditions because they imply:

(i) *Either* $\sum_j a_{ij}x_j^* = b_i,\ y_i^* \geqslant 0.$

Or $\sum_j a_{ij}x_j^* < b_i,\ y_i^* = 0.$

(ii) *Either* $\sum_i a_{ij}y_i^* = c_j,\ x_j^* \geqslant 0.$

Or $\sum_i a_{ij}y_i^* > c_j,\ x_j^* = 0.$

Proof: From the constraints $Ax \leqq b$, $yA \geqq c$, note that at x^* and y^*

$$y^*Ax^* \geqslant cx^*$$

$$y^*Ax^* \leqslant bx^*$$

so that with the duality result we must have:

$$cx^* = y^*Ax^* = y^*b,$$

Thus for (i) we have $y^* \geqq 0$, $Ax^* - b \leqq 0$, and

$$y^*[Ax^* - b] = \sum_i (\sum_j a_{ij}x_j^* - b_i)y_i = 0.$$

Clearly these require

$$y_i(\sum_j a_{ij}x_j^* - b_i) = 0, \text{ all } i.$$

Hence the conditions stated, and similarly (ii).

For sufficiency we note that conditions (i) and (ii) imply the duality result above.

Q.E.D.

This result is very important because it leads naturally to the shadow price interpretation of the dual variables y_i. Suppose we treat the quantities b_i as resource endowments and the dual variables y_i as implicit or shadow prices associated with these resources. Then the complementary slackness conditions have a simple economic interpretation. The first says that if not all of a resource is used, its shadow price is zero – it is a free good, not effectively scarce. The second says that if the cost of production of a good in terms of shadow prices exceeds the value of the good, we will not produce it at all. This interpretation is phrased in terms directly relevant to the example in section 12.1, but a similar formulation can be found for all L.P. problems and their duals. Further, it shows that the dual answers the problem of finding the lowest total value which should be attached to the available resources $\boldsymbol{b}$ given the option of converting resources into goods which can be sold at prices $\boldsymbol{c}$. Clearly this requires that the value of resources incorporated as inputs into the production of a good must be at least as great as its selling price. For optimality with x^*, y^* the value of the resources must equal the value of the goods produced for sale, i.e. $cx^* = y^*b$.

Exercise: Solve the dual of the L.P. problem in section 12.1 and interpret the results.

We will now prove two theorems which underly the interpretation of dual variables and are used in examining some linear economic models.

T.83. *Define* $S = \{i \mid \mathbf{a}^i\mathbf{x}^* = b_i\}$, *the set of constraints which are binding at the optimum of the standard L.P.: max* $\mathbf{cx}$ s.t $\mathbf{Ax} \leqq \mathbf{b}$. *Now consider the program: max* $\mathbf{cx}$ s.t $\mathbf{Ax} \leqq \hat{\mathbf{b}}$. *If this has a feasible solution* $\hat{\mathbf{x}}$ *with* $\mathbf{a}^i\hat{\mathbf{x}} = \hat{b}_i$, $i \in S$, *then it has an optimal solution with the same set of binding constraints.*

Proof: To prove this theorem we need to treat the L.P. problem in canonical form. Thus we have the canonical program: max $\boldsymbol{cx}$ $s.t$ $\boldsymbol{Ax} = \boldsymbol{b}$, $\boldsymbol{x} \geqq \boldsymbol{0}$. The dual of this is: min $\boldsymbol{yb}$ $s.t$ $\boldsymbol{yA} \geqq \boldsymbol{c}$, $\boldsymbol{y}$ unconstrained. Note that $\boldsymbol{y}$ is unconstrained because the constraints in $\boldsymbol{yA} \geqq \boldsymbol{c}$ already impose the requisite number of restrictions. In terms of this canonical program the theorem is as follows:

If the basis $\boldsymbol{B}$ (of columns from $\boldsymbol{A}$) is optimal for the canonical program and is feasible for the second problem in canonical form (i.e. $\boldsymbol{Bx} = \boldsymbol{b}$) then it is also optimal for this problem.

Now for canonical programs the complementary slackness conditions simplify to: feasible $\boldsymbol{x}^*$, $\boldsymbol{y}^*$ are optimal iff $x_j^* = 0$ whenever $\Sigma a_{ij} y_i^* > c_j$. Since $\hat{\boldsymbol{x}}$ is feasible for the second problem and $\hat{\boldsymbol{x}}$, $\boldsymbol{x}^*$ have the same basis

$$\sum_i a_{ij} y_i^* > c_j \Rightarrow x_j^* = 0 \Rightarrow \hat{x}_j = 0.$$

Thus $\hat{\boldsymbol{x}}$, $\boldsymbol{y}^*$ are optimal for the second problem and its dual. The result that we have proved for canonical programs immediately implies the theorem for standard linear programs.

Q.E.D.

This leads us directly to investigate the consequences of changing the $\boldsymbol{b}$ vector in the primal constraint. Clearly a variation in b_i is equivalent to moving the constraint boundary $\sum_j a_{ij} x_j = b_i$ inward or outward parallel to the previous position. The above theorem means that if constraints are moved in or out in this way and a given extreme point is optimal for one case, then the equivalent extreme point (that is the one defined by the same constraints) will be optimal for every other case in which it exists.

T.84. *Consider a linear program with primal constraint vector* $\mathbf{b}$, *optimal value for the objective function* V^*, *and optimal dual vector* $\mathbf{y}^*$. *Let* $\mathbf{b}$ *now be varied to* $\mathbf{b} + \Delta\mathbf{b}$ *subject to the condition that the original basis remains feasible. Then the variation* ΔV^* *in the optimal valuation is given by:*

$$\Delta V^* = \mathbf{y}^* . \Delta\mathbf{b}.$$

In particular if only the ith *component of* $\mathbf{b}$ *changes*

$$\Delta V^* = y_i^* \Delta b_i.$$

Proof: Let $\boldsymbol{x}^*$, $\hat{\boldsymbol{x}}$ be the optimal vectors for original and second cases. Then as the original basis remains feasible $\boldsymbol{y}^*$ remains the optimal dual vector. Using the duality theorem we have:

$$c\hat{x} = y^*(b + \Delta b)$$

$$cx^* = y^*b.$$

Q.E.D.

In other words $y_i^* = (\Delta V^*/\Delta b_i)$, so that the ith dual variable gives the marginal value to the program of relaxing the ith constraint This completes the shadow price interpretation of the dual variables since it tells us that it would be worth paying up to y_i^* (in terms of units of V) in order to acquire one more unit of the ith resource, provided that the extra unit does not alter the pattern of binding constraints on production.

13 Economic Applications of Linear Programming

Many branches of economic theory may be analysed with the aid of linear programming. The example in the last chapter examined the problem of a firm with fixed resources wishing to choose its best production plan. Alternatively we could have interpreted the problem as that facing a small country trading at given world prices and also wishing to choose the best combination of outputs. Thus generalising the model to many goods would enable us to formulate a theory of production to cover all such cases. In a similar manner the theory of linear programming may be applied to linear models of profit and welfare maximisation subject to constraints to give results concerning consumer behaviour, general equilibrium and welfare economics, international trade, and planning. To illustrate these applications we will examine a number of models of production and planning.

13.1 The Non-Substitution Theorem and Production Theory

In this section we will prove the static equivalent to the dynamic non-substitution theorem proved in Chapter 11 for the Von Neumann–Leontief model. We assume that there are m activities each producing one of n goods $(m > n)$ using inputs $\boldsymbol{a}_j\ (j = 1, \ldots, m)$ per unit output. Further, each activity is assumed to use direct inputs of labour per unit output of m_j. In place of the usual technology matrix $\boldsymbol{A} = [\boldsymbol{a}_1 \ldots \boldsymbol{a}_m]$ we will work with $\hat{\boldsymbol{A}} = \boldsymbol{B} - \boldsymbol{A}$ where $\boldsymbol{B}$ is the matrix whose jth column has 1 in the row corresponding to the good produced by activity j and zeroes elsewhere. In other words $\hat{\boldsymbol{A}}$ is the net output–input matrix since each column describes the net outputs and inputs of an activity with outputs being positive and inputs negative. For the usual Leontief model $(m = n)$ $\hat{\boldsymbol{A}} = \boldsymbol{I} - \boldsymbol{A}$. Now the problem is to find a set of activities which will enable us to produce some given bill of net output $\boldsymbol{c}$ using the minimum amount of the scarce primary resource labour. This gives the L.P. problem of finding an activity vector $\boldsymbol{z}^*$ as the solution to:

$$\min \boldsymbol{mz}$$

$$\text{S.T.} \quad \hat{\boldsymbol{A}}\boldsymbol{z} = \boldsymbol{c}, \qquad \boldsymbol{z} \geqq \boldsymbol{0}. \tag{13.1}$$

From the theorems in the last chapter we know that the optimal vector $\boldsymbol{z}^*$ may be taken as a basic solution to the equation system; for the sake of convenience we will assume that it is unique, though this is not essential for the argument. A basic solution will have no more than n non-zero elements, that is no more than n activities will be operated. If we assume that the system is indecomposable, all goods must be produced to fulfil any final bill of goods. Thus for the optimal solution we will be concerned only with n activities each producing one good. The matrix of columns of $\hat{\boldsymbol{A}}$ corresponding to these activities provides us with a basis for the optimal solution which we denote by $\hat{\boldsymbol{A}}_B$. If $\boldsymbol{x}$ is the activity vector with reference to the basis system – i.e. $\boldsymbol{x}$ is $\boldsymbol{z}$ with all the nonbasic activity levels omitted, then:

$$\hat{\boldsymbol{A}}_B\boldsymbol{x} = \boldsymbol{c}, \quad \text{ie.} \quad \boldsymbol{x} = \hat{\boldsymbol{A}}_B^{-1}\boldsymbol{c}.$$

Now suppose that the final bill of goods is changed from $\boldsymbol{c}$ to $\hat{\boldsymbol{c}}$. T.83 in the last chapter tells us that provided that the basis $\boldsymbol{A}_B$, which was optimal for the program with constraints $\hat{\boldsymbol{A}}\boldsymbol{z} = \boldsymbol{c}$, is still feasible for the program with constraints $\hat{\boldsymbol{A}}\boldsymbol{z} = \hat{\boldsymbol{c}}$, then this basis is also optimal for the latter. But we already know from our analysis of the Leontief model that if the activities in $\hat{\boldsymbol{A}}_B$ can produce some final output vector $\boldsymbol{c}$ they can produce any other non-negative final output vector such as $\hat{\boldsymbol{c}}$. Hence $\hat{\boldsymbol{A}}_B$ is feasible for $\hat{\boldsymbol{c}}$, and thus is optimal for $\hat{\boldsymbol{c}}$ as well as for $\boldsymbol{c}$. Formally we can state this result:

T.85. *Non-Substitution Theorem. In the general open linear model with a single scarce primary factor and no joint production the set of activities optimal for producing any one final bill of goods is optimal for producing any other final bill of goods.*

An immediate corollary of this theorem is that the price system in this model will be independent of final demand, since the relative prices of goods may be calculated in terms of their direct and indirect demand for labour in production once the basis set of activities has been established.

Suppose that we introduce a second scarce primary factor, land, as in chapter 11. With two factors we cannot formulate the valuation function of the L.P. problem as in (13.1). One approach would be to assume externally given prices for the factors – w for labour, v for land – giving us the problem of minimising the total primary factor cost of meeting a given final output demand $\boldsymbol{c}$. This yields the L.P. problem:

$$\min w\boldsymbol{m}\boldsymbol{z} + v\boldsymbol{h}\boldsymbol{z}$$

$$\text{S.T.} \qquad \hat{A}\boldsymbol{z} = \boldsymbol{c}, \qquad \boldsymbol{z} \geqq \boldsymbol{0} \tag{13.2}$$

where $\boldsymbol{h}$ is the vector of land input coefficients. Rewriting the valuation function of this problem gives us:

$$\min (w\boldsymbol{m} + v\boldsymbol{h})\boldsymbol{z}$$

so that in essence the problem is identical to that discussed above so long as the relative prices of labour and land remain unchanged. With that assumption we have a non-substitution result concerning the invariance of the best technology with respect to final demand. Further we can calculate the price of all goods in the manner outlined in section 11.2. However, if the relative factor prices are changed, not only will commodity prices change but there may also be alterations in the set of activities forming the optimal technology.

Changes in the relative prices of primary factors focus our attention on the effect of altering the valuation function when the constraints are left unchanged. Let us return for a moment to the program in (13.1) and consider the change in the solution $\boldsymbol{z}^*$ induced by altering the valuation function from $\boldsymbol{m}\boldsymbol{z}$ to $\hat{\boldsymbol{m}}\boldsymbol{z}$. Suppose that the new optimal solution is $\boldsymbol{z}^{**}$. Then, because the feasible set is unchanged, it must be the case that $\boldsymbol{z}^{**}$ has an equal or lower value than $\boldsymbol{z}^*$ for $\hat{\boldsymbol{m}}$, and vice-versa for $\boldsymbol{m}$. If this was not true neither could be the optimal solutions for their separate valuation functions.
Thus

$$\hat{\boldsymbol{m}}\boldsymbol{z}^{**} \leqslant \hat{\boldsymbol{m}}\boldsymbol{z}^*,$$

and

$$\boldsymbol{m}\boldsymbol{z}^* \leqslant \boldsymbol{m}\boldsymbol{z}^{**}.$$

Adding these and rearranging gives:

$$(\hat{\boldsymbol{m}} - \boldsymbol{m})(\boldsymbol{z}^{**} - \boldsymbol{z}^*) \leqslant 0. \tag{13.3}$$

Now consider the special case of $\hat{m}_k < m_k$, $\hat{m}_i = m_i$ all $i \neq k$; the condition implies that $z_k^{**} \geqslant z_k^*$. In words this means that a reduction in the labour requirement of one activity, *ceteris paribus*, cannot lead to a reduction in the level of operation of that activity. In terms of the example in section 12.1 an increase in the final selling price of a good with other things constant cannot result in a decline in the output of that good. In that case (13.3) would have the form:

$$(\hat{\boldsymbol{p}} - \boldsymbol{p})(\boldsymbol{x}^{**} - \boldsymbol{x}^*) \geqslant 0 \tag{13.4}$$

because the L.P. required maximisation and not minimisation.

An alternative treatment of the model with two (or more) primary factors may be formulated in terms of maximising the value of final output with a given goods price vector and endowments of the primary factors. This gives the problem:

$$\begin{aligned} &\max \boldsymbol{pAz} \\ \text{S.T.} \quad &\boldsymbol{mz} \leqslant \overline{m}; \qquad \boldsymbol{hz} \leqslant \overline{h} \\ &\boldsymbol{Az} \geqslant \boldsymbol{0}, \qquad \boldsymbol{z} \geqslant \boldsymbol{0}. \end{aligned} \tag{13.5}$$

Two observations may be made about the qualitative properties of the non-degenerate solutions to this problem. First we note that there are $(n + 2)$ constraints so that at most $(n + 2)$ of the variables – i.e. the z_i $(i = 1, \ldots, m)$ and the $(n + 2)$ slack variables – can be non-zero. But if the technology is indecomposable at least one activity producing each good must be operated, that is at least n of the z_i must be positive. Further, for each good with a positive net output, i.e. $x_i = \boldsymbol{a}^i\boldsymbol{z} > 0$, the slack variable associated with the constraint $x_i \geqslant 0$ must also be positive. Hence in the optimal solution either only one good will have a positive net output and one of the primary factors will not be fully utilised or two goods will have positive net outputs and both of the primary factors will be fully utilised. In either case only n activities will be operated at the optimum. Thus if the technology is indecomposable the number of goods with positive net output will be equal to the number of scarce primary factors. In general if degenerate solutions are possible, the number of goods produced will be less than or equal to the number of resources in the model. The second observation is that in comparing the optimal solution for two different price vectors $\hat{\boldsymbol{p}}$, $\boldsymbol{p}$ (13.4) holds for this model if we write $\boldsymbol{x}^{**} = \boldsymbol{Az}^{**}$, $\boldsymbol{x}^* = \boldsymbol{Az}^*$.

Before turning to other applications of linear programming it is worth noting that all the problems examined here are straightforward generalisations of standard economic models of production. We have already seen how the L.P. problem of maximising the value of output subject to given resource endowments generates the usual production possibility frontier. If we turn to the problem of minimising the cost of producing a given basket of final goods, we see that each set of n activities from $\hat{\boldsymbol{A}}$ capable of producing the basket $\boldsymbol{c}$ defines a vector of labour and land requirements for this production. Thus suppose the ith possible technology is represented by $\boldsymbol{T}_i$ – an nth order submatrix of $\hat{\boldsymbol{A}}$ capable of producing any final output vector. Then the labour requirement for production of the basket $\boldsymbol{c}$ will be $\boldsymbol{m}^i\boldsymbol{T}_i^{-1}\boldsymbol{c}$, where $\boldsymbol{m}^i$ is the vector of labour input coefficients corresponding to the activities in $\boldsymbol{T}_i$. So we have the vector $(\boldsymbol{m}^i\boldsymbol{T}_i^{-1}\boldsymbol{c}, \boldsymbol{h}^i\boldsymbol{T}_i^{-1}\boldsymbol{c})$ for each technology. Further, any convex linear combination of two or more technology vectors is possible for production of the net output required. Hence, as illustrated in Figure 11, we can construct an isoquant in labour – land space for the production of the basket $\boldsymbol{c}$ as the inner envelope of all possible technology vectors and their convex linear combinations. In Figure 11 we assume five technologies – $\boldsymbol{T}_1$ – $\boldsymbol{T}_5$ – of which three are efficient

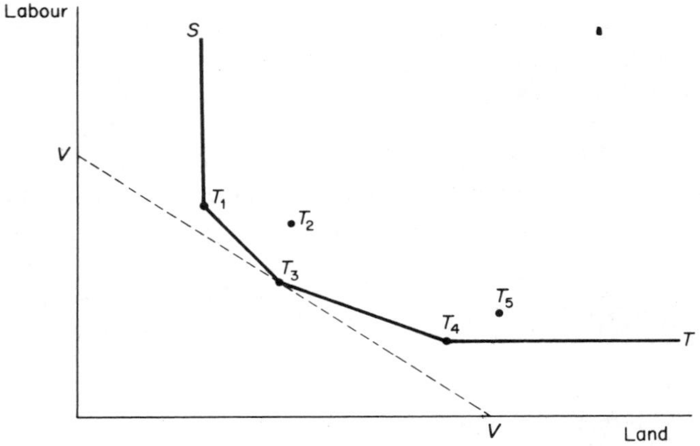

Figure 11

and appear on the isoquant $ST_1T_3T_4T$. The L.P. problem is then one of finding the innermost isocost line compatible with producing $\boldsymbol{c}$; this is given by the dotted line VV. Thus the linear programming formulation fundamentally replicates the conventional isoquant analysis of this type of problem.

13.2 Development Planning

The techniques of linear programming and input–output analysis discussed have many applications in the planning of economies, especially for less developed countries. The analyses of production subject to primary resource constraints and of the interdependence of production decisions provide insights into the consequences of investment in different sectors of the economy or of the possibility of international trade in some commodities. To illustrate another type of model in which linear programming can be useful we will examine a simple planning model for an open labour surplus economy receiving foreign aid.

The planning authorities are formulating a plan for T periods, $i = 1, \ldots, T$, with the valuation function:

$$W = \sum_{i=1}^{T} C_i \tag{13.6}$$

where C_i is aggregate consumption in period i. There are two sectors A and B producing manufactured goods for consumption or investment and agricultural goods for consumption or export. The consumption demand for each sector is a given proportion of total consumption; the remainder is spent on imported goods. Imports are also required for the production of manufactured goods and for new investment, while the country receives an amount F of aid each period. For each period in the plan agricultural production is expected to be $B(1 + g)^{i-1}$ which does not depend on any of the plan variables. On the other hand the maximum output from the manufacturing sector in any period depends on the capital available. These assumptions give us the following constraints:

Manufacturing Sector

$$\alpha C_i + \delta I_i = A_i \tag{13.7}$$

$$A_i \leqslant aK + a \sum_{j=1}^{i-1} I_j \tag{13.8}$$

where A_i is manufacturing sector output, I_i is total investment, and K is the initial capital stock.

Agricultural Sector

$$\beta C_i + E_i = B(1 + g)^{i-1} \tag{13.9}$$

where E_i is total exports.

Foreign Trade

$$(1 - \alpha - \beta)C_i + (1 - \delta)I_i + \gamma A_i \leqslant E_i + F. \tag{13.10}$$

If we use (13.7) and (13.9) to simplify these constraints, we end with the problem

$$\max W = \sum_{i=1}^{T} C_i$$

$$\text{S.T. } \theta C_i + \psi I_i \leqslant B(1 + g)^{i-1} + F \tag{13.11}$$

$$\alpha C_i + \delta I_i - a \sum_{j=1}^{i-1} I_j \leqslant aK \tag{13.12}$$

where $\theta = 1 + \alpha\gamma - \alpha$, $\psi = 1 + \gamma\delta - \delta$.

This is a straightforward linear program in the $2T$ variables $C_1, \ldots, C_T$, $I_1, \ldots, I_T$ subject to the $2T$ constraints in (13.11) and (13.12) plus non-negativity of the variables. The equality of the number of variables and of constraints tells us that if the optimal solution has positive values for all of the variables, then all of the constraints will hold with equality so that the solution could be found by solving (13.11), (13.12) as a $2T \times 2T$ equation system. In fact this is rather improbable as an optimum because, as presently specified, the valuation function gives no incentive for investment in the last period so that I_T would be as low as possible with the non-negativity constraint binding and inequality for period T in one of the constraints. This illustrates the point that an optimum for a planning problem such as this is only as sensible or helpful as the original specification allows it to be. The planning framework outlined above is clearly oversimplified. It assumes, for instance, that the country can earn as much as it wishes from exports of agricultural products. This may not be true, in which case we might add the restriction that exports cannot grow by more than a proportion μ in any period – i.e. $E_{i+1} \leqslant (1 + \mu)E_i$. In a similar manner other constraints may be added to improve the realism of the model.

The formulation and solution of the L.P. problem outlined will be of interest to planners not merely because of the paths of consumption and investment suggested, but also because of the insights provided by the dual. This will have the valuation function:

$$\min V = \sum_i p_i[B(1 + g)^{i-1} + F] + \sum_i q_i aK. \qquad (13.13)$$

Thus the dual variables will be the shadow prices in each period on:

(i) foreign exchange – since $B(1 + g)^{i-1}$ is agricultural output which if increased can immediately be used to earn more foreign exchange; and

(ii) capital in the manufacturing sector. From the complementary slackness we know that if any p_i or q_i is zero at the optimum the appropriate constraint of (13.11) or (13.12) will not be binding, i.e. will not be an effective restriction on the plan. We know from T.84 that the shadow prices are equal to the gain in W from relaxing the relevant constraint by one unit.

Now suppose that the planners consider that by the expenditure of time and resources the constraints embodied in the original model might be relaxed. For example, it might be possible to persuade donors to give more aid or to increase production in either sector by supporting research and development to encourage technical progress. Then the shadow prices provide crucial information about the return to resources spent on relaxing the various constraints, and thus guide the planners in making the best allocation. Hence even if the L.P. model is not completely realistic as a representation of the actual planning problem it can provide insights of fundamental importance into the possibilities and constraints facing the economy. Finally it should be noted that the techniques of linear programming can be modified to handle problems with non-linear valuation functions or constraints by the use of line segments approximating to the non-linear relationships.

13.3 Decentralisation and Planning

As a final application of the theory of linear programming we will demonstrate some fundamental results in the theory of decentralisation. Consider two firms with access to the same technology – represented by the resource input matrix $\boldsymbol{T}$ – and facing the same prices $\boldsymbol{p}$. The fixed endowments of each firm are given by the vectors $\boldsymbol{b}^1$, $\boldsymbol{b}^2$ and each wishes to maximise the value of its output $\boldsymbol{x}^i$. This gives:

$$\max \boldsymbol{p}\boldsymbol{x}^i \quad \text{S.T.} \quad \boldsymbol{T}\boldsymbol{x}^i \leqq \boldsymbol{b}^i, \ \boldsymbol{x}^i \geqq \boldsymbol{0}. \qquad (i = 1, 2) \qquad (13.14)$$

Further we consider the optimising problem for the two firms together as if they were consolidated: i.e.

$$\max \boldsymbol{px} \quad \text{S.T.} \quad \boldsymbol{Tx} \leqq \boldsymbol{b}, \boldsymbol{x} \geqq \boldsymbol{0} \tag{13.15}$$

where $$\boldsymbol{b} = \boldsymbol{b}^1 + \boldsymbol{b}^2.$$

First let us examine the sum of the individual decisions of the separate firms. Put $\hat{\boldsymbol{x}} = \boldsymbol{x}^1 + \boldsymbol{x}^2$ where $\boldsymbol{x}^1$, $\boldsymbol{x}^2$ are the solutions to (13.14); since each is feasible for the separate firms, $\hat{\boldsymbol{x}}$ is feasible for (13.15). Hence if the optimal solution for the latter is $\boldsymbol{x}$,

$$\boldsymbol{p}\hat{\boldsymbol{x}} \leqslant \boldsymbol{px}.$$

In other words consolidation of production cannot reduce the total value of output over the whole economy. Indeed for a sufficient difference in the firms' resource endowments – implying that different sets of resources are scarce to each firm – consolidation will increase the value of output.

The main question now is whether the same result as that achieved by consolidation can be attained by a decentralised market mechanism, that is with the firms acting independently in response to market incentives. Clearly we would expect this to involve resource trading between the firms. An examination of the solutions to the dual problems will throw further light on this. Let the dual variables be given by the vector $\boldsymbol{w}$ so that for (13.14) we get:

$$\min \boldsymbol{w}^i\boldsymbol{b}^i \quad \text{S.T.} \ \boldsymbol{w}^i\boldsymbol{T} \geqq \boldsymbol{p}, \boldsymbol{w}^i \geqq \boldsymbol{0} \tag{13.16}$$

and similarly for (13.15). As the constraints for the three dual problems are identical a solution for one must be feasible for any of them, so that:

$$\boldsymbol{w}^1\boldsymbol{b}^1 \leqslant \boldsymbol{wb}^1$$
$$\boldsymbol{w}^2\boldsymbol{b}^2 \leqslant \boldsymbol{wb}^2.$$

Thus each sector's resource vector is worth at least as much at the consolidated problem's shadow prices as at its own.

It would seem appropriate to examine the effect of permitting trade in the resources at the consolidated shadow prices. Each sector now faces the budget constraint that the value of resources used may not exceed the value of the original resource endowment, these values calculated at the consolidated shadow prices. This gives:

$$\max \boldsymbol{py}^i \quad \text{S.T.} \ \boldsymbol{wTy}^i \leqslant \boldsymbol{wb}^i, \boldsymbol{y}^i \geqq \boldsymbol{0} \qquad (i = 1, 2) \tag{13.17}$$

where we would expect the budget constraint to be fulfilled as an equality. Note that the budget constraint is a single constraint so that we have one dual variable v_i only and the dual problems are:

$$\min v_i \boldsymbol{w}\boldsymbol{b}^i \quad \text{S.T. } v_i \boldsymbol{w}\boldsymbol{T} \geqq \boldsymbol{p},\ v_i \geqslant 0. \qquad (i = 1, 2) \qquad (13.18)$$

From the dual to (13.15) it is clear that the optimal dual values in this case must be $v_1 = v_2 = 1$. Thus, from the duality theorem, we know that at the optimum $\boldsymbol{p}\boldsymbol{y}^i = \boldsymbol{w}\boldsymbol{b}^i$ $(i = 1, 2)$. Since the constraints in (13.18) with the optimal value of the dual variables are identical to those in the dual of the consolidated problem, it follows that the same activities will be used or not used in (13.15) and (13.18). Finally, if we put $\boldsymbol{y} = \boldsymbol{y}^1 + \boldsymbol{y}^2$, then

$$\boldsymbol{p}\boldsymbol{y} = \boldsymbol{w}\boldsymbol{b}^1 + \boldsymbol{w}\boldsymbol{b}^2 = \boldsymbol{w}\boldsymbol{b} = \boldsymbol{p}\boldsymbol{x}.$$

Thus we have shown that if resources may be freely traded at consolidated shadow prices the decentralised economy behaves in the aggregate exactly as it would if production had been consolidated.

This result is a rather simple example of the much more general results which may be obtained concerning the possibility of decentralising production decisions within the operations of an optimal aggregate plan. The role of shadow prices is crucial, since for efficient decentralisation resources or goods must be traded between firms at given prices and these prices will usually be the shadow prices in the optimal aggregate plan.

Appendix A
More General Vector Spaces

A vector space was defined in D.12 as follows:

D.12. *A VECTOR SPACE is a set of vectors which satisfies the following conditions:*
(i) The operation of addition is defined for any two elements of the set.
(ii) The operation of multiplication by a scalar is defined for any element of the set and any scalar.
(iii) The set is closed under these operations, i.e. the vector resulting from either of these operations is a member of the set.
(iv) The operations mentioned in (i) and (ii) have the usual associative, distributive and commutative properties.

and a vector was defined in D.7 as an ordered set of numbers.

Vectors with an infinite number of components

In all of the analysis so far, it has been assumed that the set of numbers that constitutes a vector is a finite set – that is, if $\boldsymbol{x} = (x_1, x_2, \ldots, x_n)$ is a general vector, then n is assumed to be finite. In fact there is nothing in the definition of either a vector or a vector space that actually requires that the set of numbers which are the components of a vector is a finite set. Consider the infinite sequence (0, 0, 1, 1, . . .) consisting of two zeros followed by infinitely many ones: this is clearly an ordered set of numbers which can be distinguished from (1, 0, 0, 1, 1, . . .) containing the same numbers in a different order. Infinite sequences are thus ordered sets of numbers and definitions 8 to 10 of vector equality, addition and multiplication by a scalar can be applied to them in the obvious ways – that is, let $\boldsymbol{x} = (x_1, x_2, x_3, \ldots, x_n, \ldots)$ and $\boldsymbol{y} = (y_1, y_2, y_3, \ldots, y_n, \ldots)$. Then $\boldsymbol{x} = \boldsymbol{y}$ iff $x_n = y_n$ for all n, $\lambda\boldsymbol{x} = (\lambda x_1, \lambda x_2, \lambda x_3, \ldots, \lambda x_n, \ldots)$ and $\boldsymbol{x} + \boldsymbol{y} = (x_1 + y_1,\ x_2 + y_2,\ x_3 + y_3, \ldots, x_n + y_n, \ldots)$, and the operations are associative, commutative and distributive.

Infinite dimensional vector spaces

It is clear that, if an n-component vector $\boldsymbol{x} \in V$, the vector space V is not necessarily an n-dimensional space. This is, of course, also true for the case when n is infinite; for example, the vector space V comprising vectors of the form $(x_1, 0, 0, \ldots, 0, \ldots)$ is spanned by the single unit vector $(1, 0, 0, \ldots, 0, \ldots)$ and hence has dimension 1. However, the foregoing discussion does indicate that there are vector spaces which are infinite dimensional spaces. Notice that, when discussing sequences of real numbers as components of vectors, we are actually describing the set of all infinite sequences of real numbers. The elements of this set, each being an infinite sequence, satisfy the conditions of the definition of a vector space; the set is said to be an infinite dimensional space.

There is one difference between finite and infinite dimensional vector spaces worth noting. Definition D.11 of a scalar product can in principle be applied to elements of the space just considered to yield

$$\boldsymbol{x} \cdot \boldsymbol{y} = \sum_{i=1}^{\infty} x_i y_i.$$

This is the sum of an infinite series and clearly need not be finite: thus if $\boldsymbol{x} = (1, 1, 1, \ldots)$ then $\boldsymbol{x} \cdot \boldsymbol{x} = +\infty$.

The space of all infinite sequences

Certain subspaces of the space of all infinite sequences are of interest to economists. These are:

(i) The vector space of all bounded infinite sequences of real numbers, often denoted by l_∞.

A bounded infinite sequence is a sequence $\boldsymbol{x} = (x_1, x_2, x_3, \ldots, x_n, \ldots)$ for which there exists an $M < \infty$ such that $-M \leqslant x_n \leqslant M$ for all n. Clearly the set of all such sequences is closed under the operations of addition and multiplication by a scalar, for if $\boldsymbol{x}$ satisfies $-M \leqslant x_n \leqslant M$ for all n, and $\boldsymbol{y}$ satisfies $-N \leqslant y_n \leqslant N$ for all n, then $\boldsymbol{x} + \boldsymbol{y}$ satisfies $-(M + N) \leqslant x_n + y_n \leqslant M + N$ for all n, and $\lambda\boldsymbol{x}$ satisfies $-|\lambda|M \leqslant x_n \leqslant |\lambda|M$ for all n, and any scalar λ. The second subspace sometimes encountered in economic applications is:

(ii) The vector space of all absolutely convergent sequences of real numbers, often denoted by l_1.

An infinite sequence $\boldsymbol{x}$ is absolutely convergent if $\sum_{i=1}^{\infty} |x_i| < \infty$ – i.e. if the sum of the absolute values of its elements is finite. Again it is clear that the set of such sequences is closed under the operations of addition and multiplication by a scalar since, if $\sum_{i=1}^{\infty} |x_i| = M$ and $\sum_{i=1}^{\infty} |y_i| = N$, then

$$\sum_{i=1}^{\infty} |x_i + y_i| \leqslant \sum_{i=1}^{\infty} |x_i| + |y_i| = M + N,$$

$$\text{and } \sum_{i=1}^{\infty} |\lambda x_i| = |\lambda| \sum_{i=1}^{\infty} |x_i| = |\lambda| M$$

for any scalar λ. There are of course many other spaces of this type – for example the space of all convergent infinite sequences of real numbers, or of all sequences whose limit is zero.

In addition to the above fairly obvious extensions of the idea of a vector space, there are certain other less immediate extensions. Consider for example the set of all $m \times n$ matrices. Clearly addition and scalar multiplication are defined for these, the operations are associative, distributive and commutative and the set is closed under these operations. The set of all $m \times n$ matrices therefore satisfies all the conditions of D.12 of a vector space – as do the set of all $m \times m$ matrices, and many other sets of matrices. As a further example, consider the set of all continuous functions mapping $R^1 \to R^1$. If f and g are two such functions define their sum $(f + g)$ by

$$(f + g)(a) = f(a) + g(a)$$

and define the product of f with a scalar λ, (λf), as

$$(\lambda f)(a) = \lambda f(a).$$

Since the sum of continuous functions is continuous, as is the product of such a function with a scalar, and the above operations have the usual associative, distributive and commutative properties, then the set of all continuous functions mapping $R^1 \to R^1$ is another set of objects satisfying all the conditions of D.12.

These examples show that there may be many collections of objects that are not vectors, yet which satisfy all four points of the definition of a vector space: the techniques and concepts developed for use with vectors can often be extended for use with these sets of objects.

Appendix B Differentiation in Linear Algebra

The concepts of differential calculus can be easily applied to scalars formed in linear algebra. The two examples of scalars formed from vectors and matrices which have been discussed in the text are (i) the scalar product $\boldsymbol{a} \cdot \boldsymbol{x} (= \boldsymbol{a}'\boldsymbol{x}$ or $\boldsymbol{x}'\boldsymbol{a})$ and (ii) the quadratic form $\boldsymbol{x}'\boldsymbol{A}\boldsymbol{x}$.

The scalar product S of two column n-vectors $\boldsymbol{a}$ and $\boldsymbol{x}$ is given by $S = \boldsymbol{a}'\boldsymbol{x} = \sum_{i=1}^{n} a_i x_i$. The partial derivative of S with respect to any x_i is $\dfrac{\partial S}{\partial x_i} = a_i$ for $i = 1, \ldots, n$. Thus the partial derivatives with respect to each element of the vector $\boldsymbol{x}$ are the corresponding elements of vector $\boldsymbol{a}$. It is convenient therefore to introduce the notation of a vector of derivatives $\dfrac{\partial S}{\partial \boldsymbol{x}}$ for which the ith element of vector $\boldsymbol{a}$ corresponds to the partial derivative with respect to the ith element of $\boldsymbol{x}$. Thus $\dfrac{\partial S}{\partial \boldsymbol{x}} = \boldsymbol{a}$.

Let $\boldsymbol{x}$ be a column n-vector and $\boldsymbol{A}$ a symmetric $(n \times n)$ square matrix. The quadratic form Q is given by $Q = \boldsymbol{x}'\boldsymbol{A}\boldsymbol{x} = \sum_i \sum_j a_{ij} x_i x_j$. Partially differentiating Q with respect to the ith element of $\boldsymbol{x}$, we obtain

$$\frac{\partial Q}{\partial x_i} = \sum_j a_{ij} x_j + \sum_i a_{ij} x_i$$

$$= 2\sum_{j=1}^{n} a_{ij} x_j$$

$$= 2\mathrm{a}^i \cdot \boldsymbol{x}$$

where $\boldsymbol{a}^i$ is the ith row of matrix $\boldsymbol{A}$.

Thus we can write

$$\frac{\partial Q}{\partial \boldsymbol{x}} = 2(\boldsymbol{a}^1\boldsymbol{x}, \boldsymbol{a}^2\boldsymbol{x}, \ldots, \boldsymbol{a}^n\boldsymbol{x})$$

$$= 2\boldsymbol{A}\boldsymbol{x}.$$

Note that we can also write

$$\frac{\partial Q}{\partial \boldsymbol{x}} = 2(\boldsymbol{x}'\boldsymbol{a}_1, \boldsymbol{x}'\boldsymbol{a}_2, \ldots, \boldsymbol{x}'\boldsymbol{a}_n)$$

where $\boldsymbol{a}_i$ is the ith column of $\boldsymbol{A}$ so that

$$\frac{\partial Q}{\partial \boldsymbol{x}} = 2\boldsymbol{x}'\boldsymbol{A}.$$

The choice between the two formulations depends on the context; the result $2\boldsymbol{A}\boldsymbol{x}$ is a column vector and $2\boldsymbol{x}'\boldsymbol{A}$ is a row vector.

To demonstrate how this notation can simplify discussion, consider the example of ordinary least squares regression in statistics. Let $\boldsymbol{y}$ be a column n-vector of n observed values of the dependent variable, $\boldsymbol{X}$ be an $(n \times m)$ matrix of n observed values on each of m independent variables. Consider the proposition that the dependent variable is a linear function of the m independent variables. Using as the criterion of 'best fit' the requirement that the sum of squares of the residuals is minimised, the problem is to find that linear combination of the independent variables which gives the best fit. The equation can be written as $\boldsymbol{y} = \boldsymbol{X}\boldsymbol{\beta} + \varepsilon$ where $\boldsymbol{\beta}$ is a column m-vector of the coefficients of the linear function and $\boldsymbol{\varepsilon}$ is a column n-vector of the residuals – that is, that part of each observed value of the dependent variable not accounted for by the linear combination of the independent variables. The problem therefore is:

find the values β_i $(i = 1, \ldots, n)$ which minimise $\sum_{i=1}^{n} \varepsilon_i^2$

Now

$$\sum_i \varepsilon_i^2 = \boldsymbol{\varepsilon}'\boldsymbol{\varepsilon} = (\boldsymbol{y} - \boldsymbol{X}\boldsymbol{\beta})'(\boldsymbol{y} - \boldsymbol{X}\boldsymbol{\beta})$$
$$= \boldsymbol{y}'\boldsymbol{y} - 2\boldsymbol{\beta}'\boldsymbol{X}'\boldsymbol{y} + \boldsymbol{\beta}'\boldsymbol{X}'\boldsymbol{X}\boldsymbol{\beta},$$

and hence we wish to minimise the scalar $\boldsymbol{\varepsilon}'\boldsymbol{\varepsilon}$ with respect to the elements of the vector $\boldsymbol{\beta}$. Note that $\boldsymbol{\beta}'(\boldsymbol{X}'\boldsymbol{y})$ is a scalar product and $\boldsymbol{\beta}'(\boldsymbol{X}'\boldsymbol{X})\boldsymbol{\beta}$ is a quadratic form in which $\boldsymbol{X}'\boldsymbol{X}$ can easily be shown to be symmetric. Thus

$$\frac{\partial(\boldsymbol{\varepsilon}'\boldsymbol{\varepsilon})}{\partial \beta_i} = 0 - 2\boldsymbol{x}_i'\boldsymbol{y} + 2\sum_{j=1}^{n}(\boldsymbol{x}_i'\boldsymbol{x}_j\beta_j).$$

In vector notation, we have

$$\frac{\partial(\boldsymbol{\varepsilon}'\boldsymbol{\varepsilon})}{\partial \boldsymbol{\beta}} = -2\boldsymbol{X}'\boldsymbol{y} + 2\boldsymbol{X}'\boldsymbol{X}\boldsymbol{\beta}.$$

For a minimum,

$$-2\boldsymbol{X}'\boldsymbol{y} + 2\boldsymbol{X}'\boldsymbol{X}\boldsymbol{\beta} = \boldsymbol{0}$$

$$\boldsymbol{\beta} = (\boldsymbol{X}'\boldsymbol{X})^{-1}\boldsymbol{X}'\boldsymbol{y}.$$

The elements of $\boldsymbol{\beta}$ given above as functions of the observations on the $\boldsymbol{x}_i$'s and $\boldsymbol{y}$ give the coefficients of that linear combination of the independent variables which minimises the unexplained part of the dependent variable. Under certain assumptions about the residual vector $\boldsymbol{\varepsilon}$, the vector $\boldsymbol{\beta}$ above has a number of desirable properties for statistical analysis.

Some Test Questions

1. (*a*) Evaluate

$$\text{(i)} \begin{vmatrix} a-b & b-c & c-a \\ b-c & c-a & a-b \\ c-a & a-b & b-c \end{vmatrix}; \qquad \text{(ii)} \begin{vmatrix} 1 & 1 & 1 & 1 \\ a & b & c & d \\ a^2 & b^2 & c^2 & d^2 \\ a^3 & b^3 & c^3 & d^3 \end{vmatrix}.$$

(*b*) Show that

$$\begin{vmatrix} b^2+c^2 & ab & ca \\ ab & c^2+a^2 & bc \\ ca & bc & a^2+b^2 \end{vmatrix} = \begin{vmatrix} 0 & c & b \\ c & 0 & a \\ b & a & 0 \end{vmatrix}^2.$$

(1964)

2. (*a*) Define as carefully as you can the concepts of 'linear independence' of vectors, 'vector space' and 'vector subspace'.

(*b*) Show that the vectors, $\boldsymbol{a}_1 = (1, 2, 3, 4)$, $\boldsymbol{a}_2 = (2, 3, 1, 5)$, $\boldsymbol{a}_3 = (3, 1, 2, 7)$ and $\boldsymbol{a}_4 = (1, 1, -2, 1)$ forms a linearly dependent set. Which of these vectors is not in the subspace spanned by the others?

(*c*) A linear transformation takes the vector $\boldsymbol{a}_1 = (3, 4)$ into $\boldsymbol{b}_1 = (-5, 6)$ and the vector $\boldsymbol{a}_2 = (-1, 2)$ into $\boldsymbol{b}_2 = (4, 1)$. What matrix represents this linear transformation?

(*d*) What is a fundamental set of solutions of a homogeneous system?

Find such a set for the system

$$2x + y + 3w + z = 0,$$

$$3x + y + 2w + 3z = 0,$$

$$x + y + 4w - z = 0.$$

(1967)

3. $$l_i x + m_i y + n_i z = a_i \qquad (i = 1, 2, 3)$$

are the equations of three planes in three-dimensional Euclidean space. Under what conditions will they have:

(i) just one point in common;
(ii) no point in common?

Suppose that $a_i = 0$ ($i = 1, 2, 3$). Under what conditions will the three planes have a point in common other than the origin? Show that in this case they will have an infinite number of points in common. (1964)

4. For each of the following sets of equations or inequalities, either exhibit a positive solution or show that none exists:

(i) $$\begin{aligned} x_1 + 3x_2 + x_3 &= 1; \\ x_1 - 5x_2 + 2x_3 &= -3. \end{aligned}$$

(ii) $$\begin{aligned} x_1 + x_2 + x_3 &\leqslant 1; \\ 7x_1 + 3x_2 + 5x_3 &\leqslant 4; \\ 3x_1 + 6x_2 + 9x_3 &\leqslant 2. \end{aligned}$$

(iii) $$\begin{aligned} 3x_1 + x_2 - 4x_3 &= 0; \\ x_1 - 2x_3 &= 0; \\ 3x_1 - 5x_3 &= 0. \end{aligned}$$ (1964)

5. Define a *linear transformation*. Show that a linear transformation of n-vectors into n-vectors can be represented uniquely by a square matrix with n columns. What is the interpretation in terms of the linear transformation of the case where the matrix has rank less than n?

$\boldsymbol{A}$ is a 2×2 matrix. The set of points S_1 in the co-ordinate plane contains all vectors (x, y) such that:

$$0 \leqslant x \leqslant 1,$$

and

$$0 \leqslant y \leqslant 1.$$

The set S_2 is the image of S_1 under the linear transformation represented by the matrix $\boldsymbol{A}$. Show that the area of S_2 is $|\det(\boldsymbol{A})|$, where $\det(\boldsymbol{A})$ is the determinant of the matrix $\boldsymbol{A}$, and $|.|$ indicates absolute value. (1971)

6. (*a*) If $\boldsymbol{A}, \boldsymbol{B}, \boldsymbol{C}$, are $n \times n$ matrices show that

$$(\boldsymbol{AB})\boldsymbol{C} = \boldsymbol{A}(\boldsymbol{BC}),$$

and that $\boldsymbol{AB}$ need not be equal to $\boldsymbol{BA}$.

(*b*) Suppose that the $n \times n$ matrices $\boldsymbol{A}$ and $\boldsymbol{B}$ have the property that $\boldsymbol{AB} = \boldsymbol{B}^2\boldsymbol{A}$. Show by induction that

$$(\boldsymbol{AB})^p = \boldsymbol{B}^{2^{p+1}-2}\boldsymbol{A}^p$$

for any positive integer, p.

(*c*) If $\boldsymbol{A}$ and $\boldsymbol{B}$ satisfy $\boldsymbol{AB} = \boldsymbol{B}^2\boldsymbol{A}$, and $\boldsymbol{A}$ is non-singular, show that any eigenvalue of $\boldsymbol{B}$ is also an eigenvalue of $\boldsymbol{B}^2$. Find conditions under which all the eigenvalues of $\boldsymbol{B}^2$ are eigenvalues of $\boldsymbol{B}$, and deduce that in these circumstances, all the eigenvalues are either 0 or 1. (1966)

7. Consider the $n \times n$ matrix

$$\boldsymbol{M} = \begin{bmatrix} 1-\alpha & \alpha & 0 & 0 & \dots & 0 & 0 \\ \beta & 1-\alpha-\beta & \alpha & 0 & \dots & 0 & 0 \\ 0 & \beta & 1-\alpha-\beta & \alpha & \dots & 0 & 0 \\ 0 & 0 & \beta & 1-\alpha-\beta & \dots & 0 & 0 \\ 0 & 0 & 0 & \beta & \dots & 0 & 0 \\ \cdot & \cdot & \cdot & \cdot & \dots & & \\ \cdot & \cdot & \cdot & \cdot & & & \\ \cdot & \cdot & \cdot & \cdot & & & \\ 0 & 0 & 0 & 0 & \dots & \alpha & 0 \\ 0 & 0 & 0 & 0 & \dots & 1-\alpha-\beta & \alpha \\ 0 & 0 & 0 & 0 & \dots & \beta & 1-\beta \end{bmatrix},$$

where α, β and $1 - \alpha - \beta$ are positive.

(*a*) Show that there exists a t_0 such that every element of $\boldsymbol{M}^t$ is positive for $t \geqslant t_0$.

(*b*) Find the row vector $\boldsymbol{x}$ such that its elements sum to unity and $\boldsymbol{xM} = \boldsymbol{x}$. (1964)

8. Let $\boldsymbol{J}$ be an $n \times n$ matrix, all of whose elements are unity. Show that

$$(\boldsymbol{I} + r\boldsymbol{J})(\boldsymbol{I} + s\boldsymbol{J}) = \boldsymbol{I} + t\boldsymbol{J},$$

where r, s and t are scalars, and $t = r + s + nrs$. Hence, or otherwise, show that the matrix

$$\boldsymbol{B} = \begin{bmatrix} 1 & -a & -a & \dots & -a \\ -a & 1 & -a & \dots & -a \\ -a & -a & 1 & \dots & -a \\ \dots & \dots & \dots & \dots & \dots \\ \dots & \dots & \dots & \dots & \dots \\ -a & -a & \dots & \dots & -a \\ -a & -a & \dots & \dots & 1 \end{bmatrix},$$

(having n rows and columns) defines a linear transformation whose inverse takes positive vectors into positive vectors, if

$$0 < a < \frac{1}{n-1}.$$

Deduce that, for these values of a,

(i) Det $\boldsymbol{B} > 0$.
(ii) The quadratic form $\boldsymbol{x}'\boldsymbol{B}\boldsymbol{x}$ is positive definite. (1965)

9. (*a*) Calculate $\begin{vmatrix} 1 & 2 & 3 \\ 3 & 1 & 2 \\ 2 & 3 & 1 \end{vmatrix}.$

(*b*) Find the eigenvalues and a corresponding set of orthogonal eigenvectors of

$$\begin{pmatrix} 5 & -1 & -1 \\ -1 & 3 & 1 \\ -1 & 1 & 3 \end{pmatrix}.$$

(*c*) Find a fundamental set of solutions of the equations

$$3x - 4y + z + 2w = 0,$$

$$8x + 5y - z - w = 0.$$

Are there any positive solutions? (1965)

10. (*a*) Prove that the product of the eigenvalues of a linear transformation of a finite-dimensional vector space is equal to its determinant.

(*b*) $\boldsymbol{A}$ is an $n \times n$ matrix with eigenvalues λ_i ($i = 1, 2, \ldots, n$). $\boldsymbol{x}$ is an eigenvector corresponding to the eigenvalue λ_1. $\boldsymbol{C}$ is the $(n+1) \times (n+1)$ matrix

$$\begin{bmatrix} \boldsymbol{A} & \boldsymbol{x} \\ \boldsymbol{y}' & 0 \end{bmatrix},$$

in which the first n rows and first n columns form the matrix $\boldsymbol{A}$, the first n elements of the last column form the vector $\boldsymbol{x}$, and the first n elements of the last row form an n-vector $\boldsymbol{y}'$. Prove that the eigenvalues of $\boldsymbol{C}$ are

$$\tfrac{1}{2}[\lambda_1 \pm \sqrt{(\lambda_1^2 + 4\boldsymbol{y}'\boldsymbol{x})}],\ \lambda_2, \lambda_3, \ldots, \lambda_n.$$

Calculate the determinant of $\boldsymbol{C}$. (1965)

11. (*a*) Show that a quadratic form, $\boldsymbol{x}'\boldsymbol{A}\boldsymbol{x}$, where $\boldsymbol{A}$ is a symmetric matrix, is positive definite if and only if the eigenvalues of the matrix $\boldsymbol{A}$ are all positive real numbers.

(*b*) By applying this result to the matrix $v\boldsymbol{I} - \boldsymbol{A}$ for suitable values of v, or otherwise, prove that, if $\boldsymbol{A}$ is a symmetric matrix and λ and μ are its maximum and minimum eigenvalues,

$$\lambda \geqslant \frac{\boldsymbol{x}'\boldsymbol{A}\boldsymbol{x}}{\boldsymbol{x}'\boldsymbol{x}} \geqslant \mu,$$

for all vectors $\boldsymbol{x} \neq \boldsymbol{0}$.

(*c*) Write

$$\det(v\boldsymbol{I} - \boldsymbol{A}) = a_0 + a_1 v + a_2 v^2 + \ldots + a_n v^n,$$

where $a_0, a_1, \ldots, a_n$ are scalars. Define the matrix

$$\boldsymbol{B} = a_0 + a_1\boldsymbol{A} + a_2\boldsymbol{A}^2 + \ldots + a_n\boldsymbol{A}^n.$$

By considering the linear mapping corresponding to $\boldsymbol{B}$, show that the matrix $\boldsymbol{B}$ is identically zero. (1966)

12. (*a*) Define a Linear Transformation and give two examples.

(*b*) Let

$$\boldsymbol{A} = \begin{bmatrix} 8 & 2 & 1 \\ 6 & 0 & 2 \\ 1 & 5 & 0 \end{bmatrix}$$

be the matrix representation of a linear transformation of V_3 into V_3, where the basis is $(\boldsymbol{e}_1, \boldsymbol{e}_2, \boldsymbol{e}_3)$ ($\boldsymbol{e}_i$ is the vector with unity in the ith place and zeros elsewhere). What is the matrix representation of this transformation when the vectors $\boldsymbol{q}_1 = (6, 7, 7)$, $\boldsymbol{q}_2 = (3, 7, 5)$, $\boldsymbol{q}_3 = (0, 1, 6)$ are chosen as a basis?

(*c*) Indicate briefly how you would proceed to transform the vectors $\boldsymbol{q}_1$, $\boldsymbol{q}_2$ and $\boldsymbol{q}_3$ into an *orthonormal* basis for V_3. (1963)

13. Let

$$\boldsymbol{A} = \begin{bmatrix} 1 & 2 & 3 \\ 2 & 1 & 4 \\ 3 & 4 & 1 \end{bmatrix} \text{ and } \boldsymbol{x} = (x_1, x_2, x_3)$$

a column vector.

(*a*) Find $\boldsymbol{x}^*$ such that $\boldsymbol{x}'\boldsymbol{A}\boldsymbol{x}$ is a maximum subject to

$$ax_1 + bx_2 + cx_3 = k.$$

($a = 6, b = 8, c = 1, k = 10.$)

(*b*) Evaluate

$$\frac{\partial x_1^*}{\partial k} \text{ and } \frac{\partial x_1^*}{\partial a}.$$

(1963)

14. (*a*) If $\boldsymbol{A}$ is a positive $(n \times n)$ matrix with element a_{ij} such that

$$\sum_i a_{ij} < 1 \quad \text{all} \quad j$$

prove that

$$(\boldsymbol{I} - \boldsymbol{A})^{-1} = [\boldsymbol{I} + \boldsymbol{A} + \boldsymbol{A}^2 + \ldots + \boldsymbol{A}^n] \quad \text{as} \quad n \to \infty.$$

(*b*) If $\boldsymbol{A}$ is the matrix of the above example, $\boldsymbol{x}_t$ the value of the vector $\boldsymbol{x}$ at t, $\boldsymbol{k} > \boldsymbol{0}$, a vector with n components analyse the behaviour of the set of difference equations

$$\boldsymbol{x}_t = \boldsymbol{A}\boldsymbol{x}_{t-1} + \boldsymbol{k}.$$

If $\boldsymbol{x}_0 > \boldsymbol{0}$, will $\boldsymbol{x}_t$ be positive for all t? (1963)

15. Solve the following linear programming problems, if a solution exists. Then set up and solve the dual problem in each case.

(*a*) max. $z = \frac{3}{4}x_1 + x_2$

S.T. $x_1 + x_2 \leqslant 6,$

$2x_1 + 3x_2 \leqslant 15,$

$x_1 \geqslant 1, x_2 \geqslant 2.$

(*b*) max. $z = x_1 + 5x_2$

S.T. $2x_1 + 3x_2 \leqslant 6,$

$3x_1 + x_2 \geqslant 3,$

$x_1, x_2 \geqslant 0.$

(*c*) min. $z = 2x_1 + x_2$

S.T. $x_1 + 2x_2 \leqslant 6,$

$x_1 - x_2 \leqslant 2.$

(*d*) max. $z = 3x_1 + x_2$

S.T. $2x_1 + 3x_2 + x_3 = 6,$

$4x_1 + x_2 + x_4 = 8,$

$x_1, x_2, x_3, x_4 \geqslant 0.$

16. In a linear programming problem both the primal and dual problems have feasible solutions which give the same value for their

respective objective functions. Prove that in this case each solution is optimal for its own problem.

Find values of $x_1, x_2, x_3, x_4, x_5 \geqslant 0$ which maximise

$$42x_1 + 4x_2 + 56x_3 - 48x_4 + 10x_5$$

subject to

$$-14x_1 + x_2 - 7x_3 + 6x_4 - 2x_5 \geqslant 20$$

and

$$3x_1 + 4x_2 + 8x_3 + 5x_4 + x_5 \leqslant 30. \quad (1973)$$

17. A farmer's resources are: capital – £1000; land – 80 acres; labour – 3000 man-hours. He can either produce wheat or beef; the resource requirements per unit output in each activity are given in the table below:

	Land (*acres*)	*Labour* (*man hours*)	*Capital* (£)
Wheat (per ton)	5	100	50
Beef (per cwt)	1	100	200

Find his best production plan if he can sell wheat for £40 per ton and beef for £10 per cwt. What is the maximum he would be willing to pay in order to obtain extra units of each input?

18. A farmer can produce maize, cotton, rice or sorghum. He has ten acres of land and can secure the free services of 15 man-months of dry-season labour, and 9 man-months of wet-season labour. If the yield per acre and required inputs per acre are as shown below, how can he maximise his annual revenue?

	Maize	*Cotton*	*Rice*	*Sorghum*
Yield (£ per acre)	400	350	500	250
Dry-season labour (man-months per acre)	2	3	2	2
Wet-season labour (man-months per acre)	1	1	2	0

19. Consider the standard L.P. problem with optimal solution $\boldsymbol{x}^*$. Now replace the original objective function $\boldsymbol{cx}$ by a new one $\boldsymbol{dx}$ where $d_k > c_k$, $d_i = c_i$ for all $i \neq k$. If the constraints of the program are unchanged and the new optimal solution is $\boldsymbol{x}^{**}$, show that $x_k^{**} > x_k^*$; what of x_i^{**} for $i \neq k$?

20. A farm has available resources given by a vector $\boldsymbol{k}$. These can be transformed into outputs by means of linear activities. The ith activity produces the ith good and requires a positive vector of

resources $\boldsymbol{b}_i$ ($i = 1, \ldots, n$) per unit output. $\boldsymbol{B}$ is the matrix whose ith column is $\boldsymbol{b}_i$. Suppose that the outputs sell at fixed prices given by the vector $\boldsymbol{v}$. Formulate as a programming problem the problem of producing outputs at maximum value.

Show that a decrease in the price of the ith good cannot increase optimal production of that good.

Suppose $\boldsymbol{B}$ is

$$\begin{bmatrix} 3 & 2 & 5 & 3 \\ 5 & 5 & 3 & 1 \end{bmatrix},$$

$\boldsymbol{v}'$ is (12, 10, 15, 6) and $\boldsymbol{k}'$ is (10, 10). Find the levels of output of the various goods and the imputed demand prices for extra resources.

(1972)

21. (*a*) State without proof the Nonsubstitution Theorem specifying carefully the conditions under which it is valid.

Consider the following linear production model:

	Good 1	*Good* 2	*Labour*
Activity 1	1	−0·2	−0·4
Activity 2	1	−0·5	−0·2
Activity 3	1	−0·3	−0·3
Activity 4	−0·3	1	−0·6
Activity 5	−0·6	1	−0·2

(positive numbers denote outputs, negative numbers inputs.)

Find a pair of these activities having the same output space as the original model.

(*b*) In the context of a simple Leontief model with one and only one industry producing each good and one primary factor (labour), examine the effect on the competitive equilibrium prices of (i) a uniform sales tax and (ii) a tax on labour use. (1969)

22. An economy produces a consumption good, an intermediate good and a capital good. The goods are measured in value terms and at constant prices. At the beginning of each production period the following stocks must be carried:

(*a*) Work-in-progress of each commodity equal to 20% of its gross output during the period.

(*b*) Capital goods equal to twice the value of gross output during the period.

(*c*) Intermediate goods equal to 10% of the output of consumption goods during the period.

Production of the consumption good requires a current input of the intermediate good equal to 50% of output of the consumption good, and consumption is equal to 70% of net output in each period. Find the maximum possible rate of growth of net output per period and the corresponding proportions in which net outputs should be produced. (1970)

23. In a closed model involving only two industries the output, q_1, of the first industry consists entirely of capital goods while the output, q_2, of the second industry consists entirely of consumption goods. The first industry requires k_{11} units of its own output per unit of output and the second industry requires k_{12} units of the output of the first industry per unit of its output. Capital goods do not deteriorate and labour is never a problem. A constant proportion, π of the capital goods output is allocated to the first industry.

(*a*) Derive the matrices transforming this year's output of the two industries into (i) next year's outputs and (ii) the outputs τ years from now.

(*b*) How would you choose the value of π assuming that you were (i) an elderly minister anxious to die beloved by all, and (ii) a council of egg-heads devoted to the principle of justice between the generations?

(*c*) If in either of the circumstances envisaged under (*b*) you felt in need of further information, what kind of information would you seek? (1969)

24. The numbers in the states of a demographic system, defined by combining a classification by age with a classification by activity are the elements of a vector $\boldsymbol{p}$. Two examples of such states are: being aged 15 and attending a grammar school; and being aged 20 and working in the building industry. Each year the numbers in the different states are increased by the elements of a vector $\boldsymbol{b}$ and diminished by the elements of a vector $\boldsymbol{d}$. If the population is in stationary equilibrium the elements of $\boldsymbol{p}$, $\boldsymbol{b}$ and $\boldsymbol{d}$ will remain the same from year to year; otherwise, in general, they will not.

A proportion c_{jk} of those in state j last year will be found in state k this year:

$$0 \leqslant c_{jk} \leqslant 1; \quad \sum_k c_{jk} \leqslant 1.$$

Call the matrix with elements c_{jk}, $\boldsymbol{C}$. By assumption the elements of this matrix are constants.

(*a*) Write out this year's state vector, $\boldsymbol{p}$, in terms of last year's value and this year's new entrants, $\boldsymbol{b}$.

(*b*) From (*a*) derive an expression for the state vector τ years from now; in what circumstances will this expression be independent of the present state vector?

(*c*) In the case of a population in stationary equilibrium, use the relationship under (*a*) to express $\boldsymbol{p}$ in terms of $\boldsymbol{b}$.

(*d*) Describe the form of the transforming matrix and interpret the elements in its columns.

(*e*) Compare the transforming matrix in (*c*) with the transforming matrix of an open input–output system in economics and comment on the nature of each transformation. (1969)

25. Construct counter-examples to any **three** of the following propositions:

(*a*) In a linear production model, with labour the only non-produced good, and given the rate of interest, long-run relative prices are always independent of demand.

(*b*) If an economy can grow at exponential rate g with all ratios of inputs and outputs constant, and this state is an equilibrium at constant prices and rate of interest r, and if further no other feasible balanced path has higher consumption per head, then $g = r$.

(*c*) In an optimal solution to a linear programme those activities run at zero level must necessarily show a loss at optimal shadow prices.

(*d*) Given a programme to maximise the value of output at constant prices given by a row vector $\boldsymbol{p}$ subject to available inputs given by a column vector $\boldsymbol{b}$ and an input–output matrix $\boldsymbol{A}$ (the constraints take the form $\boldsymbol{Ax} \leq \boldsymbol{b}$, where $\boldsymbol{x}$ is a column vector of activity levels) if the jth row of $\boldsymbol{A}$ is multiplied by a factor $\theta > 1$ the shadow price of the jth input must increase. (1968)

Answers to Problems

Chapter 1

1.1. (i) 1, 3, 5, 7; (ii) 2; (iii) $\varnothing$. $B \cup C$ = the numbers from 1 to 10.

1.2. For each y, find the corresponding elements of A and B. Then equate each element B with every element of A and solve for a.

y	Elements of A	Elements of B	Values of a
1	5	$-1 + a$	6, 11, 18
2	10	$2 + a$	3, 8, 15
3	17	$9 + a$	1, 17
4	26	$20 + a$	
5	37	$35 + a$	2

1.3. Sufficiency: $A \cap B = A \Rightarrow$ every element in A is contained in the intersection $\Rightarrow$ every element of A is contained in $B \Rightarrow A$ is a subset of B. Necessity: $A \subset B \Rightarrow$ intersection of A and B includes only elements of A, and that every element of A is in $B \Rightarrow A \cap B = A$. As $A \cap B = A \Leftrightarrow A \cup B = B$, $A \cup B = B$ is an alternative form of the condition.

1.4. (i) Sufficient; (ii) Necessary and Sufficient; (iii) Necessary.

1.5. Note that the rectangular hyperbola $x_1 x_2 = 1$ has segments in the first *and* third quadrants.

1.6. (i) (8, 4, 8); (ii) $(-2, 4, 6)$; (iii) (0, 14, 18). $a = 5, b = 4$.

1.7. Let $\boldsymbol{x} = (x_1, \ldots, x_n)$. Then

$$|a\boldsymbol{x}|^2 = \sum_{i=1}^{n} (ax_i)^2 = a^2 \sum_{i=1}^{n} x_i^2 = a^2 |\boldsymbol{x}|^2.$$

1.8. $a\boldsymbol{x} + \boldsymbol{y} = b\boldsymbol{x} + \boldsymbol{z}$. Then $\boldsymbol{x} \,.\, (a\boldsymbol{x} + \boldsymbol{y}) = \boldsymbol{x} \,.\, (b\boldsymbol{x} + \boldsymbol{z})$ $\therefore (a - b)\boldsymbol{x} \,.\, \boldsymbol{x} = \boldsymbol{x} \,.\, \boldsymbol{z} - \boldsymbol{x} \,.\, \boldsymbol{y}$. But $\boldsymbol{x} \,.\, \boldsymbol{y} = 0 = \boldsymbol{x} \,.\, \boldsymbol{z}$, so $a = b$ and $\boldsymbol{y} = \boldsymbol{z}$.

1.9. Show that all of the axioms are satisfied; for example the space is closed under linear combinations since:

$$(\alpha \boldsymbol{x}_1 + \beta \boldsymbol{x}_2) \cdot (1, 2) = \alpha \boldsymbol{x}_1 \cdot (1, 2) + \beta \boldsymbol{x}_2 \cdot (1, 2).$$

Every vector in the space must be of the form $(-2x, x)$.

1.10. Show in both cases that the sets are closed under addition and scalar multiplication. Clearly X is a subspace of R^n which does not include all vectors in R^n since, for any $x_1, \ldots, x_{n-1}$, there exists a scalar v such that $v \neq \sum_{i=1}^{n-1} a_i x_i$ and hence such that the vector $\boldsymbol{z} = (x_1, \ldots, x_{n-1}, v) \in R^n$ but $\notin X$. But for $\boldsymbol{z} \in R^n$ there is no scalar v such that $\boldsymbol{z} \notin Y$ since v can always be written as $\sum_{i=1}^{n} a_i x_i$ by choosing $x_n = (v - \sum_{i=1}^{n-1} a_i x_i)/a_n$ so that $\boldsymbol{z} \in Y$.

Chapter 2

2.1. (i) $|\boldsymbol{x} - \boldsymbol{a}| \geqslant \varepsilon$; (ii) $|\boldsymbol{x} - \boldsymbol{a}| < \varepsilon$ and $|\boldsymbol{x} - \boldsymbol{a}| > \varepsilon$; (iii) $\boldsymbol{a} \cdot \boldsymbol{x} \geqslant \varepsilon$; (iv) $C(X) = \{(x_1, x_2) | x_1, x_2 \geqslant 0 \text{ and } x_1 + x_2 > 0\} \cup \{(x_1, x_2) |$
$x_1 \text{ or } x_2 < 0\}$.

Sets (i), (iii) are closed; set (ii), (iv) are open.

N.B. Whether a set is open or closed has been treated here as depending solely on finite points.

2.2. Consider an ε-neighbourhood around 1. Suppose x is the greatest number less than 1. Put $1 - x = \varepsilon$; then $x < x + \varepsilon/2 < 1$. Hence x cannot be a greatest number.

2.3. Consider any two vectors $\boldsymbol{x}$, $\boldsymbol{y}$ on the hyperplane and show that the operations of addition and scalar multiplication give other vectors on the hyperplane.

2.4. Counterexample: the union of the first and third quadrants in R^2 is not convex.

2.6. Sets (i) and (iii) are convex; sets (ii) and (iv) are not since they are respectively the area below a rectangular hyperbola and that above a parabola.

2.7. The theorem is true even if the set is not closed, but the proof has to be slightly altered. It can no longer proceed by choosing a point in the set. However, using the boundary point $\boldsymbol{w}$, not necessarily in the set, the proof is fundamentally similar.

2.8. (i) $\alpha x_1 + \beta x_2 = 1$; $\alpha x_1 + \beta x_2 = 2\alpha + \beta$ with X in the open half-space $\alpha x_1 + \beta x_2 < 2\alpha \Leftrightarrow \beta$.

(ii) If $2\alpha + \beta = 3$, $2x_1 + x_2 = 3$; if $\alpha - \beta = 1$, $x_1 - x_2 = 1$. Any line for the gradient $\leqslant 1$ and $\geqslant -2$ which contains $\boldsymbol{y}$ will contain X in one half-space.

2.9. (i) $x_1 = 0$. (ii) $x_1 + x_2 = 4$; without the restriction $y_1 \geqslant 0$, Y is not convex as it contains both parts of a rectangular hyperbola. (iii) Any line through (1, 3) with slope > -1 and $< 1/2$.

2.10. Let $X = \{\boldsymbol{x} \mid \boldsymbol{x} = \sum_{i=1}^{n} \lambda_i \boldsymbol{x}_i, \sum \lambda_i = 1$ and $\lambda_i \geqslant 0 \ \forall\ i\}$, where n is finite. Consider $\boldsymbol{a} = \sum_i \lambda_i^a \boldsymbol{x}_i$, $\boldsymbol{a} \in X$ and $\boldsymbol{b} = \sum \lambda_i^b \boldsymbol{x}_i$, $\boldsymbol{b} \in X$.
Then a convex combination of $\boldsymbol{a}$ and $\boldsymbol{b}$ is written, for $0 \leqslant \alpha \leqslant 1$,

$$\alpha\boldsymbol{a} + (1 - \alpha)\boldsymbol{b} = \sum[\alpha\lambda_i^a + (1 - \alpha)\lambda_i^b]\boldsymbol{x}_i.$$

Since

$$0 \leqslant \alpha \leqslant 1 \text{ and } \lambda_i^a, \lambda_i^b \geqslant 0, \alpha\lambda_i^a + (1 - \alpha)\lambda_i^b \geqslant 0.$$

Also:

$$\sum[\alpha\lambda_i^a + (1 - \alpha)\lambda_i^b] = \alpha\sum\lambda_i^a + (1 - \alpha)\sum\lambda_i^b = 1.$$

Hence $\alpha\boldsymbol{a} + (1 - \alpha)\boldsymbol{b} \in X$.

If all the points lie on a line, the result is trivial. In general, consider the extreme points of the original set X. In each case the line segments between adjacent extreme points can be considered as sides of a triangle. There will be no triangle which lies wholly or partly outside the line segments forming the polygon of extreme points. However, every part of the area of the polygon is in some triangle. Since the line segments are in X, it follows that the polygon is the smallest convex set including all of the triangles.

Note that this set is called the *convex hull* of X and in this case is the set X itself. In general, the convex hull of a set X is the intersection of all convex sets which contain X.

Chapter 3

3.1. Any set of vectors including the null vector is L.D. since

$\lambda_1 \boldsymbol{x}_1 + \ldots + \lambda_i . \boldsymbol{0} + \ldots + \lambda_n \boldsymbol{x}_n = \boldsymbol{0}$ for $\lambda_i \neq 0$, $\lambda_j = 0$ $(j \neq i)$. Hence such a set cannot form a basis, though it may span a space as a set of basis vectors plus the null vector must, by definition, span the space.

3.2. *Sufficiency:* Suppose $\boldsymbol{x} = (x_1, \ldots, x_n)$ and $\boldsymbol{y} = (y_1, \ldots, y_n)$ are L.D. Then $\lambda_1 \boldsymbol{x} + \lambda_2 \boldsymbol{y} = \boldsymbol{0}$ and $\lambda_i \neq 0$ some i. Suppose $\lambda_1 \neq 0$, so $\boldsymbol{x} = -\dfrac{\lambda_2}{\lambda_1}\boldsymbol{y}$.

Necessity: Let $\boldsymbol{x} = \alpha \boldsymbol{y}$. Then $\boldsymbol{x} - \alpha \boldsymbol{y} = \boldsymbol{0}$. Write this as $\lambda_1 \boldsymbol{x} + \lambda_2 \boldsymbol{y} = \boldsymbol{0}$ with $\lambda_1 = 1$, $\lambda_2 = -\alpha$. But $\lambda_1 \neq 0$, so $\boldsymbol{x}$, $\boldsymbol{y}$ are L.D.

3.3. The n-component unit vectors $\boldsymbol{e}_1, \ldots, \boldsymbol{e}_m$ are L.I. and span the space including all vectors of the form: $\boldsymbol{x} = (x_1, \ldots, x_m, 0, \ldots, 0)$.

3.4. Consider

$$\alpha_1(\boldsymbol{a} + \boldsymbol{b}) + \alpha_2(\boldsymbol{b} + \boldsymbol{c}) + \alpha_3(\boldsymbol{a} + \boldsymbol{c}) = (\alpha_1 + \alpha_3)\boldsymbol{a} + (\alpha_1 + \alpha_2)\boldsymbol{b} + (\alpha_2 + \alpha_3)\boldsymbol{c}.$$

Since $\boldsymbol{a}$, $\boldsymbol{b}$, $\boldsymbol{c}$ are L.I., linear dependence of $(\boldsymbol{a} + \boldsymbol{b})$, $(\boldsymbol{b} + \boldsymbol{c})$, $(\boldsymbol{a} + \boldsymbol{c})$ requires

$$\alpha_1 + \alpha_3 = \alpha_1 + \alpha_2 = \alpha_2 + \alpha_3 = 0,$$

i.e.

$$\alpha_1 = \alpha_2 = \alpha_3 = 0.$$

Hence the vectors are L.I.

3.5. The dimension of a vector space is the number of vectors in a basis, as any other vector in the space is L.D. on the basis vectors while the basis vectors themselves are L.I. All bases contain the same number of vectors, hence the dimension must be unique.

3.6. Consider the set of m L.I. n-vectors $\{\boldsymbol{x}_1, \ldots, \boldsymbol{x}_m\}$. Choose $\boldsymbol{z}_1 \in R^n$ which is L.I. of the set $\{\boldsymbol{x}_1, \ldots, \boldsymbol{x}_m\}$. Proceeding this way show that there are exactly $n - m$ vectors $\boldsymbol{z}_i$ such that the set $\{\boldsymbol{x}_1, \ldots, \boldsymbol{x}_m, \boldsymbol{z}_1, \ldots, \boldsymbol{z}_{n-m}\}$ forms a basis for R^n.

3.7. (i) L.I.; forms a basis for R^4. (ii) L.D. (iii) L.I.; forms a basis for R^2. (iv) L.D. (v) L.D.; spans R^2.

3.8. $\lambda_1 \boldsymbol{a} + \lambda_2 \boldsymbol{b} + \lambda_3 \boldsymbol{c} + \lambda_4 \boldsymbol{d} = \boldsymbol{0}$ implies

$$\lambda_1 + \lambda_2 i + \lambda_3 i^2 + \lambda_4(1 + i + i^2) = 0$$

which is satisfied for all i if $\lambda_1 = \lambda_2 = \lambda_3 = 1$, $\lambda_4 = -1$. But, for example, $\lambda_1 \boldsymbol{a} + \lambda_2 \boldsymbol{b} + \lambda_3 \boldsymbol{c} = \boldsymbol{0}$ implies $\lambda_1 + \lambda_2 i + \lambda_3 i^2 = 0$ which cannot be satisfied for all i with $\lambda_1, \lambda_2, \lambda_3 \neq 0$.

3.9. *Sufficiency:* Clearly the set must be L.I. if it is to form a basis. Show that a set of m ($>n$) vectors in R^n must be L.D. and that a set of m ($<n$) vectors in R^n cannot span the space.

Necessity: If the set is L.I. and contains n vectors it spans R^n; therefore it forms a basis for R^n.

3.10. $\boldsymbol{x} = (x_1, \ldots, x_{n-1}, \sum_{j=1}^{n-1} a_j x_j)$ is clearly spanned by vectors of the form $\boldsymbol{v}_i = (0, \ldots, 1, \ldots, 0, a_i)$ for $i = 1, \ldots, n - 1$ where 1 is the ith element and a_i is a given scalar. This follows since $\boldsymbol{x} = \sum_{i=1}^{n-1} x_i \boldsymbol{v}_i$; the $(n - 1)$ vectors $\boldsymbol{v}_i$ form a basis for the space of $\boldsymbol{x}$, whose dimension is $(n - 1)$.

3.11. Consider $\sum_{i=1}^{n} \alpha_i \boldsymbol{x}_i = \boldsymbol{0}$, where $\boldsymbol{x}_1, \ldots, \boldsymbol{x}_n$ are mutually orthogonal. Then $\boldsymbol{x}_j \cdot \sum_{i=1}^{n} \alpha_i \boldsymbol{x}_i = 0$ implies $\alpha_j \boldsymbol{x}_j \cdot \boldsymbol{x}_j = 0$, i.e. $\alpha_j = 0$ if $\boldsymbol{x}_j \cdot \boldsymbol{x}_j \neq 0$. This is true for all α_j, $j = 1, \ldots, n$ and hence the set of vectors is L.I. If $\boldsymbol{x}_j \cdot \boldsymbol{x}_j = 0$, then $\boldsymbol{x}_j = \boldsymbol{0}$ and the set is L.D.

3.12. Consider a set of L.I. vectors $\boldsymbol{x}_1, \ldots, \boldsymbol{x}_n$. To obtain a vector orthogonal to $\boldsymbol{x}_1$, we subtract from $\boldsymbol{x}_2$ a scalar multiple of $\boldsymbol{x}_1$; define $\boldsymbol{v}_2 = \boldsymbol{x}_2 - \alpha_1 \boldsymbol{x}_1$ such that $\boldsymbol{v}_2 \cdot \boldsymbol{x}_1 = \boldsymbol{x}_2 \cdot \boldsymbol{x}_1 - \alpha_1 \boldsymbol{x}_1 \cdot \boldsymbol{x}_1 = 0$, that is, such that $\alpha_1 = \dfrac{\boldsymbol{x}_2 \cdot \boldsymbol{x}_1}{\boldsymbol{x}_1 \cdot \boldsymbol{x}_1}$.

This process is continued so that, for the kth orthogonal vector (orthogonal to $\boldsymbol{x}_1, \boldsymbol{v}_1, \ldots, \boldsymbol{v}_{k-1}$), $\boldsymbol{v}_k = \boldsymbol{x}_k - \sum_{i=1}^{k-1} \left(\dfrac{\boldsymbol{v}_i \cdot \boldsymbol{x}_k}{\boldsymbol{v}_i \cdot \boldsymbol{v}_i}\right) \boldsymbol{x}_i$ with $\boldsymbol{v}_1 = \boldsymbol{x}_1$. Thus we obtain the set of orthogonal vectors $(\boldsymbol{x}_1, \boldsymbol{v}_2, \ldots, \boldsymbol{v}_n)$. An orthonormal basis is obtained by converting each vector in the set to unit length. The orthonormal basis $\{\boldsymbol{u}_1, \ldots, \boldsymbol{u}_n\}$ is therefore obtained as $\boldsymbol{u}_1 = \boldsymbol{x}_1/|\boldsymbol{x}_1|$ and $\boldsymbol{u}_i = \boldsymbol{v}_i/|\boldsymbol{v}_i|$ for $i = 2, \ldots, n$.

Notice that we began with $\boldsymbol{x}_1$ and therefore have constructed a basis to include this vector. The choice of the starting vector is arbitrary and the orthonormal basis (corresponding to orthogonal axes in co-ordinate geometry) could have been constructed starting with any one of the original vectors $\boldsymbol{x}_1, \ldots, \boldsymbol{x}_n$.

3.13. Generalising the answer to 3.9, the set of vectors $\boldsymbol{a}_i = (0, \ldots, 1, \ldots, 0, a_{1i}, \ldots, a_{n-m,i})$ for $i = 1, \ldots, m$ where elements

$1, \ldots, m$ are zero except the ith which is 1 and the a_{ji}'s are scalars ($j = 1, \ldots, n - m$), will form a basis for V. All vectors in U are L.C.s of vectors in V and hence could be expressed as L.C.s of a set of basis vectors of V. The vector $(1, -1)$ is a basis vector for W.

Chapter 4

4.1. (*a*) $$(\boldsymbol{A}+\boldsymbol{B}) = \begin{bmatrix} 10 & 5 & 7 \\ 5 & 2 & 4 \\ 7 & 4 & 2 \end{bmatrix}, \boldsymbol{AB} = \begin{bmatrix} 30 & 18 & 37 \\ 18 & 11 & 22 \\ 37 & 22 & 46 \end{bmatrix}, \boldsymbol{BA} = \begin{bmatrix} 70 & 31 & 14 \\ 31 & 14 & 6 \\ 14 & 6 & 3 \end{bmatrix}.$$

(*b*) $\boldsymbol{B}$ is the transpose of $\boldsymbol{A}$; from this, it follows that $\boldsymbol{AB}(=\boldsymbol{AA}')$ and $\boldsymbol{BA} = (\boldsymbol{A}'\boldsymbol{A}) \neq \boldsymbol{AA}'$ are both necessarily symmetric.

4.2. $\boldsymbol{A}$ and $\boldsymbol{B}$ are conformable in the sense that the product $\boldsymbol{BA}$ exists; the product $\boldsymbol{AB}$ does not exist unless $n = p$.

$$(\boldsymbol{BA})_{ij} = \sum_{k=1}^{m} b_{ik} a_{kj}$$

and $\boldsymbol{BA}$ is a matrix of order $p \times n$.

4.3. Since $m > n$, matrix $\boldsymbol{A}$ has more rows than columns. Also, since the column and row rank of a matrix are equal, it follows that the rank of $\boldsymbol{A} \leqslant n$.

(i) $r(\boldsymbol{A}) = n$;

(ii) it is impossible for all the rows of $\boldsymbol{A}$ to be L.I. when $m > n$.

4.4. $r(\boldsymbol{A}) = 3$, $r(\boldsymbol{B}) = 2$, $$\boldsymbol{AB} = \begin{bmatrix} 19 & -1 \\ 35 & -3 \\ 98 & -4 \end{bmatrix}$$ which has rank 2.

4.5. (*a*) Write out the individual elements of the sums.

(*b*) $$((\boldsymbol{A}_1\boldsymbol{A}_2)_{ij})' = (\boldsymbol{A}_1\boldsymbol{A}_2)_{ji} = \sum_{k=1}^{n} a^1_{jk} a^2_{ki}$$

$$= \sum_{k=1}^{n} (\boldsymbol{A}'_2)_{ik}(\boldsymbol{A}'_1)_{kj} = (\boldsymbol{A}'_2\boldsymbol{A}'_1)_{ij}.$$

Hence $(\boldsymbol{A}_1\boldsymbol{A}_2)' = \boldsymbol{A}'_2\boldsymbol{A}'_1$.

Suppose it is true for $n - 1$,

i.e. $$(\boldsymbol{A}_1\boldsymbol{A}_2 \ldots \boldsymbol{A}_{n-1})' = \boldsymbol{A}'_{n-1} \ldots \boldsymbol{A}'_1$$

Then

$$(A_1A_2 \ldots A_{n-1}A_n)' = ((A_1 \ldots A_{n-1})A_n)' = A_n'(A_1 \ldots A_{n-1})'$$
$$= A_n'A_{n-1}' \ldots A_1'.$$

4.6. $(AB)_{ij} = \sum_{k=1}^{n} a_i\delta_{ik}b_k\delta_{kj} = 0$ unless $i = k = j$. If $i = k = j$, $(AB)_{ii} = a_ib_i$.

Hence AB is diagonal with elements $\| a_ib_j\delta_{ij} \|$.

Since $(BA)_{ij} = \sum_{k=1}^{n} b_i\delta_{ik}a_k\delta_{kj}$, BA is also diagonal and equal to $\| b_ia_j\delta_{ij} \|$.

Therefore $AB = BA$.

4.7. Using the argument of the proof of theorem 18, it can be shown that $n(AB) \leqslant n(A) + n(B)$ and hence that

$$n - r(AB) \leqslant n - r(A) + n - r(B).$$

4.8. Show that all of the axioms are satisfied. $AB = \begin{bmatrix} 0 & 0 \\ 0 & 1 \end{bmatrix}$ and hence $\alpha A + \beta B + \gamma I + \delta AB = \begin{bmatrix} \gamma & \beta \\ \alpha & \gamma + \delta \end{bmatrix}$. Thus A, B, I and AB span the space. It follows from the equation that $\begin{bmatrix} \gamma & \beta \\ \alpha & \gamma + \delta \end{bmatrix} = 0 \Rightarrow$ $\alpha = \beta = \gamma = \delta = 0$ and therefore that the matrices are linearly independent and so form a basis for the space.

4.9. (i) Yes, since $Ax = \sum_{i=1}^{n} x_i a_i$ where a_i is the ith column of A

$$= 0 \text{ is true for some } x \neq 0$$

since the columns of A are linearly dependent ($r(A) < n$).

(ii) If A is non-singular, $r(A) = n$ and, since all a_i will be linearly independent, the only solution is $x = 0$.

4.10.

(i) $$\begin{bmatrix} 1 & 3 & 0 & 1 \\ 0 & 1 & -7/11 & 0 \\ 0 & 0 & 1 & 55/43 \\ 0 & 0 & 0 & 1 \end{bmatrix}$$

(ii) $$\begin{bmatrix} a & b & c & d \\ 0 & b(b-a) & c(c-a) & d(d-a) \\ 0 & 0 & c(c-a)(c-b) & d(d-a)(d-b) \end{bmatrix}$$

(iii) $\begin{bmatrix} 1 & 3 & 6+2k \\ 0 & 1 & -1 \\ 0 & 0 & 2+k \end{bmatrix}$ $\begin{array}{l} k = -2, r(\boldsymbol{C}) = 2 \\ k \neq -2, r(\boldsymbol{C}) = 3 \end{array}$

4.11. Consider two matrices $\boldsymbol{A}$ and $\boldsymbol{B}$. The (i, j) element of the product $\boldsymbol{AB}$ $(=(\boldsymbol{AB})_{ij})$ is $\boldsymbol{a}^i . \boldsymbol{b}_j$ where $\boldsymbol{a}^i$ are rows of $\boldsymbol{A}$ and $\boldsymbol{b}_j$ are columns of $\boldsymbol{B}$. It is clear that $\boldsymbol{a}^i . \boldsymbol{b}_j = 0$ does not require that either $\boldsymbol{a}^i$ or $\boldsymbol{b}_j$ equal $\boldsymbol{0}$.

4.12. Write $\boldsymbol{A} = \boldsymbol{B} + \boldsymbol{C}$ where $\boldsymbol{B} = \dfrac{\boldsymbol{A} + \boldsymbol{A}'}{2}, \boldsymbol{C} = \dfrac{\boldsymbol{A} - \boldsymbol{A}'}{2}$.

Then $(\boldsymbol{B})_{ii} = \dfrac{a_{ii} + a_{ii}}{2} = a_{ii}$; $(\boldsymbol{B})_{ij} = \dfrac{a_{ij} + a_{ji}}{2} = \dfrac{a_{ji} + a_{ij}}{2} = (\boldsymbol{B})_{ji}$,

and $(\boldsymbol{C})_{ii} = \dfrac{a_{ii} - a_{ii}}{2} = 0$; $(\boldsymbol{C})_{ij} = \dfrac{a_{ij} - a_{ji}}{2} = \dfrac{-(a_{ji} - a_{ij})}{2} = -(\boldsymbol{C})_{ji}$.

Hence $\boldsymbol{B}$ is symmetric and $\boldsymbol{C}$ is skew-symmetric.

Chapter 5

5.1. If $\boldsymbol{Ax} = \boldsymbol{0}$ has no non-trivial solution, $m \leqslant n$ and $r(\boldsymbol{A}) = m$.
(i) $n = m, \mathbf{b} = \boldsymbol{0}$; there are no non-trivial solutions.
(ii) $n = m, \mathbf{b} \neq \boldsymbol{0}$; a non-trivial solution exists and is unique.
(iii) $n > m, \boldsymbol{b} = \boldsymbol{0}$; there are an infinite number of solutions.
(iv) $n > m, \boldsymbol{b} \neq \boldsymbol{0}$; there are $n!/m!\,(n-m)!$ basic solutions.
Hence, in general, there is at least one non-trivial solution to the system $\boldsymbol{y}'\boldsymbol{A} = \boldsymbol{b}$ if $b_i \neq 0$ for some i.

5.2. (i) $\boldsymbol{x} = (-1, 1, 2, -3)$; (ii) $\boldsymbol{x} = (2, 0, -2)$.

5.3. (i) $\alpha = \frac{3}{4} \Rightarrow r(\mathbf{A}) = 2$; hence there is a non-trivial solution which is unique except for scalar multiples of the solution.

$$\alpha \neq \tfrac{3}{4} \Rightarrow r(\boldsymbol{A}) = 3;$$

then there are no non-trivial solutions.
(ii) $\alpha = 0 \Rightarrow r(\boldsymbol{A}) = 3$; then there is a unique non-trivial solution for each value β with $\boldsymbol{x} = (1 - 0{\cdot}8\,\beta, -1 + 0{\cdot}4\beta, \beta)$.

$$\alpha = 5/2, \beta = 0; r(\boldsymbol{A}) = r(\boldsymbol{A}, \boldsymbol{b}) = 2$$

and hence there are an infinite number of solutions.

$$\alpha = 5/2, \beta \neq 0; r(\boldsymbol{A}) < r(\boldsymbol{A}, \boldsymbol{b})$$

and hence there are no solutions.

$$\alpha \neq 5/2 \Rightarrow r(\boldsymbol{A}) = 3;$$

then there is a unique solution for each value of β with

$$\boldsymbol{x} = \left(1 - \frac{4\beta}{5 - 2\alpha}, -1 + \frac{2\beta}{5 - 2\alpha}, \frac{5\beta}{5 - 2\alpha}\right).$$

5.4. (i) $x_1 = 0, x_3 = -1, x_4 = 1$.
(ii) $x_1 = -1 + x_4, x_2 = 1 - x_4, x_3 = -x_4$.
(iii) $x_3 = -x_4 \Rightarrow$ no vector of solutions with x_3 or $x_4 \neq 0$ can be either $> \mathbf{0}$ or $< \mathbf{0}$. If $x_3 = x_4 = 0$, $x_1 = -1$ and $x_2 = 1$. Hence there are no solutions for which $\boldsymbol{x} > \mathbf{0}$, $= \mathbf{0}$ or $< \mathbf{0}$.

5.5. Consider $\boldsymbol{Ax} = \boldsymbol{b}$. Suppose $\boldsymbol{x}_1$ and $\boldsymbol{x}_2$ are both vectors of solutions. Then $\boldsymbol{Ax}_1 = \boldsymbol{b}$ and $\boldsymbol{Ax}_2 = \boldsymbol{b}$ and hence $\boldsymbol{A}(\boldsymbol{x}_1 - \boldsymbol{x}_2) = \mathbf{0}$. Since $\mathbf{x}_1 \neq \boldsymbol{x}_2$, the rank of $\mathbf{A}$ is not maximal since the homogeneous system has a non-trivial solution. Therefore the columns of $\boldsymbol{A}$ are not L.I. and hence there are an infinite number of solutions.

5.6. Basic solution exists (i) for $x_1, x_2 = (7/4, -5/2)$, (ii) for $x_1, x_3 = (7/4, 5/2)$, (iii) for x_1, $x_4 = (0, 3)$ but is degenerate, (iv) for x_2, $x_4 = (0, 3)$ but is degenerate and (v) for $x_3, x_4 = (0, 3)$ but is degenerate. The basic solution for x_2, x_3 does not exist. This is because, for x_2, x_3, the rank of the augmented matrix exceeds the rank of the matrix comprising columns 2 and 3.

5.7. If the number of unknown variables exceeds the number of equations in the system $\boldsymbol{Ax} = \mathbf{0}$, $\boldsymbol{A}$ has more columns than rows and hence the rank of $\boldsymbol{A}$ is less than the number of columns; that is the columns of $\boldsymbol{A}$ are L.D. and there exists some $\boldsymbol{x} \neq \mathbf{0}$ such that $\boldsymbol{Ax} = \mathbf{0}$.

5.8. Since $r(\boldsymbol{A}) = r$, we can find a basic solution in r variables, the remaining $(n - r)$ variables being treated as independent variables; that is, we can find a solution $\boldsymbol{x} = (s_1, \ldots, s_r, x_{r+1}, \ldots, x_n)$ where $s_i = \sum_j \lambda_{ij} x_{r+j}$ for $i = 1, n - r$. Clearly the set of $(n - r)$ vectors $(\lambda_{1j}, \ldots, \lambda_{ij}, \ldots, \lambda_{rj}, 1, \ldots, 0), \ldots, (\lambda_{1j}, \ldots, \lambda_{rj}, 0, \ldots, 1)$span the space of vectors $\boldsymbol{x}$ and is also a linearly independent set. Hence they form a basis for the set of solutions to the system of homogeneous equations. Notice that this space is the nullity of $\boldsymbol{A}$.

5.9. For a system of m equations in n variables, the augmented $(\boldsymbol{A}, \boldsymbol{b})$ is written as

$$\begin{bmatrix} a_{11} & \dots & a_{1n} & b_1 \\ a_{21} & \dots & a_{2n} & b_2 \\ a_{m1} & \dots & a_{mn} & b_m \end{bmatrix}$$

This matrix can be reduced to echelon form by eliminating elements below successive diagonal elements; that is, the ith element in column 1 can be eliminated by replacing the ith row by $[(\boldsymbol{a}_i, b_i) - (a_{i1}/a_{11}) \times (\boldsymbol{a}_1, b_1)]$ to obtain the new matrix

$$\begin{bmatrix} a_{11} & a_{12} & \dots & a_{1n} & b_1 \\ 0 & a'_{22} & \dots & a'_{2n} & b_2 \\ 0 & a'_{m2} & \dots & a'_{mn} & b'_m \end{bmatrix}$$

where $a'_{ij} = a_{ij} - (a_{i1}/a_{11})a_{1j}$, $b'_i = b_i - (a_{i1}/a_{11})b_1$.
Similarly, we can operate on column 2 by replacing the ith row (for $i = 2, \dots, m$) by

$$\left[(\boldsymbol{a}_i, b'_i) - \frac{a'_{i2}}{a'_{22}}(\boldsymbol{a}'_2, b'_2)\right]$$

This process can be continued until we have reduced the matrix to canonical form:

(i) if $n > m$ and $r(\boldsymbol{A}) = r \leqslant m$, we have

$$\begin{bmatrix} \alpha_{11} & \alpha_{12} & \alpha_{13} & \dots\dots\dots & \alpha_{1n} & \beta_1 \\ 0 & \alpha_{22} & \alpha_{23} & \dots\dots\dots & \alpha_{2n} & \beta_2 \\ 0 & 0 & \alpha_{33} & \dots\dots\dots & \alpha_{3n} & \beta_3 \\ 0 & 0 & 0 & \dots\alpha_{rr}\dots & \alpha_{rn} & \beta_r \end{bmatrix}$$

or (ii) if $m > n$ and $r(\boldsymbol{A}) = n$, we have

$$\begin{bmatrix} \alpha_{11} & \alpha_{12} & \dots & \alpha_{1n} & \beta_1 \\ 0 & \alpha_{22} & \dots & \alpha_{2n} & \beta_2 \\ 0 & 0 & \dots & \alpha_{nn} & \beta_n \\ 0 & 0 & \dots & 0 & 0 \end{bmatrix}$$

In (i), we can then find basic solutions for $x_1, \dots, x_r$ by solving for x_r and substituting to find x_{r-1} in the row above; in (ii), we can solve for $x_n = \beta_n/\alpha_{nn}$ and substitute to find x_{n-1}, etc.

5.10. *Necessity*: Suppose all basic solutions exist and are not degenerate. Consider any set of m columns of $\boldsymbol{A}$, $\boldsymbol{a}_1, \ldots, \boldsymbol{a}_m$. We can write $\sum_{i=1}^{m} x_i \boldsymbol{a}_i = \boldsymbol{b}$ with $x_i \neq 0$ for all i. Since the basic solutions exist, every set of m columns of $\boldsymbol{A}$ are linearly independent. But since $x_i \neq 0$ for any i, we can replace $\boldsymbol{a}_i$ by $\boldsymbol{b}$ and still have a linearly independent set. Thus any set of m column vectors from the augmented matrix is also linearly independent.

Sufficiency: Suppose all set of m column vectors of the augmented matrix are linearly independent. Then, we can write $\boldsymbol{b} = \sum_{i=1}^{n} x_i \boldsymbol{a}_i$, Therefore all basic solutions exist. But the set of vectors $\boldsymbol{a}_1, \ldots, \boldsymbol{a}_{i-1}, \boldsymbol{b}, \boldsymbol{a}_{i+1}, \ldots, \boldsymbol{a}_m$ is also linearly independent for all i. Since we can replace $\boldsymbol{a}_i$ by $\boldsymbol{b}$ and still have a linearly independent set, it follows that $x_i \neq 0$. Since this is true for all i, none of the basic solutions are degenerate.

5.11. The solution to both systems is $\boldsymbol{x} = (1, 2, 3)$.

5.12. There is no difference between the values for x_k and x_{k+1} in the basic solutions but it is most unlikely that the values for $x_1, \ldots, x_{k-1}$ would be the same in the two basic solutions.

5.13. Since $\boldsymbol{Ax} = \boldsymbol{0}$ has a non-trivial solution, $r(\boldsymbol{A}) <$ number of columns of $\boldsymbol{A}$. Hence, if there exists a solution, it will not be unique.

Chapter 6

6.1. For vectors $\boldsymbol{x}_1, \boldsymbol{x}_2 \in U$, there exist $\boldsymbol{y}_1 = L_1(\boldsymbol{x}_1), \boldsymbol{y}_2 = L_1(\boldsymbol{x}_2) \in V$. Since $\boldsymbol{y}_1, \boldsymbol{y}_2 \in V$, we can apply transformation L_2 to obtain $\boldsymbol{z}_1 = L_2(\boldsymbol{y}_1)$, $\boldsymbol{z}_2 = L_2(\boldsymbol{y}_2) \in W$. Thus $\boldsymbol{z}_i = L_2(\boldsymbol{y}_i) = L_2(L_1(\boldsymbol{x}_i)) = L_2L_1(\boldsymbol{x}_i)$, $i = 1, 2$; That is, the transformation L_2L_1 operates on $\boldsymbol{x}_i \in U$ and maps it into $\boldsymbol{z}_i \in W$. Hence $L_2L_1 : U \to W$ is a transformation with domain U and range W. To show that $L_3 = L_2L_1$ is linear, consider $(\alpha_1\boldsymbol{x}_1 + \alpha_2\boldsymbol{x}_2) \in U$.

$$L_3(\alpha_1\boldsymbol{x}_1 + \alpha_2\boldsymbol{x}_2) = L_2L_1(\alpha_1\boldsymbol{x}_1 + \alpha_2\boldsymbol{x}_2) = L_2(L_1(\alpha_1\boldsymbol{x}_1) + L_1(\alpha_2\boldsymbol{x}_2))$$
$$= \alpha_1 L_2L_1(\boldsymbol{x}_1) + \alpha_2 L_2L_1(\boldsymbol{x}_2) = \alpha_1 L_3(\boldsymbol{x}_1) + \alpha_2 L_3(\boldsymbol{x}_2).$$

6.2. Since every linear transformation T can be represented by a matrix, we can write $\boldsymbol{y} = \boldsymbol{Ax}$ where $\boldsymbol{x} \in R^n$ and $\boldsymbol{y} \in R^m$ and $\boldsymbol{A}$ is $m \times n$. Thus the range of the transformation is spanned by the column vectors of A and hence the dimension of the range of A is $<m$ for $m > n$. In fact, it is clear that, when $m > n$, the dimension of the range is $\leqslant n$.

6.3. (i) for $(x_1, x_2)A = (x_1, -x_1, x_2, -x_2)$, $A = \begin{bmatrix} 1 & -1 & 0 & 0 \\ 0 & 0 & 1 & -1 \end{bmatrix}$.

(ii) for $(x_1, x_2)A = (x_1 + x_2, 0, x_1 - x_2, 0)$, $A = \begin{bmatrix} 1 & 0 & 1 & 0 \\ 1 & 0 & -1 & 0 \end{bmatrix}$.

6.4. For (i), it is clear that the rank of A is 2 since the rows are linearly independent. Also any vector in the range is of the form $(x_1, -x_1, x_2, -x_2)$ and hence the two vectors $(1, -1, 0, 0)$ and $(0, 0, 1, -1)$ span the space and are linearly independent. Hence the number of vectors in a basis for the range is 2 and the dimension of the range is 2. For (ii), the rank of A is again 2. The pair of vectors $(1, 0, 1, 0)$ and $(1, 0, -1, 0)$ span the range and are linearly independent. Thus the dimension of the range is 2.

6.5. (i) rank $= 2$; neither $1 - 1$ nor onto; the nullity $= 1$.
(ii) rank $= 3$; $1 - 1$ and onto; the nullity $= 0$.
(iii) rank $= 2$; not $1 - 1$; nullity $= 1$.
(iv) rank $= 2$; $1 - 1$ but not onto; nullity $= 0$.
(v) rank $= 3$; $1 - 1$ and onto; nullity $= 0$.
Note that the answers may be different if the matrices were operating on row vectors.

6.6 *Necessity:* Suppose T is a $1 - 1$ linear transformation from $U \to V$. Then, for $\boldsymbol{u} \in U$, $T(\boldsymbol{u}) = \boldsymbol{v} \in V$. Since T is $1 - 1$, $\boldsymbol{v}$ is unique, and hence it must be possible to find a transformation L such that $L(\boldsymbol{v}) = \boldsymbol{u}$. From this, it follows that $L(T(\boldsymbol{u})) = L(\boldsymbol{v}) = \boldsymbol{u}$ and $T(L(\boldsymbol{v})) = T(\boldsymbol{u}) = \boldsymbol{v}$. Thus the product transformations LT and TL are equivalent to the identity transformation I.

Sufficiency: Suppose there exists a transformation L such that $TL = LT = I$. Then it follows from $TL = I$ that the range of T is the domain of L and, from $TL = LT$, that the range of L is the range of T. Thus the same vector space is the range and domain of both T and L and hence T is $1 - 1$ (and also onto).

6.7. The new matrix representation is $\begin{bmatrix} 1 & -1 \\ 7 & 5 \end{bmatrix}$.

6.8. If $r(T) = 0$, then the matrix representation $= \mathbf{0}$, and the theorem is trivial. If $r(T) = 1$, then the range of T is of dimension 1 and the basis of the range can be given as a single vector $\boldsymbol{b} \neq \mathbf{0}$. Then $T(x) = \alpha\boldsymbol{b}$. Let $\boldsymbol{A} = \|a_{ij}\|$ be the matrix representation. $(\boldsymbol{Ax})_i = \sum_j a_{ij}x_j$. Let $\boldsymbol{v}_1, \ldots, \boldsymbol{v}_n$ form a basis for the domain of T. Then $\boldsymbol{x} = \sum_j \lambda_j\boldsymbol{v}_j$ and $\boldsymbol{Ax} = \boldsymbol{A}\,(\sum_j \lambda_j\boldsymbol{v}_j) = \sum_j \lambda_j\boldsymbol{A}(\boldsymbol{v}_j)$. But $\boldsymbol{A}(\boldsymbol{v}_j) = \alpha_j\boldsymbol{b}$. Hence $\boldsymbol{Ax} = (\sum_j \lambda_j\alpha_j)\boldsymbol{b}$. Hence, for the ith element, $\sum_j a_{ij}x_j = \sum_j \lambda_j\alpha_j b_i$.

It follows, therefore, that a_{ij} can be written as $a_i a_j$ with respect to any basis.

6.9. Consider the matrix representation $\boldsymbol{A}$ of T. This can be written as the sum of n matrices $\boldsymbol{A}_1, \ldots, \boldsymbol{A}_n$, where $\boldsymbol{A}_i$ has only one non-zero column corresponding to the ith column of $\boldsymbol{A}$. If the rank of the transformation (and therefore of the matrix) is r, these matrices can each be written as a linear combination of r matrices of the same form $\boldsymbol{B}_1, \ldots, \boldsymbol{B}_r$, with the jth matrix having a single non-zero column corresponding to the jth vector in a basis for the space spanned by the columns of $\boldsymbol{A}$. Hence $\boldsymbol{A} = \sum_{i=1}^{n} \boldsymbol{A}_i$ and

$$\boldsymbol{A}_i = \sum_{j=1}^{r} \lambda_{ij}\boldsymbol{B}_j.$$

Hence

$$\boldsymbol{A} = \sum_{j=1}^{r} \left(\sum_{i=1}^{n} \lambda_{ij} \right) \boldsymbol{B}_j$$

$\boldsymbol{A}$ can be written as the sum of r transformations, each of which is of rank 1 since it has one non-zero column.

6.10. For example, consider $\boldsymbol{x} \neq \mathbf{0}$ for which $\boldsymbol{Ax} \neq \mathbf{0}$. Suppose that $\boldsymbol{A}^2\boldsymbol{x} = \mathbf{0}$. Then $\boldsymbol{Ax} \in$ range of $\boldsymbol{A}$ and also, since $\boldsymbol{A}^2\boldsymbol{x}$ exists, $\boldsymbol{Ax} \in$ domain of $\boldsymbol{A}$ since $\boldsymbol{A}(\boldsymbol{Ax}) = \mathbf{0}$. Thus $\boldsymbol{Ax} \in$ null-space of $\boldsymbol{A}$. In this case, $\boldsymbol{Ax}$ is contained both within the range and null-space and hence the two are not disjoint. Note that the matrix $\begin{bmatrix} 0 & 1 \\ 0 & 0 \end{bmatrix}$ has this property.

6.11. (i) and (iii) are linear; (ii) and (iv) are non-linear.

Chapter 7

7.1. If the rank of the transformation is not maximal, then it cannot be 1 − 1. If U and V are not the same spaces, it cannot be onto. If the transformation is not 1 − 1 and onto, the question 'if $\boldsymbol{y}$ is the image of $\boldsymbol{x}$, what is the image of $\boldsymbol{y}$?' does not have an answer; hence the inverse is not defined and does not exist.

7.2. (i)
$$\boldsymbol{A}^{-1} = \begin{bmatrix} -\frac{1}{2} & -\frac{3}{8} & \frac{5}{8} \\ 1 & \frac{1}{2} & -\frac{1}{2} \\ -\frac{1}{2} & \frac{1}{8} & \frac{1}{8} \end{bmatrix}$$

(ii)
$$\boldsymbol{A}^{-1} = \begin{bmatrix} 1 & 2 & -\frac{1}{4} & 0 & -\frac{1}{2} \\ 0 & \frac{1}{2} & 0 & -\frac{1}{4} & 0 \\ \frac{1}{2} & \frac{1}{2} & \frac{1}{4} & 0 & 0 \\ 0 & \frac{1}{2} & 0 & \frac{1}{4} & 0 \\ -\frac{1}{2} & -\frac{3}{2} & 0 & 0 & \frac{1}{2} \end{bmatrix}$$

7.3. $(\boldsymbol{A}_1\boldsymbol{A}_2)^{-1} = \boldsymbol{A}_2^{-1}\boldsymbol{A}_1^{-1}$ (proof as in text).
Suppose the proposition is true for $n-1$, that is,

$$(\boldsymbol{A}_1 \ldots \boldsymbol{A}_{n-1})^{-1} = \boldsymbol{A}_{n-1}^{-1} \ldots \boldsymbol{A}_1^{-1}.$$

Then

$$\begin{aligned}(\boldsymbol{A}_1 \ldots \boldsymbol{A}_{n-1}\boldsymbol{A}_n)^{-1} &= ((\boldsymbol{A}_1 \ldots \boldsymbol{A}_{n-1})(\boldsymbol{A}_n))^{-1} \\ &= \boldsymbol{A}_n^{-1}(\boldsymbol{A}_1 \ldots \boldsymbol{A}_{n-1})^{-1} = \boldsymbol{A}_n^{-1}\boldsymbol{A}_{n-1}^{-1} \ldots \boldsymbol{A}_1^{-1}.\end{aligned}$$

7.4. It is obvious that the inverse of the transformation which interchanges rows or multiplies by a scalar will be the same form of operation; for example, if $\boldsymbol{B}$ is obtained from $\boldsymbol{A}$ by interchanging the ith and jth rows of $\boldsymbol{A}$, $\boldsymbol{A}$ can be obtained from $\boldsymbol{B}$ by interchanging the ith and jth rows of $\boldsymbol{B}$, and if $\boldsymbol{B}$ is obtained from $\boldsymbol{A}$ by replacing the ith row of $\boldsymbol{A}$ by $\alpha \times$ the ith row of $\boldsymbol{A}$, then $\boldsymbol{A}$ can be obtained from $\boldsymbol{B}$ by replacing the ith row of $\boldsymbol{B}$ by $1/\alpha \times$ the ith row of $\boldsymbol{B}$. Thus, for elementary 2×2 matrices,

$$\begin{bmatrix} 0 & 1 \\ 1 & 0 \end{bmatrix}^{-1} = \begin{bmatrix} 0 & 1 \\ 1 & 0 \end{bmatrix},$$

$$\begin{bmatrix} 1 & 0 \\ 0 & \alpha \end{bmatrix}^{-1} = \begin{bmatrix} 1 & 0 \\ 0 & 1/\alpha \end{bmatrix}, \quad \text{and} \quad \begin{bmatrix} 1 & 0 \\ 2 & 1 \end{bmatrix}^{-1} = \begin{bmatrix} 1 & 0 \\ -2 & 1 \end{bmatrix}.$$

7.5. $\boldsymbol{A}$ is non-singular $\Leftrightarrow$ $\boldsymbol{A}$ is square of maximal rank $\Leftrightarrow$ $\boldsymbol{A}$ has an inverse. ∴ (i) $\Leftrightarrow$ (ii). If $\boldsymbol{A}$ is the product of elementary matrices $\boldsymbol{A} = \boldsymbol{E}_1 \ldots \boldsymbol{E}_n$, then $\boldsymbol{A}^{-1} = \boldsymbol{E}_n^{-1} \ldots \boldsymbol{E}_1^{-1}$ exists since every elementary matrix has an inverse. If $\boldsymbol{A}$ has an inverse, it can be reduced to the identity matrix by a series of elementary operations (by multiplying $\boldsymbol{A}$ by a series of elementary matrices) and hence $\boldsymbol{A}$ is the product of elementary matrices. $\therefore$ (ii) $\Leftrightarrow$ (iii) and hence (i) $\Leftrightarrow$ (ii) $\Leftrightarrow$ (iii).

7.6. Condition (i) states that the transformation is $1-1$ and (ii) states that it is onto. Since it is $1-1$ and onto, it is non-singular, which is a necessary and sufficient condition for the inverse transformation to exist.

7.7. This follows from the answer to problem 6.6.

7.8. $\boldsymbol{A} = \boldsymbol{A}'$ if $\boldsymbol{A}$ is symmetric. Also $(\boldsymbol{A}^{-1})' = (\boldsymbol{A}')^{-1} = \boldsymbol{A}^{-1}$. Hence $\boldsymbol{A}^{-1}$ is also symmetric. If $\boldsymbol{X}$ is $m \times n$, $\boldsymbol{X}'\boldsymbol{X}$ is $n \times n$. But $(\boldsymbol{X}'\boldsymbol{X})' = \boldsymbol{X}'(\boldsymbol{X}')' = \boldsymbol{X}'\boldsymbol{X}$. Thus $\boldsymbol{X}'\boldsymbol{X}$ is symmetric and hence $(\boldsymbol{X}'\boldsymbol{X})^{-1}$ is also symmetric.

7.9. Let $\boldsymbol{B} = \boldsymbol{E}_n \ldots \boldsymbol{E}_1\boldsymbol{A}$ where $\boldsymbol{E}_n \ldots \boldsymbol{E}_1$ are elementary matrices. Then $\boldsymbol{B}^{-1} = \boldsymbol{A}^{-1}\boldsymbol{E}_1^{-1} \ldots \boldsymbol{E}_n^{-1}$.

$$\boldsymbol{B} = \begin{bmatrix} 1 & 0 & 0 \\ 0 & 2 & 0 \\ 0 & 0 & 1 \end{bmatrix} \begin{bmatrix} 0 & 1 & 0 \\ 1 & 0 & 0 \\ 0 & 0 & 1 \end{bmatrix} \begin{bmatrix} 1 & 0 & 0 \\ 0 & 1 & 0 \\ -2 & 0 & 1 \end{bmatrix} \boldsymbol{A}. \quad 2\ \boldsymbol{A}^{-1} = \begin{bmatrix} -\frac{1}{6} & -\frac{2}{3} & \frac{1}{4} \\ 1 & 1 & -\frac{1}{2} \\ -\frac{1}{2} & 0 & \frac{1}{4} \end{bmatrix}$$

$$\boldsymbol{B}^{-1} = \begin{bmatrix} -\frac{2}{3} & \frac{1}{6} & \frac{1}{4} \\ 1 & 0 & -\frac{1}{2} \\ 0 & 0 & \frac{1}{4} \end{bmatrix} = \begin{bmatrix} -\frac{1}{6} & -\frac{2}{3} & \frac{1}{4} \\ 1 & 1 & -\frac{1}{2} \\ -\frac{1}{2} & 0 & \frac{1}{4} \end{bmatrix} \begin{bmatrix} 1 & 0 & 0 \\ 0 & 1 & 0 \\ 2 & 0 & 1 \end{bmatrix} \begin{bmatrix} 0 & 1 & 0 \\ 1 & 0 & 0 \\ 0 & 0 & 1 \end{bmatrix} \begin{bmatrix} 1 & 0 & 0 \\ 0 & \frac{1}{2} & 0 \\ 0 & 0 & 1 \end{bmatrix}$$

Notice that the inverse of the elementary matrix which interchanges rows is the same matrix. Hence, if this is the only operation, the inverse of $\boldsymbol{B}$ would be obtained by interchanging the appropriate rows of $\boldsymbol{A}^{-1}$.

7.10. (i) Inverse exists and

$$= \begin{bmatrix} \frac{5}{6} & -\frac{1}{3} & \frac{1}{6} \\ -\frac{1}{3} & \frac{1}{3} & -\frac{1}{3} \\ -\frac{5}{6} & \frac{1}{3} & \frac{1}{6} \end{bmatrix}.$$

(ii) rank < 4 since row $1 =$ row $2 +$ row $3 +$ row 4.
(iii) rank < 3 since row $3 = 3 \times$ row $2 - 2 \times$ row 1.

$$7.11.\ \boldsymbol{A} = \begin{bmatrix} \cos\theta & \sin\theta \\ -\sin\theta & \cos\theta \end{bmatrix} \qquad \boldsymbol{I} = \begin{bmatrix} 1 & 0 \\ 0 & 1 \end{bmatrix}$$

$$\left[\begin{array}{cc|cc} \cos\theta & \sin\theta & 1 & 0 \\ 0 & 1 & \sin\theta & \cos\theta \end{array}\right] \qquad \begin{array}{l} \text{Row } 2 = \cos\theta \times \text{row } 2 \\ + \sin\theta \times \text{row } 1 \end{array}$$

$$\left[\begin{array}{cc|cc} \cos\theta & 0 & 1-\sin^2\theta & -\cos\theta\,.\,\sin\theta \\ 0 & 1 & \sin\theta & \cos\theta \end{array}\right] \quad \begin{array}{l} \text{row } 1 = \text{row } 1 \\ -\sin\theta \times \text{row } 2 \end{array}$$

Hence

$$A^{-1} = \begin{bmatrix} \cos\theta & -\sin\theta \\ \sin\theta & \cos\theta \end{bmatrix} = A'.$$

The operation of matrix A performs a rotation in R^2. Consider rectangular co-ordinate axes (1, 1) and (1, −1). The matrix A rotates (1, 1) to $(\cos\theta + \sin\theta, \cos\theta - \sin\theta)$ and (1, −1) to $(\cos\theta - \sin\theta, -\cos\theta - \sin\theta)$ in such a way that the resulting two axes are also rectangular. The operation of A^{-1} will simply reverse this transform.

7.12. *Necessity:* Suppose L and T are equivalent so that $L = ETF$ where E and F are non-singular. Since pre- or post-multiplication by a non-singular transformation does not alter rank, L and T have the same rank.

Sufficiency: If L and T have the same rank, both matrices can be reduced to a matrix of the form $\begin{bmatrix} I_r & 0 \\ 0 & 0 \end{bmatrix}$, where I_r is the identity matrix of order r, by a number of elementary operations. Hence

$$E_1LF_1 = E_2TF_2 = \begin{bmatrix} I_r & 0 \\ 0 & 0 \end{bmatrix}$$

where E_1, E_2, F_1, F_2 are non-singular elementary matrices. Hence $L = ETF$ and therefore L and T are equivalent.

7.13. If A and B are similar, then there exists a non-singular matrix S such that $B = S^{-1}AS$. It follows that $SB^2 = ASB = ASS^{-1}AS = A^2S$, that is, $B^2 = S^{-1}A^2S$ and $B' = (S^{-1}AS)' = S'A'(S')^{-1}$. Also, when A and B are non-singular, $S = ASB^{-1}$ and hence $B^{-1} = S^{-1}A^{-1}S$.

7.14. Let A and B be similar. Then $B = S^{-1}AS$ where S is non-singular. Hence, by definition, they are also equivlaent since the transformation $S^{-1}AS$ is an equivalence transformation. Suppose A and B are both $m \times n$ matrices and A and B are equivalent. Then we can find non-singular matrices E and F such that $B = EAF$. But E is $m \times m$ and F is $n \times n$ and hence in general (that is, for $m \neq n$)$E \neq F^{-1}$ and therefore A and B are not similar. If two matrices are equivalent, then by T.32 they represent the same transformation. By T.36, two similar matrices also represent the same transformation. The difference is simply that matrices can only be similar if they are square and thus similarity is a special case of equivalence.

7.15. Since $\boldsymbol{A}$ is square, the new matrix $\boldsymbol{B}$ will have the new vectors as a basis for both the domain and the range of the transformation. Hence $\boldsymbol{B} = \boldsymbol{Q}^{-1}\boldsymbol{A}\boldsymbol{Q}$

$$\text{where } \boldsymbol{Q}^{-1} = \begin{bmatrix} 2 & 0 & 1 \\ 0 & 1 & 1 \\ 1 & 1 & 1 \end{bmatrix} \text{ and } \boldsymbol{Q} = \begin{bmatrix} 0 & -1 & 1 \\ -1 & -1 & 2 \\ 1 & 2 & -2 \end{bmatrix};$$

$$\text{hence} \quad \boldsymbol{B} = \begin{bmatrix} -3 & -5 & 10 \\ 2 & -4 & 3 \\ 1 & -5 & 6 \end{bmatrix}.$$

$\boldsymbol{A}$ and $\boldsymbol{B}$ are clearly similar (and therefore also equivalent).

7.16. Using the notation of the text, we have $\boldsymbol{H} = \begin{bmatrix} 1 & 1 \\ 1 & 0 \end{bmatrix}$ since $\boldsymbol{y} = \boldsymbol{H}\hat{\boldsymbol{y}}$ and

$$\boldsymbol{G}^{-1} = \begin{bmatrix} 0 & 1 & 1 \\ 1 & 1 & 1 \\ 1 & 1 & 0 \end{bmatrix} \text{ since } \boldsymbol{x} = \boldsymbol{G}^{-1}\hat{\boldsymbol{x}}. \qquad \boldsymbol{H}^{-1} = \begin{bmatrix} 0 & 1 \\ 1 & -1 \end{bmatrix}$$

$$\text{and } \boldsymbol{G} = \begin{bmatrix} -1 & 1 & 0 \\ 1 & -1 & 1 \\ 0 & 1 & -1 \end{bmatrix}.$$

$$\text{The new matrix representation} = \begin{bmatrix} 2 & 0 & 1 \\ -5 & 5 & -4 \end{bmatrix}.$$

Chapter 8

8.1. If more than $n^2 - n$ elements are zero, then less than n elements are non-zero. Since there are n columns in $\boldsymbol{A}$, it is not possible to have column vectors all non-zero and hence at least one column vector must be the zero vector. Therefore the column vectors of $\boldsymbol{A}$ are linearly dependent and det $(\boldsymbol{A}) = 0$.

8.2. (i) The determinant of a diagonal matrix is the product of its diagonal elements, that is, det $\boldsymbol{A} = a_{11}a_{22} \ldots a_{nn}$.

(ii) Since all elements below (or above) the diagonal are zero, the only minors which do not vanish are leading minors. Hence the determinant of a triangular matrix depends on the smallest leading minor which depends only on diagonal elements. Thus the determinant of a triangular matrix is the same as for a diagonal matrix, that is, det $\boldsymbol{A} = a_{11}a_{22} \ldots a_{nn}$.

8.3. For a (2×2) skew-symmetric matrix, $\|a_{ij}\|$, det $\boldsymbol{A} = a_{12}^2$. For a (4×4) skew-symmetric matrix, $\|a_{ij}\|$, det $\boldsymbol{A} = (a_{13}a_{24} - a_{12}a_{34} - a_{14}a_{23})^2$. This result, that the determinant is a perfect square, does hold for all skew-symmetric matrices of even order. A proof can be found in Aitken (1956).

8.4. Since pre- or post-multiplying by a non-singular matrix does not alter the rank of a matrix, it follows that, if $\boldsymbol{AB} = \boldsymbol{0}$, then if $\boldsymbol{A}$ is non-singular, $\boldsymbol{B}$ is not and that if $\boldsymbol{B}$ is non-singular, $\boldsymbol{A}$ is not. Furthermore, if $\boldsymbol{A}$ is non-singular, the columns of $\boldsymbol{A}$ are linearly independent and, since $\boldsymbol{AB} = \boldsymbol{0}$, $\boldsymbol{B} = \boldsymbol{0}$; similarly, if $\boldsymbol{B}$ is non-singular, $\boldsymbol{A} = \boldsymbol{0}$. But neither $\boldsymbol{A}$ nor $\boldsymbol{B}$ are identically zero and hence $\boldsymbol{A}$ and $\boldsymbol{B}$ are singular and det $\boldsymbol{A}$ = det $\boldsymbol{B} = 0$.

8.5. Adjoint matrix

$$= \begin{bmatrix} 6 & -32 & -10 \\ 1 & -27 & 20 \\ -20 & 20 & -10 \end{bmatrix}$$

$\therefore$ determinant $= -130$.

Hence the inverse

$$= \frac{1}{\det} \times \text{adjoint} = \begin{bmatrix} -\dfrac{6}{130} & \dfrac{32}{130} & \dfrac{1}{13} \\[2ex] -\dfrac{1}{130} & \dfrac{27}{130} & -\dfrac{2}{13} \\[2ex] \dfrac{2}{13} & -\dfrac{2}{13} & \dfrac{1}{13} \end{bmatrix}$$

8.6. Let $\boldsymbol{A}$ be a skew-symmetric matrix of odd-order.

Then $\boldsymbol{A}' = -\boldsymbol{A}$. Now det $\boldsymbol{A}$ = det$\boldsymbol{A}'$ = det $(-\boldsymbol{A})$.

Also det $\lambda\boldsymbol{A} = \lambda^n$ det $\boldsymbol{A}$ and hence det $\boldsymbol{A} = (-1)^n$ det $\boldsymbol{A}$. Since n is odd, det $\boldsymbol{A}$ = $-$det $\boldsymbol{A}$ and hence det $\boldsymbol{A} = 0$ (that is, all skew-symmetric matrices of odd order are singular).

8.7. The proof uses induction on n, the order of the matrices.

$B = \|\alpha_i a_{ij}\|$, so that expanding by the first row gives $\det B = \sum_k \alpha_i a_{1k} B_{1k}$ where B_{1k} are the cofactors. But:

$$B(1, 1) = \begin{vmatrix} \alpha_2 a_{22} \dots \alpha_2 a_{2n} \\ \cdot \\ \cdot \\ \cdot \\ \alpha_n a_{n2} \dots \alpha_2 a_{nn} \end{vmatrix}, \text{ etc.}$$

so, if the result is true for $(n - 1)$, $\det B(1, k) = \alpha_2 \dots \alpha_n \det A(1, k)$ and thus $\det B = \alpha_1 \dots \alpha_n \det A$. But it clearly holds for $n = 1$. A similar proof by induction is possible for $B = \|\alpha_j a_{ij}\|$ using expansion by a column.

8.9. An expansion of det A by the ith row in terms of the cofactors for the kth row is $\sum_j a_{ij} A_{kj} (k \neq i)$. This is exactly the same as an expansion of a determinant with rows i and k identical. But if two rows in a determinant are the same the determinant vanishes. The only exception will be $i = k$ when $\sum a_{ij} A_{kj} = \det A$.

8.10. Consider $B = S^{-1} A S$.
Then $\det B = \det (S^{-1}) \,.\, \det (A) \,.\, \det (S)$. But $\det (S^{-1}) = (\det (S))^{-1}$. Hence $\det B = \det A$.

8.11. Since P is orthogonal, $P' = P^{-1}$. But $\det P = \det (P')$ and hence $\det P = \det (P^{-1}) = (\det P)^{-1}$.

Chapter 9

9.1. Eigenvalues of A are 1, -1, 2. Associated eigenvectors are (i) $\lambda = 1$: $(k, 3k, 0)$, (ii) $\lambda = -1$: $(0, k, 0)$, and (iii) $\lambda = 2$: $(2k, 5k, k)$. If $a_{21} = a_{23} = 0$, the eigenvalues are still 1, -1, 2 but the associated eigenvectors are (i) $\lambda = 1$: $(k, 0, 0)$, (ii) $\lambda = -1$: $(0, k, 0)$, and (iii) $\lambda = 2$: $(2k, 0, k)$. Only in special cases will it be true that the eigenvectors are the same when two matrices have the same eigenvalues.

9.2. $Ax = \lambda x$, and hence $A^2 x = A(Ax) = \lambda A x = \lambda^2 x$. Suppose $A^{n-1} x = \lambda^{n-1} x$, then $A^n x = A(A^{n-1}) x = A(\lambda^{n-1} x) = \lambda^n x$. Thus by induction $A^n x = \lambda^n x$.

Let $f(A) = \sum_{i=0}^{n} \alpha_i A^i$. Then $f(A)x = \sum_i \alpha_i \lambda^i x = f(\lambda)x$. Note this result includes the case of $A^{-1} x = (1/\lambda) x$.

9.3. A is idempotent implies $A^n x = A^{n-1} = \ldots = Ax = \lambda x$. But $A^i x = \lambda^i x$, so $\lambda^n = \lambda^{n-1} = \ldots = \lambda$ – i.e. $\lambda = 0$ or 1.

9.4. Let A be orthogonal. Then $A' = A^{-1}$. If $Ax = \lambda x$, then $x'A' = \lambda x'$, i.e. $x' = \lambda x'A$ or $x'A = (1/\lambda)x'$. But the eigenvalues for column or row eigenvectors must be the same since any square matrix and its transpose must have the same eigenvalues – because $\det B = \det B'$ and $[B - \lambda I]' = B' - \lambda I$. Hence $1/\lambda$ is also an eigenvalue of A.

9.5. Let x be the eigenvector associated with eigenvalue λ of AB, so that $ABx = \lambda x$. Pre-multiplying by B gives $BABx = \lambda Bx$, so that if $y = Bx$ we get $BAy = \lambda y$.

9.6. For any symmetric matrix A we can find n linearly independent eigenvectors, and in particular a set of orthonormal eigenvectors. Note this requires both T.49 and T.51. Let the matrix of eigenvectors be X. Then $X'AX$ is diagonal $= \| \lambda_i \delta_{ij} \|$, where λ_i are the eigenvalues. Since X is the matrix of orthonormal eigenvectors, X' and X are non-singular and rank $(X'AX)$ = rank (A). But if A has eigenvalues $= 0$ with multiplicity k, then only $(n - k)$ diagonal elements of $X'AX$ will be non-zero so that rank $(X'AX) = n - k$. Note this includes the case of non-singular A if all its eigenvalues are non-zero.

(i) Rank $= 1$; $\lambda = -3, 0, 0$. (ii) Rank $= 2$; $\lambda = 5, 3, 0$. (iii) Rank $= 3$; $\lambda = 2, -1, -1$.

9.7. $Ax = \alpha x$ and $A'y = \beta y$. Now $y'Ax = \alpha y'x$ and $x'A'y = \beta x'y$. But $(y'Ax)' = x'A'y = \beta x'y$ and $(y'Ax)' = (\alpha y'x)' = \alpha x'y$. Thus $\beta x'y = \alpha x'y$ or $(\beta - \alpha)x'y = 0$. So for $\beta \neq \alpha$, $x'y = 0$. Note that A is not necessarily symmetric.

That A and A' have the same eigenvalues is shown in answer to 9.4. In general the eigenvectors will not be the same. For $Ax = \lambda x$, $A'y = \lambda y$ and $y = x$, then $Ax = A'x$ – i.e. A must be symmetric.

9.8. A symmetric matrix A is positive/negative semi-definite iff at least one eigenvalue $\lambda_i = 0$. But in the characteristic equation $\det(A - \lambda_i I) = \det A = 0$.

9.9. Since $x'Ax$ is positive definite, all the eigenvalues of A are positive. Now the eigenvalues of A^{-1} are the inverses of those of A and hence are also positive.

9.10. *Sufficiency:* Suppose $A = X'X$ where X is non-singular and $n \times n$. Then if $y \in R^n$, $y'Ay = y'X'Xy$. But $z = Xy \in R^n$, so that

$y'Ay = z'z = \sum_i z_i^2 > 0$ – as X is non-singular. Hence A is positive definite.

Necessity: A is symmetric so that there exists an orthogonal matrix Q of eigenvectors such that $Q'AQ = \|\lambda_i\delta_{ij}\|$. As A is positive definite $\lambda_i > 0$ all i, and hence $\|\lambda_i\delta_{ij}\| = \|\sqrt{\lambda_i}\cdot\delta_{ij}\|'\,\|\sqrt{\lambda_i}\cdot\delta_{ij}\|$. Thus $A = |RQ^{-1}|'|RQ^{-1}|$ where $R = \|\sqrt{\lambda_i}\cdot\delta_{ij}\|$.

9.11. Since A is symmetric its eigenvectors are orthogonal. Consider the n orthonormal eigenvectors $y_1, \ldots, y_n$. For $x \in R^n$,

$$x = \sum_i \mu_i y_i;\; x'Ax = (\sum \mu_i y_i')\,A(\sum_i \mu_i y_i) = (\sum \mu_i y_i')(\sum \mu_i A y_i)$$

$$= (\sum \mu_i y_i')(\sum \mu_i \lambda_i y_i) = \sum_i \sum_j \mu_i \mu_j \lambda_j y_i' y_j.$$

But $y_i'y_j = \delta_{ij}$, so that $x'Ax = \sum \mu_i^2 \lambda_i$.
Further $x'x = \sum_i \sum_i \mu_i \mu_j y_i y_j' = \sum_i \mu_i^2$.

Thus

$$\frac{x'Ax}{x'x} = \frac{\sum \mu_i^2 \lambda_i}{\sum \mu_i^2} = \frac{\lambda_1 \sum \mu_i^2 \lambda_i/\lambda_1}{\sum \mu_i^2}$$

Since λ_1 is the largest eigenvalue $\lambda_i/\lambda_1 \leqslant 1$ and $\dfrac{x'Ax}{x'x} \leqslant \lambda_1$.

9.12. Let $\lambda_1, \ldots, \lambda_r$ be the distinct eigenvalues of A, each with multiplicity m_i, $i = 1, \ldots, r$. Consider the characteristic equation det $|A - \lambda I| = \alpha_0 + \alpha_1\lambda + \ldots + \alpha_n\lambda^n = 0$. For any polynomial the product of the roots is given by $(-1)^n \cdot \alpha_0/\alpha_n$. Since in the characteristic equation of an $n \times n$ matrix $\alpha_n = (-1)^n$, we have $\alpha_0 = \lambda_1^{m_1}\lambda_2^{m_2}\ldots\lambda_r^{m_r}$. But det $|A - \lambda I| =$ det A when $\lambda = 0$. Hence $\alpha_0 =$ det A.

One further result concerns the *trace* of $A (=\text{tr}\, A)$ defined as $\sum_i a_{ii}$ – that is, the sum of the diagonal elements of the matrix. From above it follows that tr $A = \alpha_{n-1}/\alpha_n = \sum_{i=1}^{r} m_i\lambda_i$ – i.e. tr A = the sum of the eigenvalues.

9.13. A is orthogonal since $A' = A^{-1}$. The eigenvalues of A are complex; $\cos\theta + i\sin\theta$ and $\cos\theta - i\sin\theta$. The associated eigenvectors are (ik, k) and (k, ik). Consider any vector $x \in R^2$. Then it is easy to show that $|Ax| = |x|$, i.e. the length of the vector is unchanged. As shown in problem 7.11 the transformation performs a rotation, keeping the axes rectangular. It is, therefore, not surprising that the eigenvalues (and hence eigenvectors) are complex since there are no vectors which $\boldsymbol{A}$ does not rotate (except for the trivial case $\boldsymbol{x} = \boldsymbol{0}$) when $0 \neq n\pi$, $n = 0, 1, 2, \ldots$. When $\theta = 0$, $\boldsymbol{A} = \boldsymbol{I}$ and the eigenvalue is 1 with multiplicity 2.

Bibliography

A. C. Aitken, *Determinants and Matrices* (Edinburgh: Oliver & Boyd, 1956).

K. J. Arrow, 'Price-Quantity Adjustments in Multiple Markets with Rising Demands' in Arrow *et al., Mathematical Methods* (1960).

K. J. Arrow, S. Karlin and P. Suppes, *Mathematical Methods in the Social Sciences* (Stanford: Stanford University Press, 1960).

R. Bellman, *Introduction to Matrix Analysis* (New York: McGraw-Hill, 1960).

E. Burmeister and A. R. Dobell, *Mathematical Theories of Economic Growth* (New York: Macmillan, 1970).

G. Debreu and I. N. Herstein, 'Non-negative Square Matrices', *Econometrica*, vol. 21 (October 1953) pp 597–606.

R. Dorfman, P. Samuelson and R. Solow, *Linear Programming and Economic Analysis* (New York: McGraw-Hill, 1958).

D. Gale, *The Theory of Linear Economic Models* (New York: McGraw-Hill, 1960).

F. R. Gantmacher, *Matrix Theory*, vol. I (New York: Chelsea Publishing Co., 1959).

G. Hadley, *Linear Programming* (Reading, Mass: Addison-Wesley, 1962).

M. D. Intriligator, *Mathematical Optimization and Economic Theory* (Englewood Cliffs, N.J.: Prentice-Hall, 1971).

L. McKenzie, 'Matrices with Dominant Diagonals and Economic Theory' in Arrow *et al., Mathematical Methods* (1960).

L. Mirsky, *An Introduction to Linear Algebra* (London: Oxford University Press, 1955).

M. Morishima, *Equilibrium, Stability and Growth* (London: Oxford University Press, 1964).

H. Nikaido, *Introduction to Sets and Mappings in Economics* (Amsterdam: North-Holland, 1970).

C. van de Panne, *Linear Programming and Related Techniques* (Amsterdam: North-Holland, 1971).

P. A. Samuelson, *Foundations of Economic Analysis* (Cambridge, Mass.: Harvard University Press, 1947).

J. T. Schwartz, *Lectures on the Mathematical Method in Analytical Economics* (New York: Gordon & Breach, 1961).

C.-S. Yan, *Introduction to Input–Output Economics* (New York: Holt, Rinehart & Winston, 1969).

Index

Adjoint matrix, 86–7
Allocation of resources, 145–7, 162–7
Associative rule, 6, 34, 38
Augmented matrix, 54

Balanced growth, 135–44
Basic feasible solutions, 149–52
Basic solution, 58
Basis, 28–31
  change of, 30–1, 77–8, 93–9
  orthonormal, 31
Bilinear mapping, 104
Boundary point, 11
Bounded, 12

Canonical form, 58
Capital goods, 134–8
Cayley–Hamilton theorem, 111
Characteristic equation, 92
Characteristic value, 90
Characteristic vector, 90
Closed set, 12
Cofactor, 84
Column operations, 40–1
Commutative rule, 6, 34, 37
Compact, 12
Compatible equations, 52
Complement, 12
Complementary slackness, 156–7
Complex eigenvalues, 92
Components of a vector, 4
Concave function, 23–5
Conformable, 37
  partitioning, 48–9
Congruence transformation, 79
Constraints, 145–9, 151, 153
Convex combination, 13
Convex function, 23–5
Convex set(s), 13
  intersection of, 14
  sum of, 15
Co-ordinates, 4
Correspondence, 62
Cramer's rule, 87

Decentralization, 167–9
Decomposable matrix, 114–16
Degenerate solution, 58
Determinant(s), 83–8
  expansion of, 83–4
  of positive/negative definite matrices, 106
  properties of, 85–8
Determinate equations, 52
Development planning, 165–7
Diagonal matrix, 39
Diagonalization, 93–103
  of quadratic forms, 105
  of symmetric matrices, 99–103
Difference of sets, 14
Differentiation, 173–5
Dimension of a vector space, 30
Direct input requirements, 131–3
Directed line segment, 4
Disjoint sets, 2
Distance between vectors, 8
Distributive rule, 6, 34, 38
Domain, 61
Dominant diagonal matrix, 123–8
Dominant root, 117–21, 124, 135–6, 138
Dual
  of linear programme, 154
  in Von Neumann model, 140
Dual stability theorems, 138

Dual variables, 154–7
  as shadow prices, 157, 167–9
Duality theorem, 155–7
Dynamic Leontief model, 134–9

Echelon matrix, 41
Efficient production, 160–4, 167–9
Eigenvalue, 90–3, 99–103, 122, 124
Eigenvector, 90–3, 99–103
Element
  of a matrix, 34
  of a set, 1
Elementary row/column operations, 40–3
Equality
  of matrices, 35
  of sets, 1
  of vectors, 5
Equilibrium prices, 126–7, 131–3, 136–8, 140–3
Equivalence transformation, 79
Euclidean distance norm, 8, 75
Euclidean vector space, 7
Expansion factor, 135, 140
Extreme point, 13–14
  in linear programming, 151–4

Feasible set of linear programme, 14, 149
Frobenius theorem, 116–21
Function, 61
Fundamental system, 54

Gaussian elimination, 56–8
Golden Rule, 138
Growth
  balanced, 135
  Leontief model, 134–9
  Von Neumann model, 139–43
  Von Neumann–Leontief model, 143–4

Half-space, 13
Hawkins–Simon condition, 128
Homogeneous equations, 53–6, 65–6
Hyperplane, 12
  normal to, 12–13
  separating, 20–2
  supporting, 17–22
Hypersphere, 11

Identity matrix, 38, 77
Image, 61
Incompatible equations, 52
Indecomposable matrix, 114–21, 142
Indeterminate equations, 52
Indirect input requirements, 131
Infinite dimensional space, 170–2
Input matrix, 50–1, 140
Input–output models, 50–1, 124–5, 129–35
  dynamic, 134–9
Inside of a hypersphere, 11
Interest rate, 136–8, 140–4
Interior point, 11
Intersection of sets, 2
Inverse matrix, 72–5
  computation of, 73–5
  of a product, 73
Isoquant, 164

Jordan canonical form, 98

Kronecker delta, 32

Labour theory of value, 131
Least-squares regression, 174–5
Length of a vector, 8
Leontief model, 50–1, 110, 124–5, 129–32
  growth, 134–9
  prices, 131, 136–9
Line segment, 12
Linear combination, 5, 26–9
Linear dependence, 27–8
Linear economic models, 129–44
  closed, 134–8, 140–4
  dynamic, 134–44
  open, 129–31, 138–9
  prices, 131–3, 136–8, 140–4
  static, 129–33, 160–4
Linear equations, 50–8, 65–6
  canonical form, 58
  equivalent systems, 57
  fundamental system, 54
  homogeneous, 53–6, 65–6

nonhomogeneous, 53–6, 65–6
non-negative solutions, 124–5, 128–9
solution by elimination, 56–8
solution set, 52
Linear independence, 27–30
Linear programming, 145–59
applications, 160–9
basic feasible solutions, 149–52
canonical form, 149
dual for canonical form, 158
dual for standard form, 154–7
dual variables, interpretation of, 157
effective/ineffective constraints, 153–4
feasible set, 149
optimal basis, 153, 157–9
primal, 154–6
simplex method, 154
slack variables, 148
Linear transformation(s), 62–73, 75–80
idempotent, 77
inverse, 70–3
matrix representation of, 63–4, 77–80, 93–9
non-singular, 67, 70–3
null space, 65
orthogonal, 75–6

Mapping(s), 61–2
bilinear, 104
one-to-one, 62
onto, 66
Markov chain, 122–3
Matrix, matrices, 34–49
addition, 35
augmented, 54
characteristic equation, 92
congruent, 79
diagonal, 39
diagonalization of, 93–103
dominant diagonal, 123–8
eigenvalues, 90–3, 99–103
eigenvectors, 90–3, 99–103
elementary transformation, 43
equality of, 34
equivalent, 79
identity, 38, 77
indecomposable, 114–16, 142
inverse, 72–5
multiplication by a scalar, 35
multiplication, 35–8
negative (semi-) definite, 105–6
non-negative, 110–28
non-singular, 45, 67, 73
null, 38
orthogonal, 76
partitioning of, 47–9
positive, 110
positive (semi-) definite, 105–6
power series, 111
rank, 43–6
scalar, 39
semi-positive, 110
similar, 80, 94
singular, 45
skew-symmetric, 40
square, 36
stable, 127–8
stochastic, 121–3
symmetric, 40, 99–103
transpose, 39
Minor, 86
Multiplier, matrix, 125

Necessary condition, 2–3
Negative (semi-) definite quadratic form, 105–6
Neighbourhood, 11
Net output, 50–1
Non-homogeneous equations, 53–6, 65–6
Non-negative constraints, 148
Non-negative matrices, 110–28
Non-singular matrix, 45, 67, 73
Non-substitution theorem
dynamic linear models, 143–4
static linear models, 131–2, 160–1
Nontrivial solution, 53
Norm of a vector, 8
Normal to hyperplane, 12–13
Normalized eigenvector, 97
Null matrix, 38
Null set, 2
Null space, 65
Nullity, 65

One-to-one, 62, 66, 70–2
Onto, 66–7, 70–2
Open set, 12
Orthogonal
  matrix, 76
  transformation, 75–6
  vectors, 8
Orthonormal basis, 31
Output matrix, 140

Partial ordering, 8
Partitioning of matrices, 47–9
Perron theorem, 116–21
Planning, 165–9
Positive (semi-) definite matrix, 105–6
Positive matrix, 110
Price adjustment, 126–8
Prices, 22, 131–3, 136–8, 140–4
Primal of linear programme, 154
Primary factors, 131–3, 160–5
Principal minor, 86
Productive matrix, 130
Profit rate, 136–8, 140–4

Quadratic form(s), 103–8
  constrained, 107–8
  matrix of, 104
  positive/negative (semi-) definite, 105–6

R^n, 7, 30
Range, 61
Rank of a matrix, 43–6
Row operations, 40–1

Scalar, 5
Scalar product of vectors, 7, 40
Separating hyperplane, 20–2
Semi-positive matrix, 110, 116–21
Set, 1
Shadow prices, 157–9
  in planning, 167–9
Similarity transformation, 80
Singular matrix, 45
Skew-symmetric matrix, 40
Slack variables, 148
Solution vector, 52
Spanning set, 28
Stable, Stability
  growth, 138
  market prices, 126–8
  matrix, 127–8
Stochastic matrix, 121–3
Strict inequality, 8
Submatrix, 47–9, 86
Subset, 1
Subspace, 8, 32
Substitution theorem, 143–4, 160–2
Subtechnology, 143
Sufficient condition, 2–3
Sum of sets, 14
Supporting hyperplane, 17–22
Symmetric matrix, 40, 99–103

Transformation, 61
Transition matrix, 121–3
Transpose
  of a matrix, 39
  of a vector, 5

Union of sets, 1
Unit vectors, 26

Valuation function, 148–9, 154, 165–6
Vector(s), 4–9
  addition, 5
  angle between, 8
  column, 5
  equality, 5
  inequalities, 8–9
  length, 8
  linear combination, 5
  multiplication by a scalar, 5
  non-negative, 9
  orthogonal, 8
  positive, 9
  product, 35–8
  row, 5
  scalar product, 7, 40
  unit, 26
Vector space, 7
  basis of, 29
  dimension, 30
  Euclidean, 7

Von Neumann model
growth, 139–43
–Leontief, 143–4
production, 160–2

Weak inequality, 8
Wealth distribution, 121–3